THE CREATIVE
COOK

THE CREATIVE
COOK

SMITHMARK

Text copyright © Richard Cawley, Lewis Esson, Janice Murfitt, Lyn Rutherford, Sally-Anne Scott, Jane Suthering
Photography copyright © Julie Fisher, Michelle Garrett, Deborah Patterson, Pia Tryde
Illustration copyright © Alison Barratt
Design and copyright © Conran Octopus 1995

Recipes selected from *The Creative Cook* series of books:
Classic Cakes, Tempting Tortes (1993), Easy and Artful Asian Cooking (1993), For the Love of Vegetables (1993), A Mediterranean Table (1993), Outdoor Affairs: Picnics and Barbecues (1994), Savory to Sweet: Pies and Tarts (1993), Splendid Herbs (1993), Traditional Country Cooking (1993).

This edition published in 1996 by SMITHMARK Publishers, a division of U.S. Media Holdings, Inc., 16 East 32nd Street, New York, NY 10016

SMITHMARK books are available for bulk purchase for sales promotion and premium use. For details write or call the manager of special sales, SMITHMARK Publishers, 16 East 32nd Street, New York, NY 100018:
(212) 532 6600

Produced by Conran Octopus
37 Shelton Street
London
WC2H 9HN

ISBN 0-7651-9951-3

Printed in China

10 9 8 7 6 5 4 3 2 1

Library of Congress CIP

Please note the following:
Quantities given in all recipes serve 4 people unless otherwise stated.
Butter and margarine are packaged in a variety of forms, including 1-pound blocks and ¼-pound sticks. A stick equals 8 tablespoons (½ cup)
Cream used is specified as light cream (containing from 18 percent to 30 percent milk fat), whipping cream (30 percent to 36 percent milk fat), or heavy cream (at least 36 percent milk fat).
Flour used is all-purpose flour, unless otherwise specified.
Preparation of ingredients, such as the cleaning, trimming, and peeling of vegetables and fruit, is presumed and the text refers to any aspect of this only if unusual, such as onions used unpeeled etc.
Citrus fruit should be thoroughly washed to remove any agricultural residues. For this reason, whenever a recipe uses the rind of any citrus such as oranges, lemon, or limes, the text specifies washed fruit. Wash the fruit thoroughly, rinse well, and pat dry. If using organically grown fruit, rinse briefly and pat dry.
Eggs used are large unless otherwise specified. Because of the risk of contamination with salmonella bacteria, current recommendations from health professionals are that children, pregnant women, people on immuno-suppressant drugs, and the elderly should not eat raw or lightly cooked eggs. This book includes recipes with raw and lightly cooked eggs. These recipes are marked by an ★ in the text.

ACKNOWLEDGMENTS
The Authors have provided the recipes on the pages indicated below:
Richard Cawley: *11, 30-1, 40, 48-53, 64 (right), 66, 73, 75, 84, 92 (right), 93 (right), 106, 108, 111, 120-36, 161, 164-5, 170-1, 178, 181 (left), 182 (left), 183 (right), 203-204, 207 (right), 230-1;* **Lewis Esson:** *34-9, 42, 56-63, 74, 76-7, 89-90, 100-102, 152 (right), 174 (bottom), 179, 185, 196-201, 228;* **Janice Murfitt:** *46-7, 85 (left), 148-51, 208-10, 223-7, 232-4;* **Lyn Rutherford:** *18-19, 25-7, 64 (left), 70-1, 78, 81-2, 86, 94-5, 103-105, 107, 110, 114-17, 141-2, 162-3 (left), 188-95;* **Sally-Anne Scott:** *10, 12-17, 20-4, 28, 45, 65, 80, 85 (right), 92 (left). 96-7, 109, 112, 140, 144-9 (left), 152 (left), 157-9, 163 (right), 166-8, 172, 174 (top), 175-6, 180, 181 (right), 182 (right), 183 (left), 184, 202, 206, 207 (left);* **Jane Suthering:** *213-21, 238-53*

The publishers thank the photographers for their kind permission to reproduce the photographs on the following pages:
Julie Fisher: *2, 32-3, 37, 43, 54-5, 58, 61, 63, 77, 88, 91, 98-9, 199, 200, 228-9;* **Michelle Garrett:** *52, 67, 118-19, 122-3, 125, 126-7, 130-1, 134-5, 137, 151, 153, 211, 212, 214, 216, 221, 222, 225, 235, 236-7, 243, 245, 248, 250, 252;* **Deborah Patterson:** *6, 8-9, 15, 23, 26, 68-9, 79, 87, 95, 104, 117, 138-9, 143, 147, 154-5, 156-7, 158, 160, 161, 169, 172-3, 177, 180, 188, 191, 192, 195;* **Pia Tryde:** *29, 41, 44, 72-3, 83, 85, 113, 204-5, 206, 230-1*

The publishers also thank Jackie Boase, Roísín Nield, Jane Newdick, Debbie Patterson, and Sue Skeen for food styling, and Richard Cawley, Meg Jansz, Janice Murfitt, Lyn Rutherford and Jane Suthering for food for photography.

CONTENTS

INTRODUCTION

Over the past few years there has been a revolution in the way that we cook. Inspired by the wonderful array of new produce available in our supermarkets and multi-ethnic markets and stimulated by more foreign travel and eating out, we have become of increasingly adventurous cooks. Even the housewife and mother who has to produce daily meals for a demanding and picky family now tends to lean on dishes like pasta and curries in a way that her parents' generation would have found unthinkable.

Health concerns have also played a big part in reshaping our eating habits. Gone are the fry-ups and stodgy puddings that were once such mainstays of our diet. Instead we are now making much more use of vegetables and fruits, rice, grains, and pulses; replacing butter, suet and lard with olive, nut, and vegetable oils; and favoring white meat and fish over red meat. To make the most of such ingredients we have broadened our horizons to embrace ideas from nations whose diets have long been based on such healthier tenets – like those of Asia and the Mediterranean region.

The Creative Cook provides an amazing wealth of recipes to help you make the most of both tried-and-tested ingredients and today's new exotica. There are recipes for traditional favorites – often given new life with an unusual and refreshing twist – alongside lots of innovative ideas, many of which are inspired by the best that the fascinating cuisines of the world have to offer.

The book begins with some basic stocks and sauces and a range of delicious soups. There are also chapters on Appetizers and Snacks: Rice, Grains, and Pasta; Vegetables and Salads; and Puddings and Desserts. Main courses are presented by ingredients, with separate sections on each different type of meat, as well as poultry and game, fish, and shellfish. To make the book even more useful for today's cook, there are substantial sections on Oriental Cooking and one on Vegetarian Main Courses. The book finishes with a section on Baking, giving an assortment of simple treats you can make at home for morning coffee and afternoon tea. Throughout, the book is also dotted with invaluable marginal notes, which provide useful hints and tips, information on more unusual ingredients, interesting serving suggestions and clever ideas for variations.

There is something for everyone and every occasion in this bible for the cooking of today. Whether you simply want some fresh ideas for family meals or are planning a special meal for a celebration or to impress your friends, you will find no end of exciting ideas every time you dip into it. With this book on your shelf, you need never again allow your cooking to get into a rut – even your family favorites can be given a new lease of life.

LEWIS ESSON

STOCKS, SAUCES, AND SOUPS

A well-flavored stock is at the heart of most good cooking, and although there are many high-quality bottled and chilled stocks readily available, you will find that making your own stock is relatively easy, very economical and gives an unbeatable freshness and depth of flavor to any dish in which it is used.

From good stocks it is one short step to making a wide range of nourishing soups, from those suitable for a dinner party, like Artichoke Soup with Lemongrass, to others, like Lentil and Ham Soup with Mushroom Toasts, which are whole meals in themselves.

Many sauces are also based on stocks, like the classic rich reductions of *haute cuisine* as well as good giblet gravy for roast poultry. This chapter, however, also features milk-based Béchamel or basic white sauce, the emulsion sauces like Mayonnaise and Hollandaise and salad dressings like French or Fruit vinaigrette, as well as some tasty relishes.

Left to right: a jar of French Vinaigrette (page 14); a plate and bowl of Low-calorie Yogurt Dressing (page 14); a spoonful of Rouille (page 100); Strawberry Vinaigrette (page 15); Mango Vinaigrette (page 15); and Homemade Mayonnaise (page 13)

Make CHICKEN STOCK as per the BASIC BOUILLON recipe, but using no beef. Use 2 or 3 chicken carcasses and some giblets or trimmings such as feet for even more flavor. Leftover carcasses from roast chickens can make good stock.

Make FISH STOCK with 1½ lb of fish heads and trimmings, 3 onions, 3 bay leaves, and a bunch of parsley. Cover with water, bring to a boil, and simmer 20 minutes only.

VEGETABLE STOCK

MAKES ABOUT 1 QUART

1 cup dried navy beans, soaked in cold water overnight
3 tbsp butter
1 tbsp sunflower or canola oil
1 garlic clove
1 stalk of celery
6 carrots, coarsely chopped
3 leeks, coarsely chopped
3 turnips, cubed
2 onions
12 whole cloves
1 parsnip
small sprig of fresh thyme
3 bay leaves
small bunch of fresh parsley
salt and freshly ground black pepper

Drain the navy beans, rinse, and put them in a saucepan. Cover them with fresh cold water and bring to a boil. Drain, rinse, and cover with more fresh cold water. Bring to a boil again and then drain.

Melt the butter with the oil in a large heavy pan over medium heat. Sauté the garlic 2 minutes.

Add the celery, carrots, leeks, turnips, onions with the cloves, and the parsnip. Cook 5-7 minutes, stirring constantly.

Remove from the heat and add the drained beans, followed by 3 quarts of water, the thyme, bay leaves, and the parsley, complete with stems. Bring to a boil, cover, and simmer gently 1½ hours.

Remove from the heat and let cool about 2 hours.

Return the pan to low heat and simmer 15 minutes. Strain the stock, return it to the pan and boil rapidly to reduce it by about half.

Cool any stock not being used immediately and then store it in the refrigerator.

BASIC BOUILLON OR ENRICHED MEAT STOCK

MAKES ABOUT 3½ CUPS

1½-2 lb beef shank
carcass of 1 fresh chicken
1 onion, coarsely chopped
3 carrots, coarsely chopped
bouquet garni
2 stalks of celery, coarsely chopped
8 black peppercorns

Chop the meat and chicken into manageable pieces and place them in a large pan. Cover with 2¼ quarts of cold water and bring to a boil.

Reduce the heat and add the other ingredients. Cover and cook gently about 1½ hours, skimming as necessary.

Remove all the larger solids from the pan, then strain the stock through a cheesecloth-lined strainer.

Return the liquid to the heat and boil it rapidly to reduce it by about half. Strain it through cheesecloth again before use.

Cool any stock not being used immediately and then store it in the refrigerator.

PEANUT AND PEPPER RELISH

MAKES ABOUT 1 CUP

¾ cup chopped salted peanuts
½ red or yellow sweet pepper, seeded and minced
½ tsp curry powder
1 small garlic clove, minced
3 tbsp thick plain yogurt
2 tbsp chopped fresh flat-leaf parsley

Mix all the ingredients and chill at least 1 hour, or up to 24, to let the flavors develop fully.

MANGO SAMBAL

MAKES ABOUT 1½ CUPS

½ large ripe mango, peeled and coarsely chopped
2 scallions, thinly sliced
⅛ English cucumber, coarsely chopped
1 hot chili pepper, seeded and minced
juice of 1 lime or lemon
1 heaping tbsp chopped fresh cilantro

Combine all the ingredients except the cilantro and chill at least 1 hour, or up to 24, to let the flavors develop fully. Just before serving, mix in the cilantro.

COCONUT SAMBAL

MAKES ABOUT 1½ CUPS

1 cup freshly grated coconut (not packed)
½ small mild onion, thinly sliced
1 hot chili pepper, seeded and minced
juice of 1 lime or lemon
¼ tsp salt

Mix all the ingredients well and chill at least 1 hour, or up to 24, to let the flavors develop fully.

CUCUMBER AND CARROT RELISH

MAKES ABOUT 1½ CUPS

2 tbsp sugar
juice of ½ lime
¼ English cucumber, minced
2 shallots, thinly sliced
1 small carrot, grated
1 large hot red or green chili pepper or more to taste, seeded and minced

In a small bowl, dissolve the sugar in 2 tablespoons of hot water. Mix in all the other ingredients.

Chill for at least 1 hour to let the flavors develop fully, but use within 24 hours.

PLUM SAUCE

MAKES ABOUT 5 CUPS

2 oz Asian pickled plums
2¼ cups sugar
2-3 large hot red chili peppers, seeded and minced
1 red sweet pepper, seeded and minced
¼ cup rice or white wine vinegar

Rub the plums through the fingers to break up the flesh, but do not discard the pits.

Put the sugar and 1¼ cups of water in a saucepan and bring to a boil over medium heat. When the syrup is boiling well, add the chili peppers, the sweet pepper, and the plums with their pits. Bring back to a boil and boil 2-3 minutes, then stir in the vinegar. The resulting sauce will be sweet-and-sour.

Let cool, then remove and discard the pits. Pour into warmed sterilized bottles or jars and seal or stopper tightly. This sauce will stay fresh for several weeks in the refrigerator.

Thick sweet-spicy PLUM SAUCE *is traditionally served by the Chinese as a dip with dumplings or seafood and with poultry dishes, especially duck.*

ASIAN PICKLED PLUMS, *preserved in a spiced vinegar, are available from Asian markets. A blender or food processor easily gets the peppers minced to the correct degree of fineness.*

SAMBALS *are Indonesian relishes, usually spiced with chili peppers.*

Variations on
BÉCHAMEL *include*
AURORE SAUCE,
*which contains
added tomato pulp
or purée and*
MORNAY, *which
is flavored with
grated cheese.*

QUICK TOMATO SAUCE

MAKES ABOUT 1 CUP

*¼ cup olive oil
2 garlic cloves, minced
1 tbsp finely chopped parsley
small pinch of hot red pepper flakes
one 14-oz can tomatoes
salt and freshly ground black pepper*

Heat the oil over medium heat and cook the garlic, parsley, and red pepper flakes stirring constantly, until soft, 1-2 minutes.

Crush or purée the tomatoes and add to the pan. Bring to a boil, season to taste, mix well, and remove from heat.

BECHAMEL SAUCE

MAKES ABOUT 1¼ CUPS

*1¼ cups milk
1 small onion
¼ tsp freshly grated nutmeg
1 bay leaf
sprig of fresh thyme
2 tbsp butter
2 tbsp flour
salt and freshly ground black pepper*

Place the milk in a saucepan together with the onion, nutmeg, bay leaf, and thyme. Very slowly bring to a boil. Immediately remove from the heat and let infuse 20 minutes.

Melt the butter in a heavy saucepan. Stir in the flour and cook thoroughly, stirring constantly, about 4 minutes.

Strain the infused milk and then gradually add it to the butter and flour in the pan. Mix thoroughly and then bring to a boil, stirring constantly.

Reduce the heat and simmer 3-4 minutes, still stirring. Season with salt and pepper and a little more nutmeg, if desired.

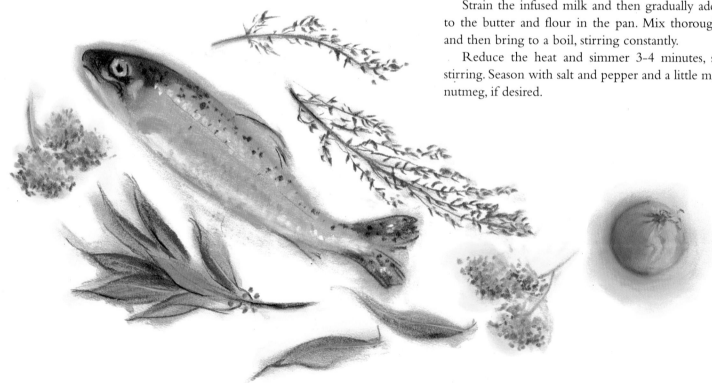

HOLLANDAISE SAUCE★

MAKES ABOUT 1¼ CUPS

14 tbsp unsalted butter
3 egg yolks★
(★see page 2 for advice on eggs)
1 tbsp lemon juice
1 tbsp dry white wine
salt and freshly ground black pepper

Melt 12 tbsp of the butter in a heavy pan over low heat. Transfer to a warmed measuring jug.

Place the egg yolks in the same pan and beat them quickly with a whisk. Add half the lemon juice, the wine, and a pinch of salt. Beat again. Add half the remaining unmelted butter and place the pan in a water bath or double boiler.

Whisking steadily, cook gently until the egg yolks are creamy in texture and beginning to thicken. Immediately remove the pan from heat and stir in the remaining unmelted butter until it is all absorbed.

Drizzle the melted butter into the yolk mixture, whisking fast. Add the butter more rapidly as the sauce thickens. When the sauce is the consistency of thick cream, add the remaining lemon juice and adjust the seasoning.

NOTES: if the sauce is too thick, it can be thinned with 1 tablespoon of water.

Hollandaise not being used immediately should be stored in the refrigerator a day or two only.

Try adding 3 tablespoons of freshly grated Parmesan cheese to the sauce for extra flavor.

HOMEMADE MAYONNAISE★

MAKES ABOUT 1 CUP

1 egg yolk★
(★see page 2 for advice on eggs)
½ tsp salt
½ tsp dry mustard
freshly ground black pepper
⅔ cup olive oil
1 tbsp white wine vinegar or lemon juice
pinch of sugar (optional)

In a bowl beat the egg yolk until thick. Then beat in the salt, mustard, and black pepper to taste.

Add the oil very slowly, drop by drop, whisking constantly so the oil is absorbed evenly. When the mayonnaise thickens and becomes shiny, add the oil in a thin steady stream. Finally, blend in the vinegar or lemon juice and sugar, if using.

NOTES: if all the mayonnaise is not being used immediately, any left should be stored in the refrigerator a day or two only.

Try flavoring the mayonnaise with 2 or 3 garlic cloves, 2 tablespoons chopped fresh minced herbs, or 1 tablespoon grated orange or lemon zest.

Make BÉARNAISE SAUCE in the same way as HOLLANDAISE, but first flavor the vinegar by boiling it with some chopped shallots, fresh tarragon, and black peppercorns.

For really exciting salad dressings, use the wide variety of flavored oils and vinegars now readily available. As appropriate, more exotic items, such as nut oils - like sesame, walnut, and hazelnut - soy sauce, tahini (sesame-seed paste), and Japanese rice vinegar are also very useful. It is also quite easy to make flavored oils and vinegars at home by adding flavoring ingredients such as fresh herbs like tarragon or rosemary, 3 or 4 garlic cloves, 1 or 2 small hot chili peppers, or some berry fruit to good-quality oil or white wine vinegar, and leaving it in a cool place several weeks.

LOW-CALORIE YOGURT DRESSING★

MAKES 2 CUPS

3 egg yolks★
(★see page 2 for advice on eggs)
2 cups thick plain yogurt
2 tsp lime or lemon juice
2 tsp Dijon-style mustard
salt and freshly ground black pepper
1 tbsp minced fresh parsley

In a bowl, beat the egg yolks, yogurt, and lemon juice together until creamy.

Stand the bowl in a pan of very gently simmering water and cook, stirring constantly, until dressing has thickened to a coating consistency, about 15 minutes.

Add the mustard, season with salt and pepper, and let cool. Stir in the parsley just before use.

Store any not being used immediately in a screw-top jar in the refrigerator a day or two only.

FRENCH VINAIGRETTE

MAKES ABOUT ⅔ CUP

2-3 garlic cloves, minced
2 tbsp wine vinegar
2 tsp Dijon-style mustard
salt and freshly ground black pepper
pinch of sugar (optional)
6 tbsp olive oil

In a bowl, whisk together the minced garlic, vinegar, mustard, salt and pepper, and sugar, if using. Add the oil and whisk together well.

If not using immediately, transfer to a screw-top jar and store in the refrigerator.

NOTE: use more or less garlic to taste. Try flavoring the dressing with the additions listed for Basic Vinaigrette.

BASIC VINAIGRETTE

MAKES ABOUT ⅔ CUP

6 tbsp olive oil
2 tbsp wine vinegar
salt and freshly ground black pepper

Pour the oil and vinegar into a screw-top jar. Seal and shake vigorously. Season and shake again.

NOTES: add 2 teaspoons of minced fresh herbs, such as parsley, chervil, or chives, for an herb vinaigrette.

Instead of these herbs, the vinaigrette can be flavored with 2 tablespoons of chopped fresh tarragon, 1 tablespoon of tomato paste with a pinch of paprika, 2 tablespoons each of minced onions and parsley, or 1 tablespoon of minced anchovy.

STRAWBERRY VINAIGRETTE

MAKES ABOUT ¼ CUP

⅓ cup strawberries
1½ tbsp strawberry vinegar or lemon juice
6 tbsp grapeseed oil
salt and freshly ground black pepper

Put the strawberries in a blender or food processor with the vinegar or lemon juice. Pulse briefly until the mixture is smooth.

With the machine running, gradually add the oil until it is all incorporated and the mixture is thick and smooth. Strain out the seeds, if desired. Season.

NOTE: serve with a cucumber salad or with cold poached chicken or salmon.

MANGO VINAIGRETTE

MAKES ABOUT ¼ CUP

1 very ripe mango, peeled
1½ tbsp red wine vinegar or lemon juice
5 tbsp sunflower or canola oil
1 tbsp minced fresh parsley
salt and freshly ground black pepper

Slice away the mango flesh coarsely from the seed.

Put the mango flesh in a blender or food processor with the vinegar or lemon juice. Pulse briefly until the mixture is smooth.

With the machine running, gradually add the oil until it is all incorporated and the mixture is thick and smooth. Stir in the parsley and season.

NOTE: serve with smoked chicken salads, or flavor with chopped fresh dill or mint and serve with smoked fish. Try flavoring it with some mustard, too.

Left: Strawberry Vinaigrette; right: Mango Vinaigrette

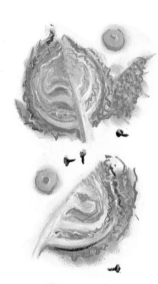
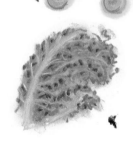

Other blue cheeses, such as Gorgonzola, Stilton, or Danish Blue, can be substituted for Roquefort in this soup, but the flavor will not be quite the same.

LEEK AND POTATO SOUP

SERVES 6-8

4 tbsp butter
2 lb leeks, sliced into ¼-inch pieces
1 lb thin-skinned potatoes (preferably red), unpeeled and coarsely diced
2 large stalks of celery, chopped
2½ cups chicken stock
2½ cups low-fat milk
½ tsp freshly grated nutmeg
salt and freshly ground black pepper
1¼ cups whipping cream
minced fresh parsley, for garnish

Melt the butter in a large heavy pan over medium heat. Add the leeks and potatoes and cook gently 7-10 minutes, stirring constantly.

Add the celery. Stir in the stock and milk and bring to a boil. Add the nutmeg and season with salt and pepper. Reduce the heat and simmer 30 minutes.

If serving cold, let cool completely and then purée in a blender or food processor. Stir in the cream and chill at least 2 hours. Adjust the seasoning, if necessary, and serve garnished with parsley.

If serving hot, stir in the cream and warm through gently, without letting it boil. Adjust the seasoning, if necessary, pour into warmed bowls, and garnish with the parsley.

NOTE: for a hot smooth soup, let the mixture cool before blending and then reheat.

ROQUEFORT AND SAVOY CABBAGE SOUP

SERVES 6-8

½ lb Canadian bacon, cut into strips
10 whole cloves
2 onions, quartered
3 leeks, chopped
4 carrots, chopped
1 large head of Savoy cabbage
4 potatoes, diced
6-8 slices of whole wheat bread, lightly toasted
½ lb Roquefort cheese
salt and freshly ground black pepper

Put 2 quarts of cold water in a pan and place over medium heat. Add the bacon and bring to a boil. Skim, then simmer 15 minutes. Skim again.

Stick the cloves into the onion quarters, and add these to the stock together with the leeks and carrots. Simmer 30 minutes longer.

Quarter the cabbage, cutting out the core and any thick ribs on outer leaves. Blanch 3 minutes in a large pan of boiling water. Drain and refresh under cold running water, then cut into strips.

Add the cabbage strips to the stock and cook 20 minutes over medium heat. Add the potatoes and simmer 30 minutes or so longer, until they are tender. Remove the cloves, if preferred.

Place a slice of toast in the bottom of each of the warmed bowls and crumble the cheese over it.

Season the soup with pepper (no salt should be necessary due to the high salt content of the cheese), pour it into the bowls and serve.

BEEFSTEAK TOMATO AND OKRA SOUP

SERVES 4

4 tbsp butter
6 scallions (including the green tops), sliced
½ lb okra, sliced
1 garlic clove, minced
3 large beefsteak tomatoes, peeled, seeded, and sliced
1 tbsp light brown sugar
1 tsp soy sauce
3½ cups vegetable stock
1 tsp grated zest amd 1 tbsp juice from a washed lemon
1 heaped tbsp chopped fresh cilantro, for garnish
salt and freshly ground black pepper

Melt the butter in a heavy pan over medium heat. Add the scallions, okra, garlic, and tomatoes and sauté gently 7 minutes. Add the remaining ingredients, cover, and simmer 10 minutes longer.

Season, and add the cilantro just before serving.

PETITPOIS AND LEMONGRASS SOUP

SERVES 4

2 stalks of lemongrass
3½ cups vegetable stock
4 tbsp butter
1 large onion, diced
2 large potatoes, diced
¾ lb (2⅓ cups) frozen small green peas, thawed
salt and freshly ground black pepper

Using a rolling pin, crush the bulbous part of the lemongrass stalks and place them in a pan. Add one-third of the stock. Cover, bring just to a simmer, and cook over very low heat 30 minutes.

Meanwhile, melt the butter in a large pan over

medium heat and toss the onion and potatoes 5 minutes. Add the remaining stock and bring to a boil. Cover and simmer 30 minutes.

Remove the pan with the lemongrass from the heat. Discard the lemongrass, then add the peas. Let them sit 15 minutes, off the heat.

Add the contents of this pan to the other. Season and let cool, then purée in a blender or food processor. Reheat the soup gently for serving.

LENTIL SOUP WITH FRESH GINGER

SERVES 4

1¼ cups red lentils, soaked overnight
1 large onion, diced
1 large purple garlic clove, minced
2 tbsp corn or canola oil
1¼ cups vegetable stock
1¼ cups low-fat milk
1 oz peeled fresh gingerroot, grated
salt and freshly ground black pepper
⅓ cup sesame seeds, toasted
1 tbsp chopped fresh parsley, to garnish

Drain the lentils thoroughly, then bring them to a boil in 2 cups of water over medium heat. Simmer until tender, 20-30 minutes.

In a large heavy pan, sauté the onion and garlic in the oil until translucent. Add the vegetable stock and milk. Bring to a boil and simmer 10 minutes. Add the lentils with their stock and the ginger. Season, then simmer 15 minutes longer. Let cool, then purée in a blender or food processor.

Reheat for serving, being careful not to let it boil. Put some of the sesame seeds in the base of each of the warmed serving bowls, but reserving some for garnish. Fill the bowls with soup and garnish with the remaining sesame seeds and the parsley.

BUTTERNUT SQUASH, *with its buff skin and yellow-orange flesh, makes a delicious soup. If unavailable, any winter squash, particularly pumpkin, will work in this recipe.*

SPICED GOLDEN SQUASH SOUP

SERVES 6

2 lb butternut squash
4 tbsp butter
white parts of 4 leeks, thinly sliced
1 tbsp coriander seeds, crushed
⅛ tsp ground allspice
⅛ tsp freshly grated nutmeg
3 cups chicken stock
salt and freshly ground black pepper
1¼ cups milk
6 tbsp light cream, for garnish

Peel the squash, cut the flesh into 1-inch cubes and discard the seeds.

Melt the butter in a large saucepan over medium heat. Add the leeks and cook, stirring, until they are soft and beginning to color, 5-6 minutes. Stir in the squash, coriander seeds, allspice, and nutmeg and cook 1 minute.

Stir in the stock, season with salt and pepper, and bring to a boil. Cover and simmer until the squash is very soft, about 35 minutes.

Purée the soup, in batches, using a blender or food processor. Return the puréed soup to the pan and stir in the milk. Reheat gently and adjust the seasoning to taste.

Serve garnished with swirls of cream.

TOMATO AND RICE SOUP WITH BASIL

SERVES 4-6

1 tbsp olive oil
1 large onion, minced
1 garlic clove, minced
1 small red sweet pepper, seeded, and chopped
1½ oz Milano or other Italian salami, chopped
2 lb ripe tomatoes, peeled, seeded, and chopped
1 tbsp tomato paste
sprig of fresh oregano
1 cup dry white wine
2½ cups chicken or vegetable stock
salt and freshly ground black pepper
⅓ cup risotto rice, preferably arborio
3 tbsp chopped fresh basil
bread sticks or crusty Italian bread, for serving

Heat the oil in a large heavy saucepan over medium heat, add the onion and garlic and cook 5 minutes, without browning. Stir in the red pepper and salami and cook 2 minutes longer.

Add the tomatoes, tomato paste, and oregano, and stir in the wine and stock. Season. Bring to a boil, then lower the heat, cover, and simmer 20 minutes.

Add the rice and basil to the pan, cover again, and continue cooking until the rice is tender, about 15 minutes.

Serve accompanied by bread sticks or crusty Italian bread.

CREAM OF MUSHROOM SOUP WITH MARSALA

SERVES 4

3 tbsp butter
1½ lb mushrooms, roughly chopped
1 shallot, minced
½ garlic clove, minced
2 tbsp flour
½ cup Marsala wine
3 cups well-flavored chicken or vegetable stock
salt and freshly ground black pepper
¾ cup whipping cream
chopped fresh flat-leaf parsley or chervil, for garnish

Melt the butter in a large heavy saucepan. Add the mushrooms, shallot, and garlic and cook 4 minutes, stirring constantly.

Stir in the flour and continue cooking 1 minute. Gradually stir in the Marsala and stock. Season and bring to a boil. Lower the heat, cover, and simmer 20 minutes.

Purée the soup in a blender or food processor, in batches if necessary, until smooth and then return it to the pan.

Just before serving, stir in all but 4 tablespoons of the cream and reheat the soup gently. Adjust the seasoning and serve garnished with swirls of the reserved cream and the parsley or chervil.

NOTE: if available, fresh wild mushrooms will give a much better flavor than cultivated ones. A mixture of mushroom varieties is best, particularly if it includes a few cèpes.

BORSCHT

SERVES 6

¾ lb cooked beets, peeled and grated
2 carrots, grated
1 onion, minced
1 celery stalk, minced
3½ cups beef stock
strip of zest and 1 tbsp juice from a washed lemon
bouquet garni
salt and freshly ground black pepper
¾ cup sour cream

Put the beets in a large pan with the carrots, onion, and celery. Stir in the stock, lemon zest, and bouquet garni. Season with salt and pepper. Bring to a boil, then lower the heat, cover, and simmer 40 minutes.

Remove the lemon zest and bouquet garni. Purée the soup, in batches, in a blender or food processor. Strain into a bowl or serving tureen and let cool.

When the soup is completely cold, stir in the lemon juice and all but 6 tablespoons of the sour cream. Adjust the seasoning to taste. Cover and chill at least 2 hours.

Swirl the reserved sour cream into the soup before serving.

Versions of
BORSCHT, *or beet soup, are traditional throughout Eastern Europe, especially in Poland and Russia. The soup can be served either hot or cold, with sour cream swirled into it.*

HERBED CREAM OF CARROT SOUP

SERVES 4–6

1 lb carrots, chopped
2 cups vegetable stock
2 tbsp butter
1 large onion, diced
1 tsp celery salt
1¼ cups light cream
freshly ground black pepper
½ tbsp each minced watercress, parsley, and chives

Put the carrots and vegetable stock in a large saucepan and slowly bring to a boil. Reduce the heat, cover, and simmer until the carrots are tender, about 15 minutes. Remove from the heat and let cool.

Melt the butter in a frying pan over medium heat and sauté the onion until translucent. Add the celery salt and stir thoroughly. Remove from the heat and let cool.

Transfer the carrots and their stock to a blender or food processor. Add the onion and blend until smooth.

Return this to the saucepan and bring almost to a boil. Remove from the heat and add the cream. Season with pepper only and stir over low heat just to warm through. Do not allow to boil or the cream will curdle.

Pour the soup into warmed bowls and sprinkle a little of each of the 3 herbs over each serving.

HERBED VEGETABLE SOUP WITH VERMICELLI

SERVES 6

1 tbsp butter
1 large onion, diced
2 crisp celery stalks, chopped
2 large carrots, chopped
2 heads of broccoli, chopped
1 large potato, diced
1 tbsp chopped fresh oregano
1½ quarts vegetable stock
3 oz vermicelli
salt and freshly ground black pepper
1 tbsp chopped fresh flat-leaf parsley
1 tbsp chopped fresh chives

Melt the butter in a large heavy saucepan over medium heat and sauté the onion until translucent.

Add the other vegetables and sauté 5 minutes, stirring constantly. Add the oregano and sauté 2 minutes longer.

Add the stock and bring it slowly to a boil. Cover and simmer 10 minutes over low heat.

Add the vermicelli, increase the heat to medium again, and cook until the vermicelli is tender.

Adjust the seasoning. Add the parsley and chives just before serving.

CHILLED CELERY ROOT AND APPLE SOUP WITH CHIVES

SERVES 4

4 tbsp butter
1½ large onions, sliced
½ tsp freshly grated nutmeg
3 firm, tart, green-skinned apples, unpeeled
and coarsely chopped
1 celery root, peeled and cut into small cubes
3 chicken bouillon cubes
2 tsp lime juice
salt and freshly ground black pepper
bunch of fresh chives

Melt the butter in a large heavy saucepan over medium heat and sauté the onions until translucent, 2-4 minutes.

Sprinkle in the nutmeg and cook 1 minute longer. Add the apples and celery root and cook 5 minutes more, stirring constantly.

Dissolve the chicken bouillon cubes in 5 cups of hot water and add this to the pan. Reduce the heat, cover, and simmer 30 minutes.

Remove the pan from the heat and let cool a little before adding the lime juice. When cold, purée the soup in a blender or food processor. Then chill overnight.

Adjust the seasoning of the chilled soup and pour it into serving bowls. Finely snip the chives over the bowls to garnish.

CHILLED AVOCADO SOUP WITH CILANTRO

SERVES 4

2 ripe avocados
juice of ½ lemon
1 tsp chili oil
3 tbsp minced fresh cilantro
1 cup thick plain yogurt
1¼ cups crème fraîche or sour cream
1¼ cups fresh tomato juice
2 cups vegetable stock
½ onion, finely shredded
salt and freshly ground black pepper

Halve and pit the avocados. Peel them and place the flesh in a large bowl with the lemon juice. Mash until smooth. Stir in the chili oil and two-thirds of the cilantro. Cover and chill 30 minutes.

Gently blend in the yogurt and crème fraîche, followed by the tomato juice and finally the stock. Stir in the shredded onion and season. Chill 2 hours.

Adjust the seasoning, if necessary, and garnish with the remaining cilantro before serving.

CELERY ROOT, *or* CELERIAC, *is a variety of celery grown for its large, spherical, fleshy white root. Long a favorite in France, it has become more widely available in this country. Usually boiled and puréed with potatoes, it is also popular shredded raw in salads.*

As in FIVE-BEAN SOUP WITH GARLIC AND GOOSEBERRY, *an alternative to spooning swirls of cream decoratively into soups before serving is to add fruit and vegetable purées with complementary colors and flavors. Try avocado purée in tomato soup, tomato purée in spinach soup, and applesauce in pea and ham soup.*

CHILLED BEET AND HORSERADISH SOUP

SERVES 6-8

6 raw beets (see below)
1½ quarts chicken stock
8 scallions (including green tops), chopped
½ cucumber, peeled, halved lengthwise, and seeded
juice of ½ lime
1 tsp dark brown sugar
2 tsp freshly grated horseradish root
⅔ cup light cream
salt and freshly ground black pepper
6-8 tbsp sour cream
2 large dill pickles, thinly sliced, for garnish
½ tbsp minced fresh dill leaves, for garnish

Try to buy beets which still have their stems and leaves and an intact skin. It is also a good idea to buy ones of a uniform size so that they will cook in the same time.

Put the stock in a large pan and bring to a boil. Place the beets gently in the stock, cover, and simmer until they are completely tender, 15-20 minutes.

Trying to avoid breaking the skins, remove the beets from the stock. Let cool completely and reserve the stock.

Once cool, peel and coarsely dice the beets and leaves. Purée in a blender or food processor, together with the scallions and cucumber.

Mix with the reserved stock, lime juice, sugar, horseradish, and light cream. Chill at least 3 hours.

To serve: adjust the seasoning and pour the chilled soup into bowls. Place a spoonful of sour cream in the middle of each bowl, then garnish with the slices of pickle and some minced dill leaves.

FIVE-BEAN SOUP WITH GARLIC AND GOOSEBERRY

SERVES 6

3 tbsp butter
1 tbsp olive oil
3 garlic cloves, sliced
1 large onion, sliced
2 leeks, cut into ½-inch slices
3½ cups vegetable stock
½ lb potatoes, cut into small chunks
1½ cups fresh gooseberries, halved
3 cups mixed cooked beans: kidney, flageolet, lima, navy, and black-eyed pea
salt and freshly ground pepper

Melt the butter with the oil in a large heavy pan over low heat. Add the garlic and cook gently 3 minutes, stirring constantly. Add the onion and leeks and sauté 5 minutes.

Add the stock and bring to a boil. Reduce the heat, add the potatoes, and simmer until they are tender, 15-20 minutes.

Place the gooseberries in a small pan with a few spoonfuls of water and bring to a boil. Simmer until they are reduced to a pulp. Remove from the heat, let cool a little, and then push them through a strainer to make a coulis.

Add the cooked beans to the potato and vegetable broth. Heat through but do not bring to a boil.

Season and pour into warmed soup bowls. Drizzle some of the gooseberry coulis into each and serve immediately.

Left: Five-Bean Soup with Garlic and Gooseberry; right: Chilled Beet and Horseradish Soup

The very fine green LENTILS FROM LE PUY in France are actually almost purple in color. They have an incomparable flavor and cook very quickly. If none are available use any green lentils, but they will need longer cooking.

GREEN LENTIL SOUP WITH HERBES DE PROVENCE

SERVES 4

1¼ cups green lentils, preferably Le Puy
2 tbsp butter
1 large onion, coarsely chopped
½ lb tomatoes, coarsely chopped
1 tbsp herbes de Provence
salt and freshly ground black pepper
1 tbsp chopped fresh flat-leaf parsley, for garnish

Wash the lentils thoroughly, then put them in a large heavy saucepan with 3½ cups of water. Bring to a boil, then simmer gently until the lentils are tender, 15–20 minutes. Set them aside in their stock.

Melt the butter in a frying pan over medium heat and add the onion. Sauté until translucent, then add the tomatoes and herbs and stir constantly for 5 minutes. Transfer the contents of the frying pan to the lentil pan. Season, cover, and let cool.

When cool, purée the soup in a blender or food processor or push it through a strainer. Return to a medium heat and gently warm it through.

Serve in warmed bowls, sprinkled with parsley.

CREAM OF BLACK-EYED PEA SOUP

SERVES 6-8

2⅓ cups black-eyed peas, soaked overnight in cold water
6 tbsp butter
3 onions, chopped
¾ cup chopped carrots
¾ cup chopped celery
2 garlic cloves, minced
1½ quarts vegetable stock
bouquet garni
1 tsp lemon juice
salt and freshly ground black pepper
1 cup light cream
1-2 tbsp cranberry sauce
1 tbsp minced fresh parsley, for garnish

Drain the peas, put them in a pan, and cover with fresh cold water. Bring to a boil, drain, and cover again with fresh water. Bring to a boil once more, cover, and simmer until tender, about 40 minutes.

Melt the butter in a frying pan over medium-low heat. Add the onions, carrots, celery, and garlic and sauté 10 minutes. Transfer the vegetables to a large pan, and add the vegetable stock, cooked peas, and the bouquet garni. Bring to a boil, cover, and simmer 20 minutes.

Discard the bouquet garni. Add the lemon juice and season the soup to taste. Let cool.

When cool, purée the soup in a blender or food processor. Stir in the cream, then heat through, being careful not to let it boil.

Ladle the soup into 6-8 warmed bowls and spoon some of the cranberry sauce in the center of each. Garnish with parsley and serve.

LENTIL AND HAM SOUP WITH MUSHROOM TOASTS

SERVES 6

2 tbsp butter
1 large onion, chopped
1 garlic clove, minced
1 carrot, finely diced
1 celery stalk, finely diced
1¼ cups red lentils
1 bay leaf
sprig of fresh thyme
salt and freshly ground black pepper
1 tbsp chopped fresh parsley (optional)
FOR THE HAM STOCK
1 meaty smoked ham hock, weighing about 1½ lb
1 onion, quartered
1 carrot, quartered
6 black peppercorns
FOR THE MUSHROOM TOASTS
3 tbsp butter
½ cup finely chopped mushrooms
2 tsp chopped fresh parsley
½ garlic clove, minced
6 small slices of French bread

First prepare the ham stock: put the ham hock in a large pot, cover it with water, and bring to a boil. Boil 1 minute, then discard this salty cooking water.

Add 1¼ quarts of fresh cold water to the pot with the onion, carrot, and peppercorns. Return to a boil, then lower the heat, cover, and simmer until the ham is tender, about 1½ hours.

Transfer the hock to a plate and let it cool. Then cut the meat into small dice or flake it with a fork and set aside. Let the stock cool, then remove the fat that rises to the surface. Strain the stock and reserve.

Melt the butter in a large saucepan over medium heat. Add the onion, garlic, carrot, and celery and cook, stirring, for 3-4 minutes. Stir in the lentils, bay leaf, and thyme and add the reserved ham stock. Bring to a boil, then lower the heat, cover, and simmer 1-1½ hours.

About 10 minutes before serving, make the mushroom toasts. Preheat the broiler.

Melt the butter in a small heavy pan over medium-high heat. Add the mushrooms, parsley, and garlic and cook, stirring frequently, until all the liquid that exudes from the mushrooms is evaporated. Season with salt and pepper.

Toast the bread slices on one side under the broiler. Then turn them over and divide the mushroom mixture among them. Broil 1 minute longer, until well heated.

Season the soup with salt and pepper. Remove and discard the bay and thyme and stir in the parsley, if using. Serve piping hot, accompanied by the mushroom toasts.

The MUSHROOM TOASTS *make good appetizers or snacks on their own. Just double or triple the quantities, depending on appetites.*

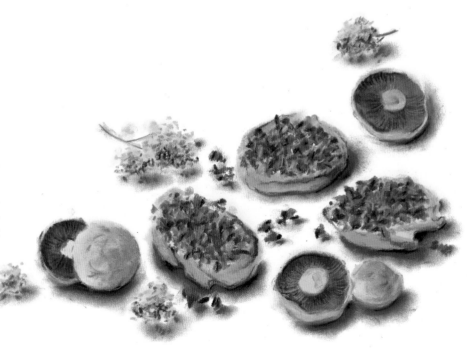

MINESTRONE SOUP

SERVES 6-8

6 oz piece of pancetta, chopped
1 large onion, minced
1 garlic clove, minced
3 carrots, diced
3 celery stalks, thinly sliced
½ lb potatoes, diced
1 lb tomatoes, peeled and chopped
1 cup dried white kidney beans, soaked overnight
in cold water
5 cups stock or water
½ head of small green cabbage, finely shredded
2 zucchini, thinly sliced
1 cup shelled fresh or frozen green peas
5 oz macaroni or other small pasta
2 tbsp chopped fresh flat-leaf parsley
handful of fresh basil leaves, shredded
salt and freshly ground black pepper
½ cup freshly grated Parmesan cheese, for serving

Put the pancetta in a large, heavy-based saucepan over medium heat and cook until the fat begins to melt, about 3-4 minutes. Add the onion and cook until soft, about 5 minutes.

Stir in the garlic, carrots, celery, potatoes, tomatoes, and drained beans. Pour in the stock and bring to a boil. Lower the heat, cover, and simmer until the beans are tender, about 2 hours.

Add the cabbage, zucchini, peas, macaroni, and parsley to the pan, cover and cook 20 minutes longer.

Just before serving, stir in the basil and season with salt and pepper. Serve piping hot, sprinkled with freshly grated Parmesan.

Clockwise from the top center: Minestrone Soup, Lentil and Ham Soup (page 25) and Cream of Mushroom Soup with Marsala (page 19)

SPRING CHICKEN AND LEEK SOUP

SERVES 4

5 tbsp olive oil
1 large onion, chopped
2 bay leaves
sprig of fresh thyme
2 dressed Cornish game hens, each weighing about 1 lb
⅔ cup dry white wine
1 lb leeks, diced
¼ lb potatoes, diced
⅛ tsp freshly grated nutmeg
salt and freshly ground black pepper
⅔ cup whipping cream

Heat 2 tablespoons of the oil in a large heavy pot over medium heat, add the onion, and cook, stirring, until it is pale golden in color, about 10 minutes .

Add the bay leaves, thyme, and Cornish game hens to the pan and pour over the wine. Add just enough water to cover the birds (about 3½ cups). Bring to a boil, then lower the heat, cover and simmer until the birds are cooked, 30-40 minutes, .

Remove the birds from the stock and set aside until cool enough to handle. Strain the stock into a large bowl, discarding the herbs and onion.

Heat the remaining oil in the pot. Add the leeks and potatoes and sauté 2-3 minutes. Pour over the reserved stock and bring to a boil. Season with freshly grated nutmeg, salt, and pepper. Cover and simmer 25-30 minutes, stirring occasionally.

Meanwhile, remove the meat from the birds, and cut it into dice or strips. Add these to the soup.

Just before serving, stir the cream into the soup and warm through gently. Adjust the seasoning to taste, if necessary.

The exact recipe for MINESTRONE, *the classic vegetable soup of Italy, varies from region to region. Generally, however, it is garnished with pasta and sprinkled with grated Parmesan cheese.*

LEMONGRASS *is native to Southeast Asia, and its citrus tang is a basic flavor in much of the cooking of the area, especially Thai cuisine. It remains fibrous even after lengthy cooking so it is best removed after it has imparted its flavor. Once available only from specialty markets, or in its powdered form, known as* SEREH, *the long pale green stalks with bulbous bases are now a common sight in many supermarkets.*

FINNAN HADDIE *is smoked haddock. Originally a British specialty, it is also produced in New England.*

ARTICHOKE SOUP WITH LEMONGRASS

SERVES 6

2 stalks of lemongrass
1 lb large Jerusalem artichokes (sunchokes), unpeeled and coarsely chopped
6 tbsp butter
2 large onions, sliced
1 garlic clove, minced
5 cups chicken stock
¼ cup light cream (optional)
salt and freshly ground black pepper
1 tbsp minced fresh parsley, for garnish

Bring a large pan of water to a boil.

Crush the bulb ends of the lemongrass stalks, then place them in the pan of water with the artichokes and simmer 10 minutes. Drain the artichokes, reserving the lemongrass.

Melt the butter in a large heavy saucepan over medium heat. Add the onions and garlic and sauté about 3 minutes. Reduce the heat, cover, and simmer 5 minutes.

Add the pieces of artichoke and stir them into the onions and garlic. Then add the stock and bring to a boil. Add the reserved lemongrass, cover, and simmer 20 minutes. Remove from heat and let cool. Remove and discard the lemongrass.

Purée the mixture in a blender or food processor. Return it to the pan and reheat gently. Stir in the cream, if using, and adjust the seasoning.

Pour the soup into warmed serving bowls and garnish with parsley.

FISH CHOWDER WITH HORSERADISH

SERVES 6

1 lb skinned cod fillet
1 lb skinned finnan haddie fillet
5 cups milk
1 lb potatoes, peeled and diced
2½ cups fish stock
4 tbsp butter
½ lb onions, sliced
1 tbsp finely grated fresh horseradish
juice of ½ lemon
salt and freshly ground black pepper
½ cup drained canned whole-kernel corn (optional)

Put the fish in a large saucepan and cover with the milk. Bring to just below a boil over medium heat and simmer gently 20 minutes, or until the flesh flakes readily.

In another pan, put the potatoes and the fish stock. Bring to a boil and simmer 15 minutes.

Melt the butter in a frying pan over medium heat and sauté the onions until translucent, about 5 minutes,

Pour the potatoes and their stock into the fish pan, then add the onions in their butter. Sprinkle the horseradish on top and mix gently. Add the lemon juice.

Slowly bring the contents of the pan to a simmer and cook very gently for 15 minutes over very low heat. Season and add the corn, if using.

Pour into warmed bowls and serve immediately.

Clockwise from the left: Herbed Cream of Carrot Soup (page 20), Artichoke Soup with Lemongrass, and Fish Chowder with Horseradish

The flavor of THAI SHRIMP SOUP *relies on fragrant* LEMONGRASS *and* KAFFIR LIME LEAVES, *which add a strong citrus note without acidity. These are available, fresh or dried, from Asian markets. Lemon or lime zest can be used instead, but will not give the same distinctive taste.* GALANGAL, *a spice related to ginger, is available from Asian markets. Fresh gingerroot can be substituted.*

QUICK CHICKEN AND COCONUT SOUP

SERVES 4

2 cups chicken stock
grated zest of ½ washed lime,
juice of 1½ limes
3 tbsp fish sauce
1 tsp ground ginger
½ tsp chili powder
1¼ cups thick canned coconut milk
6 oz skinless boneless chicken breasts, cut across into thin slices
chopped fresh cilantro, for garnish
sliced hot chili peppers, for garnish (optional)

Put the stock in a saucepan with the lime zest and juice, the fish sauce, ginger, and chili powder and simmer 5 minutes.

Add the coconut milk and chicken slices and simmer until the chicken is just cooked through, 2-3 minutes longer.

Pour into 4 warmed bowls and garnish with cilantro and chili slices, if using.

THAI SHRIMP SOUP

SERVES 4

¾ lb raw medium shrimp in their shells
3 hot chili peppers
1 tbsp vegetable oil
2 stalks of lemongrass, thinly sliced
3 Kaffir lime leaves
3 slices of galangal, each about ½-inch thick
2 garlic cloves, chopped
2 tbsp fish sauce, or more to taste
juice of ½ lime
1 tbsp chopped fresh cilantro, for garnish
3 chopped scallions, for garnish

Remove the shells from the shrimp; put the shrimp to one side and reserve the shells. Seed the chili peppers. Coarsely chop 2 of them and thinly slice the third into rings.

Heat the oil in a saucepan over medium heat and fry the shrimp shells until they turn pink, 1-2 minutes.

Add 1½ quarts of water, the coarsely chopped chili peppers, the lemongrass, Kaffir lime leaves, galangal, garlic, and fish sauce. Bring to a boil, then reduce the heat, and simmer 20 minutes. Strain into a clean pan and discard the solids.

Add the shrimp and cook until they become pink and opaque, 3-4 minutes. Do not overcook or the shrimp will become tough and tasteless.

Add the lime juice and, if the soup seems too bland, add a little more fish sauce to taste.

Pour into 4 warmed bowls and garnish with the rings of chili pepper, the cilantro, and the chopped scallions.

CORN AND CRAB SOUP★

SERVES 4

3½ cups chicken stock
½-inch cube of peeled fresh gingerroot, crushed through a
garlic press or minced
1 tsp soy sauce
1 tsp sugar
1½ cups canned or frozen whole-kernel corn, drained or
thawed
1 tbsp cornstarch
3 tbsp dry sherry
1½ cups flaked crab meat
1 egg white★, lightly beaten
(★see page 2 for advice on eggs)
1 tsp Asian sesame oil
6 tbsp chopped cooked ham, for garnish (optional)
1 thinly sliced scallion, for garnish

Put the chicken stock in a saucepan with the ginger,
soy sauce, sugar, and corn. Bring to a boil, then reduce
the heat and simmer 2-3 minutes.

In a small bowl, mix the cornstarch with the
sherry. Remove the pan from the heat and whisk the
cornstarch mixture into the soup. Simmer until the
soup thickens, about 2 minutes longer.

Add the crab meat and cook another minute or so
to warm it through.

Remove the soup from the heat once more.
Whisk the egg white with the sesame oil and then
vigorously whisk this into the soup so that it forms
white strands.

Pour into 4 warmed bowls and sprinkle with
chopped ham, if using, and the sliced scallion.

HOT AND SOUR SOUP

SERVES 4

4 dried Chinese mushrooms
5 cups chicken stock
¼ lb skinless boneless chicken breast, cut into thin slivers
3 oz peeled cooked small shrimp
4 oz tofu, cut into ½-inch cubes
¼ cup chopped canned bamboo shoots, drained
½ cup frozen peas
2 scallions, chopped
2 tbsp soy sauce
3 tbsp rice or white wine vinegar
2 tbsp cornstarch
salt and freshly ground black pepper
1 tsp Asian sesame oil, for serving

Soak the dried mushrooms in warm water for 30
minutes. Drain them, remove and discard the stems,
and slice the caps thinly.

Bring the stock to a boil in a saucepan, add the
mushrooms and chicken, and simmer 10 minutes.

Add the shrimp, tofu, bamboo shoots, peas, and
scallions and simmer 2 more minutes.

In a bowl, mix together the soy sauce, vinegar,
cornstarch, and 6 tablespoons of water. Season with
salt and plenty of pepper to give the soup its
characteristic "hot" flavor.

Stir this mixture into the soup and simmer until
the soup thickens, about 2 mintues longer.

Pour the soup into warmed bowls and add a few
drops of sesame oil to each before serving.

A wide variety of
bottled FISH SAUCES
is made from
fermented fish by
various Asian
countries. This salty
condiment, used as a
flavor-enhancer and
not just in fish
dishes, is available
from Asian
supermarkets.

TOFU, or soybean
curd, is available
from most
supermarkets and
health-food stores as
well as Asian
markets.

APPETIZERS AND SNACKS

*T*he worldwide popularity and influence of Mediterranean-style cuisine have made us all familiar with the *tapas* of Spain and the *mezze* of the Aegean and Middle East. These assortments of little tidbits can be served just to accompany drinks, as first courses prior to a simple main dish of plainly cooked fish or meat, or they can even make meals in themselves.

What characterizes the dishes in this chapter is their flexibility. Some, like Bresaola with Lemon Vinaigrette or the devilishly easy Smoked Mackerel Pâté with Horseradish, make perfect first courses for formal meals. Others, like Spicy Hummus with Tahini and Assorted Phyllo Pastry Parcels, are classic *mezze*. Many, like Bruschette with Tomatoes and Crostini with Wild Mushrooms, make elegant and satisfying snacks at any time of the day. All may be used singly or in conjunction with others to make meals for any occasion.

Clockwise from the left: Pissaladière (page 34), Crostini with Wild Mushrooms (page 35), and Bruschette with Tomatoes (page 34).

PISSALADIÈRE

SERVES 4

FOR THE DOUGH
1½ tsp active dry yeast
1⅔ cups all-purpose flour, plus more for dusting
1 egg, lightly beaten
½ tsp salt
1 tbsp olive oil

FOR THE TOPPING
5 tbsp olive oil
2¼ lb onions, very thinly sliced
3 garlic cloves, minced
1 bay leaf
1 tsp chopped fresh thyme or ½ tsp dried thyme
1 tsp chopped fresh basil or ½ tsp dried basil
1 tsp chopped fresh rosemary or ½ tsp dried rosemary
salt and freshly ground black pepper
3 tbsp red wine
1 tbsp capers, drained and mashed
1 cup canned plum tomatoes, drained and chopped
24 canned anchovy fillets, drained and cut in half
lengthwise
24 small pitted black olives

PISSALADIÈRES, a specialty of the Provence region of France, are flat, open tarts not dissimilar to Italian pizzas.

First make the dough: dissolve the yeast in ⅓ cup of warm water. Sift the flour into a warm bowl and form a well in the center of it.

When the yeast mixture is spongy, pour it into the middle of the well together with the egg and salt. Gradually mix in the flour from the edges until the mixture forms a smooth dough.

Turn it onto a floured surface and knead until smooth and elastic, about 5 minutes.

Generously grease a bowl with the oil, place the ball of dough in it, and turn the ball well to coat it thoroughly with the oil. Cover with a damp cloth and let rise in a warm place until it has risen to about twice its original bulk, about 1 hour.

Meanwhile make the topping: put 4 tablespoons of oil in a large frying pan (preferably with a lid) over medium heat and add the onions, garlic, bay leaf, and other herbs. Season well and cook until the onions are translucent, about 5 minutes. Add the wine, capers, and tomatoes. Stir well, cover, and cook over low heat   until the onions are very soft, about 30 minutes longer.

Preheat the oven to 475°F and grease a 10-inch pie or pizza pan, or a baking sheet, with a little of the remaining olive oil.

Remove the risen dough from the bowl and knead it briefly on a lightly floured surface. Then roll it out and use it to line the pie or pizza pan, or simply press it into the pan so that it is higher at the edges and there is a hollow in the center. Alternatively, form the dough into a similar round container on the prepared baking sheet.

Adjust the seasoning of the onion mixture and spoon it into the center of the pie, leaving a broad rim around the edge. Using the strips of anchovy, make a lattice pattern on top of the filling and press the olives into the spaces between. Brush the uncovered rim with the remaining olive oil. Let the pissaladière rise in a warm place, about 15 minutes.

Bake until the dough is crisp and brown, 20-25 minutes. Serve hot or warm.

NOTE: defrosted frozen bread dough, pizza dough, or pie pastry also works well in this recipe.

BRUSCHETTE WITH TOMATOES

SERVES 4

2 loaves of flat Italian bread (ciabatta)
2 large garlic cloves, minced
¼ cup extra virgin olive oil
4 large, very ripe tomatoes, halved
salt and freshly ground black pepper
tiny basil or tarragon leaves, for garnish (optional)

Preheat the broiler.

Split each loaf in half lengthwise (start by cutting the crusts with a knife, but try to pry the halves apart and not to slice all through cleanly, as it is necessary to create a rough surface). Then cut each of these pieces crosswise in half.

Toast the pieces of bread under the broiler, rough sides uppermost, until just beginning to brown.

While the bread is still very warm, spread each piece with some minced garlic, brush generously with oil, and then rub a tomato half all over the surface to spread the tomato pulp on it. Season well.

Return to the broiler briefly just to warm through and then garnish with the herbs, if using.

BRESAOLA WITH LEMON MUSTARD VINAIGRETTE

SERVES 4

2 washed lemons
⅓ cup extra virgin olive oil
2 tsp English mustard
salt and freshly ground black pepper
20 slices of bresaola
2 tbsp minced fresh flat-leaf parsley
about 12 tiny cherry tomatoes, for garnish
radicchio leaves, for garnish

Finely grate 2 teaspoons of zest from one of the lemons and extract 1 tablespoon of its juice. Cut the other lemon into wedges.

In a small bowl, blend the lemon zest and juice with the oil, mustard, and seasoning to taste.

Fan the slices of beef decoratively on a plate. Just before serving, mix the dressing together well again and drizzle it over the slices of beef.

Sprinkle with the parsley, garnish with the cherry tomatoes nestling in radicchio leaves, and serve with the lemon wedges.

CROSTINI WITH WILD MUSHROOMS

SERVES 4

4 tbsp extra virgin olive oil
4 garlic cloves, minced
½ lb mixed fresh wild mushrooms, preferably including some cèpes, sliced
3 tbsp lemon juice
2 tbsp chopped fresh flat-leaf parsley
salt and freshly ground black pepper
8 thick slices of crusty white Italian bread
1 tbsp anchovy paste
1 buffalo or fresh mozzarella cheese, thinly sliced
cayenne pepper

Preheat the broiler or the oven to 350°F.

In a large frying pan, heat 2 tablespoons of the oil over medium heat and sauté the garlic gently until translucent. Add the mushroom slices and sauté over medium-high heat until the mushrooms are just beginning to give off their liquid.

Increase the heat and cook briskly 3-4 minutes until the liquid has evaporated and the mushrooms are beginning to brown. Stir in the lemon juice and most of the parsley. Season with salt.

Meanwhile lightly toast the slices of bread under the broiler or in the oven.

Spread the toasted slices of bread sparingly with the anchovy paste and then brush them with the remaining oil. Spoon the sautéed mushroom mixture in heaps in the center, reserving some of the better-looking mushroom slices for garnish.

Cover the mushrooms with slices of mozzarella and sprinkle some pepper over the cheese. Broil or bake until the cheese is bubbling.

Garnish with the reserved mushrooms and parsley and dust lightly with cayenne before serving piping hot.

BRESAOLA *is a specialty of Italy's Lombardy province. Best quality beef is sliced very thinly and air-cured. It is available from Italian groceries.*

BRUSCHETTE *could be described as Italian garlic bread while* CROSTINI *are more like a type of toasted sandwich.*

If fresh wild mushrooms are difficult to obtain, use equal parts button mushrooms, oyster mushrooms or fresh shiitake, and dried cèpes (porcini), soaked in warm water 20 minutes.

SPICY HUMMUS WITH TAHINI

SERVES 4

1¼ cups dried chickpeas (garbanzos), soaked overnight, or
2½ cups canned chickpeas, drained
3 or 4 large garlic cloves, minced
juice of 3 lemons
3 tbsp extra virgin olive oil
2 tsp ground cumin
salt
cayenne pepper
⅔ cup tahini paste
2 tbsp minced fresh flat-leaf parsley
1 tbsp toasted pine nuts, for garnish (optional)
pita bread, cut into strips, for serving

Rinse the chickpeas thoroughly (carefully removing any debris and shed skins). Cover the chickpeas with water, bring to a boil, and simmer them until quite tender: just over 1 hour for dried chickpeas and only 10-15 minutes for canned chickpeas.

Drain thoroughly, reserving a little of the liquid, and purée the chickpeas into a food processor or mash them in a bowl. Add the garlic, lemon juice, 2 or 3 tablespoons of the cooking liquid, 1 tablespoon of oil, 1 teaspoon of cumin, a generous pinch of salt, and a pinch of cayenne.

Add most of the tahini and mix again to a thick, creamy consistency. Adjust the consistency, if necessary, with more tahini, cooking liquid or lemon juice. Adjust the seasoning with salt and cayenne. Turn the mixture out into a shallow serving dish. Mix the remaining oil with a pinch of cayenne and a pinch of the remaining cumin. Drizzle this over the top of the hummus.

Sprinkle with the parsley and decorate with the remaining cumin and some more cayenne (a star pattern is traditional). Dot with the pine nuts, if using. Serve with pita strips or crudités.

Now familiar all over the world, the Middle-Eastern chickpea purée, HUMMUS, traditionally appears on most mezze tables. Such purées may simply be flavored with garlic and salt, or - as here - with lemon juice, cumin, and tahini paste, made from crushed sesame seeds, to give a fine nutty flavor. The earthy taste of tahini is also essential to the classic Turkish eggplant dip, BABA GHANOUJ. The eggplants must first be charred to impart the right degree of smokiness. Serve both these dips with strips of pita bread or crudités, such as celery stalks, sticks of cucumber and zucchini, and sweet pepper strips.

BABA GHANOUJ

SERVES 4

2-3 large eggplants
3 large garlic cloves, minced
1 small onion, grated
salt
pinch of paprika
juice of 2 large lemons
7 tbsp tahini paste
2 tsp minced fresh mint, cilantro or flat-leaf parsley, for garnish
tiny pitted black olives, for garnish
1 tbsp olive oil, for serving
pita bread or crudités, for serving

Preheat the broiler or the oven to 450°F.

Either broil the eggplants, turning them regularly, or bake them in the oven, until the skins are black and blistered, about 30 minutes.

Let them cool slightly and then peel off the charred skin. Rinse the eggplants and squeeze them firmly to extract their bitter juices.

Chop the eggplant flesh coarsely and put into a blender or mash it in a bowl. Add the garlic, onion, a large pinch of salt, paprika, and some of the lemon juice. Blend lightly and then add alternating small amounts of the tahini paste and remaining lemon juice. The final consistency should be thick and smooth. Adjust this and the seasoning with more salt, tahini, or lemon juice.

Turn into a serving bowl and garnish with the herbs and olives. Just before serving with pita bread or crudités, drizzle the oil over the top.

Clockwise from the top left: Assorted Phyllo Pastry Parcels (page 38), Grape Leaves Stuffed with Seafood Mousse (page 39), Baba Ghanouj, baby eggplants, black olives, and Spicy Hummus with Tahini served with crudités

ASSORTED PHYLLO PASTRY PARCELS

MAKES ABOUT 48

1 lb phyllo pastry, thawed if frozen
olive oil, for greasing
salt and freshly ground black pepper
FOR THE CHEESE FILLING
½ lb feta cheese
2 tbsp finely chopped walnuts
2 tbsp minced fresh chervil or chives
1 extra large egg, separated
FOR THE SHRIMP FILLING
½ cup crab meat
2 garlic cloves, minced
2 scallions, minced
3 tbsp mayonnaise
2 tbsp minced fresh flat-leaf parsley
juice of 1 lemon
15 large cooked shrimp, shelled and deveined
FOR THE SAUSAGE FILLING
4 small chorizo sausages, cut across into quarters
2 tbsp minced fresh flat-leaf parsley
cayenne pepper

Preheat the oven to 375°F and grease 2 baking sheets with oil.

First make the fillings. For the cheese filling, crumble the cheese into a bowl and stir in the nuts, herbs, and lightly beaten egg yolk. Season and add just enough lightly beaten egg white to give a mixture with a thick but spoonable consistency.

For the shrimp filling, in a bowl mix all the ingredients except the lemon juice and shrimp. Season and add just enough of the lemon juice to give a good sharp flavor and a thick but spoonable consistency.

Remove the sheets of phyllo pastry from their package only 2 or 3 at a time, reseal the package and return to the refrigerator. Use a damp cloth to cover those sheets not being worked with at any given time to prevent them drying out.

For the shrimp purses: cut out 45 x 4-inch squares of phyllo. Oil lightly. For each purse, arrange 3 squares on top of one another so that the corners form a star shape. Put the filling in the center, press a shrimp into it, and then pull up the edges and twist around to form a coinpurse. Make sure the pastry is not too tightly wrapped around the filling. Brush the outsides of the purses lightly all over with oil.

For the cheese triangles: cut the phyllo in long strips about 3 inches wide and brush these lightly with oil. Place a generous spoonful of the cheese filling on one end of each strip about 1 inch from that end and slightly off-center. Lifting the corner of the end farther from the filling, fold the pastry in to cover it and form a triangle. Then fold this stuffed triangle on its side parallel to the short edge of the strip of pastry up and over on the strip. Next fold this triangle on its diagonal slide over onto the strip of pastry. Continue until all the strip is used. Press the edges lightly to seal the triangle well, and brush the outside lightly with oil.

For the sausage "cigars": cut the phyllo into the same long strips as for the cheese triangles and lightly oil them. Place a piece of sausage at one end parallel to the short ends, sprinkle with a little cayenne and some parsley, and simply roll up, tucking in the edges as you go. Brush the finished "cigars" lightly with oil.

Arrange on the baking sheets and bake until just golden, about 25 minutes. Serve hot or warm with cocktails or as part of a buffet meal.

GRAPE LEAVES STUFFED WITH SEAFOOD MOUSSE

MAKES 18

2 washed lemons
4 large garlic cloves
1 tbsp oil
1 onion, minced
2 tsp minced fresh gingerroot
2 tbsp minced bulb fennel
½ lb white fish fillets, skinned
1 celery stalk, chopped into small dice
3 tbsp minced fresh cilantro
1 egg, separated
½ cup cooked rice
3 oz cooked shelled bay or tiny shrimp
3 oz canned shucked baby clams, drained
salt and freshly ground black pepper
about 24 large grape leaves
2 cups canned plum tomatoes, chopped
2 tbsp minced fresh flat-leaf parsley
1 tbsp tomato paste
lemon slices, for serving

Finely grate 1 teaspoon of zest from one of the lemons and extract the juice from both. Cut 1 of the garlic cloves into fine slivers and mince the rest.

Put the oil in a sauté pan over medium heat. Add the onion, three-quarters of the minced garlic, the ginger, and fennel and sauté until the onion is soft but not browned.

In a food processor, purée the fish, celery, cilantro, egg yolk, grated lemon zest, half the lemon juice, and the sautéed mixture. Be careful not to over-process! Stir in the rice, shrimp, and clams. Season generously.

Beat the egg white to stiff peaks and then stir a spoonful into the stuffing to loosen it. Gently fold the remaining egg white into the mixture.

If using grape leaves preserved in brine, cover with boiling water, stir well, and let soak about 30 minutes.

Drain and rinse with cold water. Repeat the process. If using fresh leaves, blanch about 15 minutes in boiling water and then drain well.

Arrange 18 of the best leaves (don't use any with holes or tears) with vein sides up. Put a generous spoonful of stuffing on each leaf, near its base. Roll up the leaf from the base, tucking in the sides as you go. Take care not to wrap the filling too tightly as it needs a little room to expand. Squeeze the parcel gently in the palm to secure it.

Line a large heavy-based saucepan with the remaining grape leaves and arrange the rolled leaves on them with the tips tucked underneath to keep them rolled during cooking. Combine the remaining lemon juice and minced garlic, tomatoes and their liquid, parsley, garlic slivers, and tomato paste. Season and pour over the parcels. Cover and simmer over very low heat 30 minutes.

Serve the stuffed grape leaves hot, with a little of the cooking juices and garnished with lemon slices.

Sweet peppers broiled as in the MARINATED PEPPERS *recipe develop a unique smoky flavor. Do not peel them under running water (as some other recipes suggest!) or you will lose all the flavorful juices.*

MARINATED PEPPERS WITH PINE NUTS AND CAPERS

SERVES 4

*4-6 (depending on size) red or yellow sweet peppers,
quartered and seeded
1 tbsp pine nuts
1 tbsp capers, rinsed and drained
crusty sourdough or French bread for serving*
FOR THE GARLIC VINAIGRETTE
*1 tbsp vinegar
3 tbsp extra virgin olive oil, plus more for greasing
1 garlic clove, minced
salt and pepper*

Preheat the broiler. Line the broiler pan with foil and lightly grease it with olive oil.

Place the pepper quarters, skin side up, in a single layer in the prepared pan and broil until all the skin is blackened.

Put the pepper quarters in a plastic bag. Seal the bag and let the peppers cook in their own steam for 5 minutes. Then remove the blackened skin, but do not rinse the peppers as this will wash away the precious tasty juices.

Make the garlic vinaigrette by combining the ingredients in a bowl with some seasoning. Add the pepper pieces and toss gently but thoroughly to coat them well. Cover the bowl with plastic wrap and let marinate at room temperature 1-2 hours, or in the refrigerator up to 24.

To serve: arrange the pepper pieces in one layer on an attractive serving plate and drizzle over any dressing remaining in the bowl. Scatter the pine nuts and capers on the top. Accompany with crusty bread to mop up the juices.

AÏOLI WITH QUAIL EGGS, SHRIMP, AND CRUDITÉS★

SERVES 4

*12 quail eggs
about 1 lb mixed raw vegetables (such as carrots, celery,
cucumber, radishes, cherry tomatoes, seeded
sweet peppers, broccoli, cauliflower, zucchini, sugar snap
peas, snow peas, and button mushrooms), cut into sticks or
bite-sized pieces as necessary
12 shelled cooked large shrimp*
FOR THE AÏOLI
*2 garlic cloves, minced
1 egg★
(★see page 2 for advice on eggs)
salt and pepper
¾ cup sunflower or corn oil
1 tsp white wine vinegar or lemon juice*

First make the aïoli: put the garlic and egg in the bowl of a blender or food processor and season generously with salt and pepper.

With the motor running, add the oil in a slow trickle. The sauce will thicken. Add the vinegar or lemon juice and process for a couple of seconds more.

Transfer the aïoli to a serving bowl and set it aside for at least 30 minutes before serving, to let the rich flavors develop fully.

Meanwhile, boil the quail eggs 3 minutes, then cool them under cold running water.

To serve: place the bowl of aïoli in the middle of a large plate and surround it with the vegetable crudités, quail eggs, and shrimp for dipping.

*Top: Aïoli with Quail Eggs, Shrimp, and Crudités;
bottom: Marinated Peppers with Pine Nuts and Capers.*

For the AÏOLI WITH QUAIL EGGS, SHRIMP, AND CRUDITÉS *you can make your own selection of vegetables according to what are the freshest and best available.* AÏOLI *is the Provençal garlic-flavored mayonnaise that is a traditional accompaniment to many fish and seafood dishes.*

ZUCCHINI TORTILLA WITH HERB SALSA

SERVES 4-6

2 large potatoes, diced small
2 tbsp butter
2 tbsp olive oil
2 onions, minced
3 garlic cloves, minced
3 large zucchini, thinly sliced
salt and freshly ground black pepper
8 eggs, beaten
2 tbsp chopped fresh flat-leaf parsley
FOR THE HERB SALSA
5 tbsp olive oil
1 tbsp red wine vinegar
1 tsp whole-grain mustard
⅓ cup chopped canned plum tomatoes, drained
pinch of chili powder
2 tbsp each chopped fresh chives and flat-leaf parsley

In a large pan of boiling salted water, blanch the potato dice 2-3 minutes. Refresh under cold running water, drain well, and pat dry.

In a 10-inch frying or omelette pan, preferably with a lid, melt the butter with the oil over medium heat.

Sauté the onions and garlic until the onion is translucent and soft. Add the zucchini and potatoes and sauté a few minutes more, taking care that the onion and garlic do not get too brown.

Season the eggs and stir in most of the parsley. Stir into the pan, cover, and cook over low heat until the eggs are just set, about 10 minutes.

Meanwhile, preheat the broiler. Finish cooking the omelette under the broiler to brown the top.

While the tortilla is cooking, make the salsa by mixing all the ingredients and seasoning to taste.

Serve the tortilla warm or cold, sprinkled with the remaining parsley. Serve the salsa separately.

GORGONZOLA AND ANCHOVY SOUFFLÉ

SERVES 4

3 tbsp unsalted butter
2 oz canned anchovy fillets, drained
1 tbsp flour
⅔ cup milk
3 eggs, separated
3 oz gorgonzola cheese, crumbled or cubed
freshly ground black pepper
cayenne pepper

Preheat the oven to 375°F and heat a baking sheet in it. Grease a 6-inch soufflé dish with 1 tablespoon of the butter. Make sure that the rim is well greased to prevent the soufflé sticking as it rises.

Rinse the anchovies to remove excess saltiness, pat them dry, and cut them into small strips.

In a large heavy-based pan, melt the remaining butter over low heat and stir in the flour. Cook 1-2 minutes, stirring constantly. Gradually add the milk, still stirring, and cook until smooth and thick.

Off the heat, stir the egg yolks into the sauce, one at a time. Then stir in the cheese and anchovies. Adjust the seasoning with pepper and cayenne pepper (the seasoning should be quite forceful as it will be cut by the unseasoned egg white). Set aside.

Beat the egg whites to stiff peaks. Spoon a little of the beaten egg white into the cheese mixture and stir well to loosen the mixture. Carefully fold the remaining egg white into the mixture.

Pour the mixture into the prepared soufflé dish. Tap the base on a work surface, then put the dish in the oven on the hot baking sheet.

Bake until well risen and golden, 20-25 minutes. Serve immediately, dusted with cayenne.

Zucchini Tortilla with Herb Salsa.

CEVICHE

SERVES 4

2 whole mackerel, cleaned, or 4 skinned mackerel fillets
⅓ cup lime juice
⅓ cup lemon juice
salt and freshly ground black pepper
3 tbsp extra virgin olive oil
1 tbsp red wine vinegar
1 large onion, minced
1 tsp chopped fresh cilantro
2 tbsp chopped fresh flat-leaf parsley
1 fresh hot chili pepper, seeded and finely chopped
2 large tomatoes, peeled and chopped
1 ripe avocado
tortilla chips, for serving

If using whole fish, press out the backbone of each and remove. Cut the fish or the fillets into chunks about ½-inch across.

Place the pieces of fish in a shallow dish and pour over the lime and lemon juices. Season, cover, and let marinate 6 hours, turning once or twice.

Put the oil, vinegar, onion, cilantro, parsley, chili, and tomatoes in another bowl and mix together thoroughly.

Drain the fish, reserving the juice. Mix the fish with the herb and tomato mixture and transfer to a serving dish.

Halve and pit the avocado. Peel and slice the flesh thinly, then arrange the slices on top of the fish mixture. Using a pastry brush, coat the avocado with the reserved juice to prevent discoloration.

Season with salt and pepper and serve with tortilla chips.

Top: Smoked Trout and Dill in Whitefish Cornets; bottom: Ceviche.

SMOKED MACKEREL PÂTÉ WITH HORSERADISH

SERVES 4

4 smoked mackerel fillets, skinned
2 tbsp butter, softened
⅔ cup light cream
3 tbsp coarsely chopped hazelnuts
1 tbsp lime juice
1 tbsp cream-style horseradish
salt and freshly ground black pepper
slices of warm toast, for serving

Put all the ingredients into a blender or food processor with some seasoning. Process until smooth, then transfer to a bowl. Serve with toast.

SMOKED TROUT AND DILL IN WHITEFISH CORNETS

SERVES 4

6 oz smoked trout fillets, skinned and flaked
1 tbsp minced fresh dill
1 tbsp cream-style horseradish
salt and freshly ground black pepper
¾ lb very thin slices of smoked whitefish
2 slices of whole wheat toast
small bunch of fresh chervil
juice of ½ lemon and 1 lime

Place the smoked trout, dill, and horseradish in a small bowl. Season and mix together thoroughly.

Lay the whitefish slices on a flat surface and cut them into 8 strips. Spread each piece with the smoked trout mixture, then roll up into a cornet.

Cut each slice of toast into 4 rectangles. Place on a serving platter, then sit the cornets on top of them.

Garnish with chervil. Drizzle the fruit juices over and sprinkle with pepper just before serving.

CEVICHE *is a dish native to South America in which raw fish "cooks" in a lime juice marinade.*

You can substitute SMOKED SALMON *or* SMOKED EEL *for the whitefish.*

When buying Camembert cheese for the CAMEMBERT AND CRANBERRY BARQUETTES, try to buy a slightly under-ripe cheese as this will slice more easily.

For the GOAT CHEESE AND HERB TARTLETS, buy a goat cheese that has no flavored coating and is quite soft in texture.

PROSCIUTTO is a traditional Italian ham. The pigs are fed on a diet of whey left over from making the local Parmesan cheese and the ham is dry-cured under weights and left to mature for one year. It is very thinly sliced and served raw as an appetizer or used as a flavoring in cooking.

CAMEMBERT AND CRANBERRY BARQUETTES

MAKES 16

FOR THE PASTRY
¾ cup flour
½ tsp salt
½ tsp dried English mustard
6 tbsp butter, cut into small pieces
1 egg yolk
FOR THE FILLING
2 tbsp orange juice
1 tbsp sugar
½ cup fresh or frozen cranberries
¼ lb Camembert cheese, thinly sliced

To make the pastry: sift the flour, salt, and mustard powder into a bowl, add the butter and rub it in finely with your fingertips. Stir in the egg yolk and mix together with a fork to form a firm dough.

Knead the dough on a lightly floured surface until smooth. Roll it out thinly and use to line sixteen 4-inch fluted barquette molds. Chill 30 minutes.

Preheat the oven to 400°F.

Bake the pastry shells "blind" until lightly browned at the edges and cooked, about 10 minutes.

While they are baking make the filling: place the orange juice, sugar, and cranberries in a small saucepan. Heat gently, shaking the pan occasionally, until the cranberries are tender and the liquid has evaporated. Let the cranberries cool.

Arrange a little cheese in each pastry shell. Just before serving, place the pastry boats in the oven until the cheese has just melted, 2-3 minutes. Remove them from the oven and arrange a few cranberries on each barquette. Serve immediately.

GOAT CHEESE AND HERB TARTLETS★

MAKES 4

FOR THE PASTRY
¾ cup flour
½ tsp salt and ¼ tsp freshly ground black pepper
6 tbsp butter, cut into small pieces
1 egg yolk
FOR THE FILLING
¼ lb soft goat cheese
2 tbsp chopped mixed fresh herbs,
including basil, marjoram, and parsley
2 tbsp minced scallion
1 egg★
(★see page 2 for advice on eggs)
⅔ cup light cream
½ tsp freshly ground black pepper

To make the pastry: sift the flour, salt, and pepper into a bowl. Add the butter and rub it in finely with your fingertips. Stir in the egg yolk and mix together with a fork to form a firm dough.

Knead the dough on a lightly floured surface until smooth. Roll it out thinly and use to line four 4½-inch round loose-bottomed fluted tartlet molds. Chill 30 minutes.

Preheat the oven to 400°F.

Bake the cases "blind" until lightly browned at the edges and cooked on the bottom, about 10 minutes. Reduce the oven temperature to 375°F.

While they are baking make the filling: place the cheese, herbs, and scallion in a bowl and beat together until well blended. Add the egg, cream, and pepper and beat again until well blended.

Pour the filling into the pastry shells and return them to the cooler oven to bake until the filling has just set, 10-15 minutes longer. Serve warm or cold.

GRUYÈRE AND PROSCIUTTO BARQUETTES★

MAKES 6

FOR THE PASTRY
¾ cup flour
½ tsp salt and ¼ tsp freshly ground pepper
6 tbsp butter, cut into small pieces
1 egg yolk
1 tbsp chopped fresh basil
FOR THE FILLING
3 oz Gruyère cheese, thinly sliced
2 oz prosciutto, cut into strips
⅔ cup light cream
1 egg★
(★see page 2 for advice on eggs)
½ tsp Dijon-style mustard
¼ tsp freshly ground pepper

To make the pastry: sift the flour, salt, and pepper into a bowl, add the butter and rub it in finely with your fingertips. Stir in the egg yolk and basil and mix together with a fork to form a firm dough.

Knead the dough on a lightly floured surface until smooth. Roll it out thinly and use to line six 6-inch barquette molds. Chill 30 minutes.

Preheat the oven to 400°F.

Bake the shells "blind" until lightly browned at the edges and cooked on the bottom, about 10 minutes. Reduce the oven temperature to 375°F.

While they are baking make the filling. In a bowl, whisk together the cream, egg, mustard, and pepper.

Arrange the cheese slices in the pastry shells with the strips of prosciutto on top. Spoon the egg mixture into the pastry shells and return them to the cooler oven to bake until the filling has just set, about 15 minutes. Serve warm or cold.

POTSTICKER
DUMPLINGS *are a
popular Chinese
snack often included
in the "dim sum"
menus traditional to
family Sunday
brunches, which
feature dumplings of
all types - steamed,
broiled, and fried.*

SESAME SHRIMP TOASTS

MAKES 24

*½ lb raw shrimp in their shells
2 heaping tbsp canned Chinese water chestnuts, drained
2 bacon slices, chopped
½ tsp salt
1 tsp cornstarch
white of 1 medium egg
6 slices of white bread, crusts removed
¼ cup sesame seeds
vegetable oil, for frying*

Remove the shells from the shrimp. Using a sharp knife, make an incision along the length of the back of each shrimp (the outside curve). Remove and discard any dark vein.

Place the shrimp, water chestnuts, bacon, salt, cornstarch, and egg white in the bowl of a blender or food processor and reduce to a smooth purée.

Alternatively, reduce the ingredients to a purée in a large mortar with a pestle, or simply mince them as finely as possible with a sharp knife.

Spread the purée evenly over the slices of bread.

Spread an even layer of sesame seeds on a large plate and then press in the spread sides of the bread to coat them evenly with seeds.

Fill a frying pan or wok with oil to a depth of about 1 inch. Heat until nice and hot, then fry the toasts, coated-side down, until the seeds are crisp and golden, 1 minute or so. Turn and fry on the other side until the bread is crisp and golden. Drain on paper towels.

Cut each slice into 4 even strips and serve as soon as possible.

POTSTICKER DUMPLINGS

MAKES 16

*1¼ cups flour
2 tbsp vegetable oil
⅔ cup chicken or vegetable stock
Asian sweet chili sauce or other dipping sauce, for serving*
FOR THE FILLING
*¾ cup flaked white crab meat
3 tbsp minced green cabbage
1 small scallion, minced
1-inch cube of peeled fresh gingerroot, minced
1 tbsp dry sherry
1 tbsp soy sauce
¼ tsp salt
1 tsp Asian sesame oil
¼ tsp sugar*

In a bowl, mix the flour with ½ cup of very hot water to make a dough. Knead 10 minutes, adding a little more water if the dough seems too dry or a little more flour if it seems too sticky. Cover with a damp cloth and let rest 30 minutes.

Meanwhile, make the filling: mix all the ingredients together in a bowl.

Knead the rested dough 5 minutes longer and then divide it into 16 equal balls. On a floured surface, roll out the balls to make rounds of dough with a diameter of about 3 inches. Keep the balls and rounds of dough covered with a damp cloth while working to prevent their drying out.

Place a small teaspoon of stuffing in the center of each round. Moisten the edges with water. Fold each circle over in half to make a half-moon and pinch the edges to seal. Using the thumb and forefinger, "frill" the edges to make each dumpling into a small pasty shape, with a frilly seam on top and a flat base.

Heat the oil in a frying or sauté pan that is large enough to take the dumplings snugly in one layer and that preferably has a tight-fitting lid. Fry the dumplings over very low heat until their flat bottoms are crisp and golden.

Pour in the stock, cover, and simmer over very low heat until all the liquid has been absorbed, 12-15 minutes. Remove the lid and cook 2 minutes longer.

Serve hot, accompanied by sweet chili sauce or another dipping sauce.

THAI FISH CAKES

MAKES 8

½ lb skinless white fish fillets, coarsely chopped
1½ tsp Thai red curry paste
1 tbsp cornstarch
1 tbsp fish sauce
1 medium egg, beaten
1 large hot red or green chili pepper, seeded and chopped
2 shallots, minced
3 oz green beans, minced
2 tbsp vegetable oil
Cucumber and Carrot Relish (see page 11) or a dipping
sauce, for serving

In a blender or food processor, blend the fish until just smooth. Add the curry paste, cornstarch, fish sauce, and egg and process briefly until mixed. Be careful not to over-process, or the fish will lose all texture! Transfer to a small bowl and mix in the chili pepper, shallots, and beans.

Divide the mixture into 8 portions and shape them into round cakes about ¼-inch thick.

Heat the oil in a frying pan over medium heat and fry the cakes until uniformly golden, 3-4 minutes on each side.

Serve immediately with Cucumber and Carrot Relish or a dipping sauce.

DEEP-FRIED "SEAWEED"

SERVES 4

½ lb cabbage or collard greens, very finely shredded
vegetable oil, for deep-frying
sugar, for sprinkling

Heat the oil in a wok until just beginning to smoke, then deep-fry the cabbage, in small batches, for a few seconds only, until it turns dark and crispy.

Remove each batch with a slotted spoon, drain on paper towels, and keep warm while the remaining batches are being cooked. Sprinkle with a little sugar as soon as all the greens are cooked and serve.

THAI RED CURRY PASTE *is flavored with lime zest, lemongrass, galangal, and trassi — the Southeast Asian condiment made from fermented shrimp — and is available from Asian markets.*

As here, the DEEP-FRIED "SEAWEED" *served in many Chinese restaurants is not seaweed at all but shredded greens. Use a food processor to shred them very finely.*

Popular in Singapore, Malaysia, and Indonesia, SATAY dishes consist of tiny "kebabs" and may contain meat, poultry, or fish.

Japanese TERIYAKI SAUCE, made from soybeans and wine and used as a marinade and basting sauce, is available bottled from Asian markets, as are small wooden skewers.

CHICKEN SATAY

MAKES 8 SMALL SKEWERS

½ lb skinless boneless chicken breast, cut into
¾-inch cubes
FOR THE MARINADE
1 tbsp brown sugar
2 tbsp soy sauce
juice of ½ lemon
1 tbsp vegetable oil
FOR THE DIPPING SAUCE
1 tbsp vegetable oil
1 small onion, minced
1 garlic clove, minced
1 tbsp crunchy peanut butter
1 tbsp Asian sweet chili sauce
1 tsp soy sauce
3 tbsp boiling water

First make the marinade: in a small bowl, dissolve the sugar in 1 tablespoon of hot water and then add the remaining ingredients and mix well. Add the chicken pieces and stir until well coated, then let marinate at least 1 hour, or up to 24 hours in the refrigerator.

Meanwhile make the dipping sauce: in a small pan, heat the oil over medium heat and cook the onion until softened. Then add the remaining ingredients and simmer 3 minutes. Transfer to a serving bowl and let cool.

Soak 8 small wooden skewers in water for 30 minutes or more, to prevent their scorching too much during cooking. Preheat the broiler, a grill, or barbecue.

Thread the marinated meat onto the prepared skewers and cook them under the broiler or on the grill or barbecue for 4-5 minutes, turning once.

Serve accompanied by the dipping sauce.

NOTE: for an unusual and attractive presentation, use bay twigs instead of skewers.

TERIYAKI CHICKEN

MAKES 12 SKEWERS

2 tbsp vegetable oil
⅓ cup teriyaki sauce
1 tbsp dry sherry
1 tbsp brown sugar
1 garlic clove, minced
1-inch cube of peeled fresh gingerroot, crushed in a garlic press or minced
½ small red sweet pepper, seeded and cut into
½-inch squares
½ lb skinless boneless chicken breast, cut into
½-inch cubes
strips of scallion and cucumber, for serving

Soak 12 small wooden skewers in water for 30 minutes or more, to prevent their scorching too much during grilling.

Place all the ingredients except the chicken, scallion, and cucumber in a bowl and mix them well to combine.

Drop the pieces of chicken into the marinade and toss them well to ensure that they are coated on all sides. Cover and let marinate at least 30 minutes, or up to 3 hours, shaking the bowl occasionally.

Preheat the broiler, a grill, or barbecue.

Thread the pieces of chicken and red pepper onto the skewers and grill or barbecue for about 5 minutes, or until cooked through, turning 2 or 3 times and brushing each time with marinade.

Serve immediately, accompanied by the scallion and cucumber.

SPRING ROLLS

MAKES 12

12 spring roll wrappers
vegetable oil, for deep-frying
FOR THE FILLING
5 dried Chinese mushrooms
1 tbsp vegetable oil
½ tsp Asian sesame oil
½ lb ground pork
2 scallions, minced
2 garlic cloves, minced
1 small carrot, grated
6 canned Chinese water chestnuts, drained and chopped
2½ oz peeled cooked shrimp, chopped
1 tbsp soy sauce
1 egg, beaten

Soak the dried mushrooms in warm water for 30 minutes. Drain, remove and discard the stems, and slice the caps thinly.

Make the filling: heat the oils in a wok or frying pan over medium heat and stir-fry the pork 5 minutes. Add the scallions, garlic, carrot, mushrooms, and water chestnuts and stir-fry 2 minutes longer. Let the mixture cool.

Add the shrimp, soy sauce, and most of the egg, saving a little egg to seal the wrappers.

Divide the mixture into 12 portions and place one on the edge of each egg-roll wrapper. Fold in the sides of each and roll it up, brushing the seam with a little of the reserved egg to seal.

Deep-fry the rolls, in batches, in hot oil in a wok until golden and crispy, 4-5 minutes. Be careful not to have the oil too hot or the wrappers will burn before the filling is cooked through. Drain on paper towels and keep warm while the rest are being cooked. Serve as soon as all are cooked.

NOTE: serve with a dipping sauce made from equal parts soy sauce and rice or wine vinegar.

WATER CHESTNUTS IN CRISPY BACON

SERVES 4

about ½ lb sliced bacon
1¼ cups canned Chinese water chestnuts, drained

Soak some wooden toothpicks in water for 30 minutes or more to prevent their burning during cooking. Preheat the broiler, a grill, or barbecue.

Using the back of a knife, scrape each slice of bacon to stretch it a little and then cut it in half.

Wrap each water chestnut in a piece of bacon and secure it with a toothpick.

Broil or grill, turning once, until the bacon is crisp, 5-7 minutes.

Serve immediately.

EGG-ROLL *wrappers are available fresh or frozen from Asian markets and many supermarkets, as are* CHINESE DRIED MUSHROOMS.

ASIAN SESAME OIL, *made from toasted sesame seeds, is aromatic and flavorful.*

THAI STUFFED CHICKEN WINGS

MAKES 12

12 chicken wing portions (see below)
¼ lb ground pork
⅓ cup canned bamboo shoots, drained
⅓ cup canned Chinese water chestnuts, drained
1 oz button mushrooms
2 garlic cloves, minced
2 tsp dark soy sauce
1 tsp sugar
salt and freshly ground black pepper
1 egg, lightly beaten
¼ cup flour
vegetable oil, for deep-frying and greasing
Plum Sauce (see page 11), for serving

Buy whole wing portions: two sections plus the wing tip. Sever the joint between the two sections. Skin and bone the meatiest section. Grind the meat and add it to the pork in a large bowl.

Mince the bamboo shoots, water chestnuts, and mushrooms in a food processor and add to the meat mixture, together with the garlic, soy sauce, sugar, and a good seasoning of salt and pepper. Mix well together, add the egg to bind and mix well again.

Using a small, sharp-pointed knife, bone the second section of the wings, working from the cut end. There are two bones, one bigger than the other, which will be joined together at that cut end. Separate them first with the point of the knife. The bigger bone will also be firmly attached to the meat on the side opposite to the small bone – carefully detach this with the knife.

Now using the edge of the knife, scrape the meat downward from the bones, being careful not to cut the skin. Work down to the joint, then twist and snap

Top: Sesame Beef Balls; bottom: Thai Stuffed Chicken Wings

off each bone in turn. Discard these bones or reserve them for stock. This will leave wing tips with a hollow pocket of skin and meat attached.

Using a teaspoon and your fingers, fill the cavities with the meat mixture. They should be filled until they are almost overflowing.

Place the stuffed wings in the lightly oiled upper part of a steamer and steam over boiling water until firm, about 20 minutes. Let cool.

Season the flour with salt and pepper. Coat the cooled wings in it and deep-fry them in batches in hot oil in a wok until the skin is golden brown and crisp. Drain on paper towels and keep warm while the rest are being cooked.

Serve immediately with Plum Sauce.

SESAME BEEF BALLS

SERVES 4

¾ lb ground round steak
3 bacon slices, chopped
1 tbsp chopped celery
1 tbsp chopped carrot
1 tbsp minced mushroom
2 scallions, chopped
1 tbsp cornstarch
1 tbsp soy sauce
1 tbsp dry sherry
½ tsp salt
freshly ground black pepper
flour, for dusting
1 egg, beaten
vegetable oil, for deep-frying
2 tbsp hoisin sauce
2 tsp sugar
1 tbsp sesame seeds
hoisin sauce, Plum Sauce (see page 11) or other dipping sauce, for serving

Put the beef, bacon, chopped vegetables, mushrooms, scallions, cornstarch, two-thirds of the soy sauce, the sherry, salt, and some pepper in a blender or food processor and process until well mixed. Be careful not to over-process.

Using floured hands, form the paste into walnut-sized balls. Coat these thoroughly and evenly in the beaten egg.

Deep-fry the coated balls in hot oil in a wok until well browned all over. Drain the cooked balls on paper towels.

Remove all but 2 tablespoons of the oil from the wok and add the remaining soy sauce, the hoisin sauce, sugar, and sesame seeds.

Heat the wok over medium heat. Add the beef balls and cook a few minutes, shaking the wok occasionally, until the balls are coated with the sauces and sesame seeds and turn a deep mahogany brown all over.

Serve immediately, with more hoisin sauce, Plum Sauce, or other dipping sauce.

Fresh CHINESE WATER CHESTNUTS *are occasionally available from Chinese markets.*

HOISIN SAUCE, *one of the most popular dipping sauces in China, is available in bottles from most better supermarkets.*

RICE, GRAINS, AND PASTA

O ne of the greatest changes in our eating habits in the last few years has been the increasing displacement of the potato by rice and pasta in our meal-making. As much as being a matter of convenience, this reflects our new interest in the foods of other cultures, especially Asia and the Mediterranean. Perhaps the peak of creativity in Mediterranean cooking is reached in their cunning uses of rice and grains. Scarcely ever served as mere accompaniments, they are cooked slowly with flavoring ingredients to make such dishes as risotto, paella, and lasagne. Less common grains such as couscous, polenta, and bulghur wheat are also cooked with rich sauces or made into refreshing salads. The myriad different pasta shapes available can be combined with literally innumerable sauces to make anything from light snacks to substantial meals – and even interesting desserts.

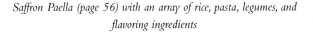

Saffron Paella (page 56) with an array of rice, pasta, legumes, and flavoring ingredients

There are endless variations on the Spanish rice dish, PAELLA – only rice, oil, and saffron are essential. Other ingredients may include green beans, green peas, and artichoke hearts, lobster, duck, and rabbit.

SAFFRON PAELLA

SERVES 6-8

*1 chicken, weighing about 3 lb, cut into 12 pieces,
backbone and giblets retained
4 onions
3 large garlic cloves, chopped
white part of 1 leek, chopped
1 celery stalk, thinly sliced
1 bouquet garni
12 black peppercorns
salt and freshly ground black pepper
¾ lb squid, sliced into rings
about 18 mussels
¼ cup olive oil
½ lb chorizo sausage, sliced
1 large red sweet pepper, seeded and cut into thick strips
1 large green sweet pepper, seeded and cut into thick strips
few strands of saffron
6 large tomatoes, peeled and chopped
cayenne pepper
2 cups long-grain rice
6-8 jumbo shrimp or any large shrimp (optional)
lemon wedges, to serve*

Put the chicken giblets and backbone in a pot with 2 of the onions coarsely chopped, the garlic, leek, celery, bouquet garni, peppercorns, and a large pinch of salt. Barely cover with water and bring to a boil. Skim and then simmer for about 1 hour.

Meanwhile, put the squid in a pan and cover with cold water. Bring to a boil and simmer 5 minutes, then drain and set aside. Scrub the mussel shells well, discarding any open ones that do not close when tapped. Finely chop the remaining onions.

Heat the oil in a large frying or paella pan over medium heat and brown the chicken pieces. Remove them with a slotted spoon and set aside.

In the same oil, cook the chorizo, squid, pepper strips, and chopped onions 3-4 minutes. Stir in the saffron and cook 5 minutes longer. Add the tomatoes, and bring to a boil. Season well and add 1-2 pinches of cayenne.

Stir in the rice. Place the chicken pieces, mussels, and shrimp, if using, on top. Pour in the strained chicken stock and bring to a boil.

Cover and simmer gently until the rice is tender, about 20 minutes. Keep checking: if it looks too dry at any time, add a little water. Serve with lemon wedges.

SALAMI AND BLUE CHEESE RISOTTO

SERVES 4

*3 tbsp butter
2 tbsp olive oil
1 large onion, minced
2 large garlic cloves, minced
1½ cups risotto rice, preferably arborio
3¾-4 cups hot chicken or veal stock
½ lb Italian salami, peeled and cubed
½ lb gorgonzola or other blue cheese
2 celery stalks, chopped
1 large red sweet pepper, seeded and cut into thin strips
⅛ tsp dried sage
2 tbsp minced fresh flat-leaf parsley
salt and freshly ground black pepper
cayenne pepper
chopped fresh chives, for garnish*

In a large heavy pan that has a tight-fitting lid, melt the butter with the oil over medium heat. Add the onion and garlic. Cook until soft and just beginning to color, 1-2 minutes.

Add the rice and sauté over medium-high heat for 2 minutes. Add 1¼ cups of stock, stir well, and bring to a boil. Reduce the heat and simmer gently until the stock is absorbed, about 5 minutes.

Continue to add the remaining stock, one-quarter at a time, stirring well and waiting until it has all been absorbed before adding more. The whole process should take about 30 minutes and the final result should be rice that is richly creamy and slightly sticky – but not mushy.

About halfway through, add half the salami and cheese with the celery, red pepper, and sage.

With the final addition of stock, add the remainder of the salami and cheese and the parsley. Adjust the seasoning with salt, pepper, and cayenne. Serve garnished with chives.

CHICKEN AND LAMB COUSCOUS

SERVES 6-8

2 tbsp oil
1 large chicken, cut into 12 pieces, backbone retained
½ lb boned lamb, cut into large cubes
3 onions, chopped
4 garlic cloves, minced
3 turnips, cut into chunks
3 large carrots, chopped
salt and freshly ground black pepper
few strands of saffron
½ tsp each of ground cumin, ginger, and turmeric
4 large ripe tomatoes, chopped
4 zucchini, chopped
½ cup raisins
bunch of fresh flat-leaf parsley, minced
bunch of fresh cilantro, minced
1 cup canned chickpeas (garbanzos), drained
1 lb (2⅔ cups) instant couscous
2 tsp harissa or other chili sauce
2 tbsp butter
2-3 tbsp rose water
⅓ cup dates, cut into slivers
more harissa sauce, for serving

In the bottom part of a couscoussier or a large heavy saucepan, heat the oil over medium-high heat and brown the pieces of chicken and lamb.

Add the onions, garlic, turnips, carrots, and the chicken backbone. Cover with water, season, and stir in the saffron and other spices. Bring to a boil and simmer about 1 hour, skimming as necessary.

Remove and discard the backbone. Add the tomatoes, zucchini, raisins, most of the herbs, and two-thirds of the chickpeas. Simmer 30 minutes more.

Prepare the couscous either by simply pouring boiling water over it, letting it steep about 10 minutes, and draining it, or by steaming it about 20 minutes in the top part of the couscoussier.

Remove 2 ladlesful of the broth and season it with the harissa. When the couscous is fluffed up and ready, stir in one-third of this seasoned broth along with the butter, the remaining chickpeas, the rose water, and dates.

Serve the couscous on a large warmed serving platter with the pieces of meat and vegetables piled in the center and some of the broth poured over. Sprinkle with the remaining herbs and pass the remaining seasoned broth and more harissa separately.

Fiery-hot HARISSA SAUCE from Tunisia can be bought in Middle-Eastern stores.

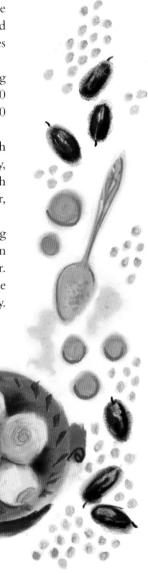

LENTIL AND BULGHUR PILAF WITH YOGURT

SERVES 4

1 cup + 3 tbsp green lentils, preferably le Puy
1 bay leaf
1 tsp cumin seeds, finely crushed
1 tsp coriander seeds, finely crushed
1⅓ cups bulghur wheat
pinch of cayenne
salt and freshly ground black pepper
6 tbsp olive oil
2 onions, thinly sliced
2 garlic cloves, minced
juice of ½ lemon
⅔ cup thick plain yogurt
2 tbsp minced fresh cilantro

Soak the lentils in cold water about 1 hour. Drain and put them in a pan. Pour in 5 cups of fresh water and add the bay leaf and spices. Bring to a boil and simmer until just tender, about 20 minutes.

Remove the bay leaf and add the bulghar wheat with the cayenne and seasoning to taste. Stir well, cover, and remove from the heat. Let sit until the bulghur is tender, about 20 minutes. Check from time to time to see if it has become too dry and add a little more water as necessary.

Meanwhile, heat one-third of the oil in a frying pan over medium heat and cook the onion and the garlic until brown and just beginning to caramelize.

Transfer the lentil and bulghur mixture to a warmed serving dish. Drizzle over the remaining oil and top with the onion and garlic mixture. Stir the lemon juice into the yogurt and pour it over the middle. Sprinkle the dish with the cilantro.

Serve hot, warm, or cold, with a green salad.

Top: Chicken and Lamb Couscous (page 57); bottom: Lentil and Bulghur Pilaf with Yogurt

GAME LASAGNE

SERVES 4-6

2 large partridges, or other game birds
1 lb apples, peeled, cored, and thickly sliced
1¼ cups dry hard cider
1¼ cups game consommé
9 tbsp butter
¼ cup flour
1¼ cups milk
⅔ cup light cream
2 cups sharp grated Cheddar cheese
salt and freshly ground black pepper
1 tsp ground allspice
1 tbsp vegetable or olive oil
about 1 lb fresh lasagne, preferably a mixture of colors
¼ cup freshly grated Parmesan cheese

Preheat the oven to 375°F.

Put the birds in a roasting pan with the apples, cider, and consommé. Cover with foil and bake 20 minutes. Remove from the oven and let cool.

When the birds are cool enough to handle, remove all the meat and slice it thinly. Using a slotted spoon, transfer the apples to a bowl and reserve the cooking liquid.

Heat a large pot of water for the lasagne.

Melt 4 tablespoons of the butter in a saucepan over medium heat. Sprinkle in 2 tablespoons of flour and cook 1-2 minutes, stirring constantly. Gradually add the milk, stirring to make a smooth liquid. Bring nearly to a boil, still stirring, and simmer gently until thickened. Stir in the cream and Cheddar and continue to stir until the cheese has melted. Season.

In another pan make another sauce as above, starting with 4 tablespoons of the remaining butter and the remaining flour, but adding about 1½ cups of the reserved game cooking liquid instead of milk.

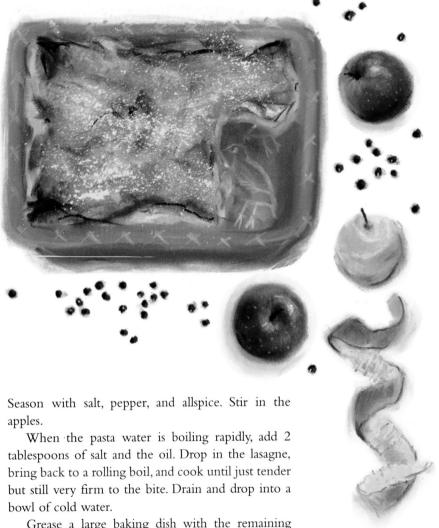

Season with salt, pepper, and allspice. Stir in the apples.

When the pasta water is boiling rapidly, add 2 tablespoons of salt and the oil. Drop in the lasagne, bring back to a rolling boil, and cook until just tender but still very firm to the bite. Drain and drop into a bowl of cold water.

Grease a large baking dish with the remaining butter. Spoon some cheese sauce over the bottom and arrange some of the drained lasagne over that. Layer some partridge meat over the lasagne and spoon some game sauce and apples over that. Continue layering in this way, finishing with cheese sauce.

Sprinkle with Parmesan and bake until bubbling and well browned on top, about 30 minutes.

TAGLIATELLE WITH ROAST GARLIC

SERVES 4

about 30 large garlic cloves, preferably the fresh summer variety, unpeeled
1 bay leaf
6 tbsp olive oil
⅔ cup pine nuts
salt and freshly ground black pepper
1 lb dried tagliatelle
small bunch of fresh basil leaves
1 tbsp balsamic vinegar
freshly grated Parmesan cheese, for serving

The delicious Italian fresh double-cream cheese, MASCARPONE, *is available in Italian markets and specialty food stores. More usually served with sugar or fruit at the end of a meal, its subtle flavor and buttery texture are also incomparable in savory dishes.*

Preheat the oven to 425°F.

Put the garlic cloves and bay leaf in the center of a large sheet of foil. Add 2 tablespoons of oil, wrap in a loose package, and put in a baking dish.

Bake until the garlic is tender but not mushy, 20 minutes. About halfway through, add the pine nuts to the oven, scattered on a baking sheet.

Meanwhile, put about 4½ quarts of water in a pasta pan or a large pot Add 2 tablespoons of salt and 1 tablespoon of oil and bring to a boil.

When the water is boiling rapidly, put the pasta in and bring it back to a rolling boil as quickly as possible. Boil rapidly, uncovered, until the pasta is tender but still firm, testing regularly.

Remove the foil package and toasted pine nuts from the oven. Take the garlic from the foil and let cool slightly. Squeeze the cloves out of their skins, first snipping off one end if necessary. Keep the pine nuts and garlic cloves warm. Finely chop most of the basil, reserving 12 small leaves.

As soon as the pasta is ready, drain well and stir in the remaining oil, with most of the garlic and pine nuts, the chopped basil, vinegar, and seasoning. Dot the remaining garlic, pine nuts, and basil leaves over the top. Serve accompanied by Parmesan.

PASTA SHELLS WITH MASCARPONE AND NUTS★

SERVES 4

6 oz (¾ cup) mascarpone cheese
2 tbsp butter, melted
1 tbsp balsamic vinegar
½ tsp freshly grated nutmeg
salt and freshly ground black pepper
1 lb pasta shells
1 tbsp olive oil
2 egg yolks★
(★see page 2 for advice on eggs)
½ cup freshly grated Parmesan cheese
¾ cup coarsely chopped walnuts

Put the mascarpone in a large serving bowl and stir in the butter, vinegar, half of the nutmeg, and seasoning. Set in a warm place in the kitchen.

Cook the pasta in boiling salted and oiled water as described for the tagliatelle (left). While the pasta is cooking, in another large bowl lightly beat the egg yolks with half the Parmesan and season.

Drain the pasta quickly so that some water still clings to it and immediately stir it well into the egg mixture. The egg should cook on contact.

While the pasta is still very hot, add it to the cheese mixture together with two-thirds of the walnuts and toss to coat uniformly.

Sprinkle over the remaining walnuts, Parmesan, and nutmeg, and serve.

Clockwise from the top: Tagliatelle with Roast Garlic; Pasta Shells with Mascarpone and Nuts; Spaghettini with Chicken and Eggplant (page 62)

Throughout Italy many types of PASTICCIO, *or pasta pies, are served on special occasions. Usually topped with a pastry lid, they can be filled with a wide variety of types of pasta and other ingredients, including eggplant, ricotta cheese, and pigeon.*

SPAGHETTINI WITH CHICKEN AND EGGPLANT

SERVES 4

1 large eggplant, cut into ½-inch cubes
6 tbsp olive oil
1 onion, minced
4 garlic cloves, minced
¼ lb chicken breast meat, cut into ½-inch cubes
about 30 pitted black olives
2 cups canned plum tomatoes, chopped
salt and freshly ground black pepper
pinch of sugar
1-2 tbsp tomato paste
1 lb dried spaghettini
chopped fresh basil, parsley, or tarragon, for garnish

First make the sauce: sprinkle the eggplant with salt and let drain in a colander about 20 minutes. Rinse well and pat dry.

Heat 2 tablespoons of oil in a sauté pan over medium heat and cook the onion 1-2 minutes. Add the garlic and cook 1 minute more. Using a slotted spoon, transfer the onion and garlic to a bowl.

Add the cubes of chicken to the pan and sauté them briskly, until beginning to brown, 1-2 minutes. Transfer to the bowl.

Add 2 more tablespoons of oil to the pan and sauté the eggplant until browned.

Halve some olives for garnish and chop the rest.

Return the chicken, garlic, and onion to the pan along with the chopped olives and the tomatoes with their liquid. Season and add the sugar. Simmer gently about 10 minutes. It should be a good thick sauce: adjust the consistency with some tomato paste, as necessary.

Meanwhile, cook the pasta in boiling salted and oiled water until just tender but still firm to the bite, as described for tagliatelle (page 60).

Stir 1 tablespoon of oil into the cooked and drained pasta and pour the sauce over it. Garnish with the halved olives and the herbs.

NOTES: add some chopped cooked ham or bacon or a spoonful of brandy when sautéing the chicken, for more flavor. This dish is also good for vegetarians without the chicken. Sprinkle with shredded mozzarella cheese to make it more substantial.

OPEN PASTICCIO WITH CHICKEN LIVERS

SERVES 6

FOR THE PASTRY
2 cups flour
10 tbsp butter, softened, plus 2 tbsp for greasing
FOR THE FILLING
1 lb tagliatelle, preferably a mixture of colors
7 tbsp olive oil
salt and freshly ground black pepper
1 large onion, minced
3 garlic cloves, minced
3 oz chicken livers, trimmed
3 tbsp Marsala or sweet sherry wine
⅔ cup crème fraîche or heavy whipping cream
¼ lb frozen spinach leaves, thawed and squeezed dry
⅛ tsp freshly grated nutmeg
1 buffalo mozzarella cheese
2 tbsp freshly grated Parmesan cheese

To make the pastry dough: sift the flour with a pinch of salt and rub the butter into it gently with your fingertips. When it has a crumb-like consistency, add enough cold water, a little at a time, to make a smooth dough. Roll into a ball and chill 1 hour. Roll out the dough to a thickness of about ½ inch and fold it in thirds. Roll out and repeat this process twice more and then roll back into a ball and chill 30 minutes more.

Preheat the oven to 425°F and generously grease a deep 9-inch round spring form pan with butter. Roll out the dough and use to line the mold.

To make the filling: cook the pasta in boiling salted and oiled water as for the tagliatelle recipe (page 60), but stop cooking when just slightly underdone. Drain thoroughly. Stir in 2 tablespoons of oil and season.

While the pasta is cooking, heat 2 tablespoons of the remaining oil in a sauté pan over medium heat and sauté the onion 2-3 minutes. Add the garlic and cook 1 minute more. Then add the chicken livers, and as soon as these change color, add the Marsala or sherry. Sauté 1 minute more. Stir in the cream and season. Set aside. Season the spinach with salt, pepper, and nutmeg.

Arrange a layer of half the tagliatelle in the bottom of the pastry shell, so that there is a depression in the middle. Pour the chicken liver mixture into the center. Arrange half the mozzarella slices on top and then cover these with half the spinach. Put half the remaining tagliatelle on top of this, followed by layers of the remaining mozzarella, spinach, and tagliatelle. Sprinkle over the remaining oil and the Parmesan.

Bake until the pastry is firm and the top golden, about 30-35 minutes. Let cool 2-3 minutes before removing from the mold.

Top: Open Pasticcio with Chicken Livers; bottom: Mozzarella and Tomato Salad with Avocado (page 174)

RISOTTOS *of all types are found in Italian cuisine, from those simply flavored with cheese or herbs to those containing rich assortments of fish, shellfish, meat, or poultry. It is important to use a good stock and the right type of rice, such as arborio, which absorbs a great deal of liquid and gives the desired creamy texture.*

HERB AND WILD MUSHROOM RISOTTO

SERVES 4

1 oz dried cèpes (porcini mushroom)
¼ lb fresh mushrooms, preferably wild
1 stick (8 tbsp) butter
1 small onion, minced
1½ cups risotto rice, preferably arborio
⅔ cup dry white wine
5 cups hot chicken stock
2 tbsp chopped fresh parsley
2 tbsp chopped fresh sage
salt and freshly ground black pepper
3 tbsp freshly grated Parmesan cheese, plus shavings for garnish

Put the dried mushrooms in a small bowl and cover with warm water. Let soak 20 minutes, then rinse thoroughly, drain, and chop, reserving a few whole pieces for garnish. Halve, slice, or quarter the fresh mushrooms according to their size.

Melt half of the butter in a heavy saucepan over medium heat. Add the onion and cook until soft, about 5 minutes.

Stir in the rice and the fresh mushrooms and cook until the rice is translucent, 2-3 minutes. Add the wine and chopped dried mushrooms and cook until all the liquid is absorbed, about 3 minutes longer.

Add 2½ cups of the stock, lower the heat, cover, and simmer until the stock is absorbed, about 10 minutes. Keep adding stock, a ladleful at a time, until the rice is tender. Total cooking time will be 20-30 minutes.

Stir in the chopped herbs with the remaining butter, seasoning, and grated Parmesan.

Serve garnished with the reserved pieces of dried mushroom and Parmesan shavings.

PASTA WITH OVEN-BAKED TOMATOES, CHICKEN LIVERS, AND WATERCRESS

SERVES 4

2 tbsp extra virgin olive oil, plus more for greasing
½ cup whole hazelnuts
1 lb large cherry tomatoes, or other flavorsome variety, halved
salt and pepper
1 tsp herbes de Provence
¾ lb pasta
1 onion, chopped
1 garlic clove, minced
1 lb chicken livers, cut into bite-sized pieces
½ bunch (about 2½ oz) watercress, coarsely chopped
fresh basil leaves, for garnish

Preheat the oven to 400°F and lightly grease a baking sheet with oil.

In a frying pan, fry the hazelnuts 1-2 minutes. Let cool slightly and then rub off and discard the skins.

Arrange the tomato halves, cut-side up, on the baking sheet. Sprinkle with salt, pepper, and herbs and bake until hot and bubbling, about 15 minutes.

Meanwhile, cook the pasta in plenty of boiling salted water until just tender but still firm. Drain and return to the pan, and keep warm.

While the pasta is cooking, heat the oil in a frying pan or wok over medium heat and cook the onion, stirring frequently, until soft and translucent, about 5 minutes. Add the garlic and livers and stir-fry until the livers are just cooked, 3-4 minutes. Add the chopped watercress and stir-fry for a few seconds longer or until it just begins to wilt.

Add the tomatoes, chicken liver mixture, and the nuts to the pan of pasta. Toss gently but thoroughly and divide among 4 warmed plates or soup dishes. Serve immediately, garnished with basil leaves.

GRAPE LEAVES STUFFED WITH CILANTRO RICE

SERVES 4–6

½ lb preserved grape leaves or 40 fresh leaves
2¾ cups cooked brown rice
2 tbsp tomato paste
2 onions, diced
2 garlic cloves, minced
1 tsp ground cinnamon
2 tbsp minced fresh cilantro
1 tbsp currants
1 tbsp sliced almonds
salt and freshly ground black pepper
2 tbsp walnut oil
juice of 2 limes
2 cups vegetable stock

Place the fresh grape leaves in a large bowl and scald them thoroughly with boiling water. If using preserved leaves, let them soak 10 minutes.

Drain the leaves, refresh under cold water, and lay flat on paper towels, dull-side up.

In a bowl, combine the rice, tomato paste, onions, garlic, cinnamon, cilantro, currants, almonds, and seasoning.

Place 10 leaves in the bottom of a Dutch oven. Cut any stems from the other leaves and place a scant tablespoon of the filling in the center of each leaf. Fold the stem end of the leaf over the filling, then fold in the sides and continue to roll up the leaf carefully from the stem end to form a firm package about 2 inches long.

Place these side by side, seam-side down, in the Dutch oven. Sprinkle with the walnut oil and lime juice, and add just enough vegetable stock to cover them. If necessary, add a little water.

Cover the pot and bring to a gentle simmer. Simmer over low heat about 1 hour. Throughout this time check that the grape leaves remain moist.

Transfer to a warmed serving dish and serve any excess liquid as a sauce.

If serving cold, let cool in the covered pot, then transfer to a serving dish.

If GRAPE LEAVES are difficult to obtain, use large spinach or Swiss chard leaves. The rice stuffing can also be flavored with ground lamb or chicken.

Translucent CELLOPHANE NOODLES *are made from mung bean starch or rice flour rather than wheat and have a very delicate flavor. Bottled* CHINESE BLACK BEAN SAUCE, *made from fermented beans, is a widely used condiment in Chinese kitchens and is available from Asian markets and many supermarkets.*

CELLOPHANE NOODLES WITH BLACK BEAN SAUCE

SERVES 4 AS AN ACCOMPANIMENT

6 oz cellophane noodles
1 tbsp vegetable oil
1 large onion, thinly sliced
2 garlic cloves, minced
1¼ cups chicken stock
1 heaping tbsp Chinese black bean sauce
4 tsp light soy sauce
½ tsp chili powder
¾ tsp Asian sesame oil

Soak the noodles in hot water for 10 minutes and then drain them well.

Heat the oil in a wok or large frying pan and stir-fry the onion 2 minutes. Add the garlic, stock, sauces, and chili powder and simmer 5 minutes.

Add the noodles and cook 2 minutes, stirring constantly. (They absorb most of the liquid.) Sprinkle over the sesame oil, toss, and serve at once.

SPICY COCONUT RICE

SERVES 4-6

2⅔ cups basmati rice
1 tbsp vegetable oil
1 large onion, chopped
2 garlic cloves, minced
1 tsp ground coriander seed
1 tsp ground cumin
¼ tsp chili powder
1½ tsp salt
2½ cups thin canned coconut milk
chopped fresh cilantro or other herbs, for garnish

Rinse the rice thoroughly and drain well.

In a large heavy saucepan that has a tight-fitting lid, heat the oil over medium heat and fry the onion until softened. Add the garlic, spices, and salt and stir well. Add the rice and mix well until every grain is coated.

Add the coconut milk and bring to a boil. Turn the heat down to the lowest possible setting, put the lid tightly on the pan, and cook undisturbed about 15 minutes.

Without removing the lid, take the pan from the heat and set aside for 30 minutes to let the rice finish cooking in the steam.

Transfer to a serving dish and serve garnished with herbs.

Top: Spicy Coconut Rice; bottom: Cellophane Noodles with Black Bean Sauce

MEAT, POULTRY, AND GAME

*U*ntil quite recently the usual treatment we gave meat, poultry, or game was roasting, broiling, or casseroling. The influence of other cuisines has had an effect on even this bastion of our culinary traditions. Perhaps because of its expense, people are generally now much more inventive with meat – using it more as a flavoring ingredient. With current concerns for health there has also been a general move away from red meat – with its high saturated fat and cholesterol content – towards white meat. At the same time, worries about the effects of intensive rearing of both meat and poultry have helped restore the popularity of game.

In the spirit of these movements, we again look for our influence towards the cooking of Asia, the Middle-east and the Mediterranean, where small amounts of meat and poultry are used to such good effect in combination with rice, pasta, and vegetables to produce memorable dishes such as kofta, kebabs, or moussaka. There is also much to be learned from our own country traditions in the range of stews flavored with lamb or pork chops and, of course, the delights of the savory pastry – from Old-fashioned Poultry Pie and Steak and Mushroom Pudding to the glories of Game Pie.

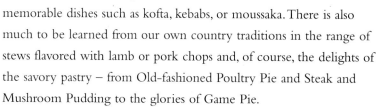

Left: Steak and Mushroom Pudding (page 71); right: Beef and Stout Pie (page 70)

BEEF IN BACON WITH MUSTARD SAUCE

SERVES 6

2 tbsp butter
2 shallots, minced
1 garlic clove, minced
1 lb mushrooms, minced
salt and freshly ground black pepper
1 tbsp chopped fresh parsley
4 oz smooth liver pâté or liver sausage
10 slices of bacon
2 lb piece of beef tenderloin, trimmed of fat
1 onion, chopped
2 carrots, chopped
1 celery stalk, chopped
1 tbsp flour
2 tbsp Dijon-style mustard
⅔ cup red wine
⅔ cup beef stock

Preheat the oven to 400°F. Melt the butter in a heavy pan over medium heat. Add the shallots and garlic and cook until translucent, about 3 minutes.

Add the mushrooms and season with salt and pepper. Continue cooking, stirring, for a few minutes. Increase the heat and cook rapidly to evaporate almost all the liquid, until the contents of the pan are fairly dry.

Remove from the heat and add the parsley and pâté to the pan. Mix thoroughly and let cool.

Lay the bacon slices, overlapping slightly, on a board. Spread the mushroom-pâté mixture over the bacon, then place the beef on top. Season with a little more pepper and wrap the bacon up and around the beef, securing it in place with wooden toothpicks or string.

Put the chopped onion, carrot, and celery in the bottom of a roasting pan and place the wrapped beef on top. Roast the beef, allowing 40 minutes for rare, 50 minutes for medium.

Make the sauce: strain the cooking juices into a small saucepan. Add the flour and mix until smooth. Cook over medium heat for 2 minutes, stirring. Stir in the mustard followed by the wine and stock. Bring to a boil, stirring, and simmer 5 minutes. Season to taste and serve with the beef.

BEEF AND STOUT PIE

SERVES 4

2 tbsp flour, plus more for dusting
½ tsp dried English mustard
salt and freshly ground black pepper
1½ lb chuck steak, cubed
¼ cup olive oil
12 baby onions, peeled
1 cup stout or dark beer
1 cup beef stock
sprig of fresh thyme
2 tbsp Worcestershire sauce
1 lb Quick Puff Pastry (see page 94)
1 egg, beaten
milk, for glazing

Mix the flour, mustard powder, and some salt and pepper in a large bowl. Add the meat and toss to coat it well with the seasoned flour.

Heat the oil in a Dutch oven or large heavy pan over high heat. Add the onions and brown them lightly, 3-4 minutes. Using a slotted spoon, remove the onions and set aside.

Add the cubes of meat to the pan, in batches if necessary, and brown them on all sides.

Stir in the stout, stock, thyme, and Worcestershire sauce. Bring to a boil, then lower the heat, cover, and simmer until the meat is tender, about 2 hours. After 1½ hours, stir in the reserved onions and remove the thyme.

Preheat the oven to 425°F. Transfer the filling to a

round deep baking dish, piling the meat in the center to prevent the crust from sinking.

On a floured surface, roll out the pastry dough to a round big enough to cover the pie generously. Dampen the rim of the baking dish with water and cut a long strip of pastry dough to fit it. Once this is firmly in place, dampen its top with a little more water. Use the remaining pastry dough to cover the pie, trim the edges and crimp to seal.

Make a slit in the center of the crust to let the steam escape and brush with a mixture of beaten egg and milk to glaze. Use the pastry trimmings to decorate the crust, if desired, and glaze again.

Bake until the pastry is well risen and golden brown, 25-30 minutes.

STEAK AND MUSHROOM PUDDING

SERVES 4

¼ cup vegetable oil
1½ lb chuck steak, cubed
1 onion, chopped
2 tbsp flour
sprig of fresh thyme
sprig of fresh marjoram
1 tbsp Worcestershire sauce
⅔ cup beef stock
5 tbsp port wine
salt and freshly ground black pepper
¼ lb small button mushrooms
FOR THE SUET-CRUST PASTRY
2⅓ cups self-rising flour
1 tsp salt
6 oz shredded beef suet

Heat the oil in a large heavy saucepan over high heat. Brown the meat, in batches if necessary, stirring to color on all sides. Transfer to a plate.

Add the onion to the pan and cook over medium heat until softened, about 5 minutes. Stir in the flour and cook 1 minute longer. Add the herbs and Worcestershire sauce to the pan and gradually stir in the stock and port. Cook until thickened.

Return the meat to the pan and bring to a boil. Season, cover, and simmer gently 45 minutes.

Meanwhile, prepare the suet-crust pastry: sift the flour and salt into a large mixing bowl and stir in the suet. Gradually stir in 1-1¼ cups of cold water to form a soft, but not sticky, dough.

Grease a 5-cup pudding basin. Turn the dough onto a lightly floured surface and knead gently. Roll it out to form a large round about ¼-inch thick. Cut a quarter wedge from the dough and set it aside to be used for the lid. Use the remaining dough to line the prepared pudding basin, pressing the edges to form a seal. Spoon alternate layers of the filling and mushrooms into the basin.

Re-roll the reserved pastry and use it to cover the pudding. Crimp the edges to seal and trim away any excess pastry. Cover with a pleated piece of wax paper and the same of foil and secure tightly with string.

Put the basin in a large saucepan that has a tight-fitting lid. Pour in enough hot water to come about three-quarters of the way up the basin, cover, and steam the pudding about 2 hours, adding more water occasionally to prevent its boiling dry.

THE BEEF AND STOUT PIE *can be made with any strong dark beer. Try adding some canned oysters - fresh oysters were once a traditional part of the filling. A round or oval deep baking dish with a rim is needed for the pie.*

The traditional deep, slope-sided PUDDING BASIN *for steamed puddings is made of glazed ceramic. A steamed-pudding mold with lid could also be used.*

GREEN GINGER WINE, *available from better liquor stores or wine shops, was once popular in England added to glasses of wine. It is now most often mixed with Scotch. It is a useful flavoring as it retains much of the original warmth of gingerroot. If unavailable, macerate 2 or 3 1-inch cubes of gingerroot for a few days in ½ cup of cider vinegar with 1 tablespoon of sugar. Strain and use in place of the wine.*

MARINATED STEAKS WITH GINGER BUTTER

SERVES 4

½ tsp salt
½ tsp pepper
1 garlic clove, minced
juice of ½ lime
½ cup green ginger wine
4 boneless sirloin steaks, each about 6-7 oz
FOR THE GINGER BUTTER
juice from 1-inch cube of fresh gingerroot, crushed through a garlic press
4 tbsp butter, softened

In a bowl, mix together the salt, pepper, garlic, lime juice, and ginger wine. Add the steaks and toss thoroughly so that they are well coated. Cover the bowl with plastic wrap and let marinate about 1 hour at room temperature, or up to 3 hours in the refrigerator, shaking from time to time.

Meanwhile, mix the ginger juice with the softened butter and put this on a small piece of plastic wrap. Wrap tightly, forming into a small fat log shape. Chill in the freezer about 30 minutes.

Preheat the barbecue until coals are quite hot.

Remove the steaks from the marinade and cook to the desired doneness, basting frequently with the marinade. Exact cooking times will depend on how thick the steaks are and the temperature of the coals. Start by cooking for 2-3 minutes on each side, then cut a little piece off. If it isn't cooked enough, return it to the barbecue for another minute or two.

Just before serving, unwrap the chilled ginger butter and cut the log across to form 4 circular pats. Serve the steaks on hot plates with a pat of ginger butter on top of each

Top: Marinated Steaks with Ginger Butter; bottom: Butterflied Quails with Tomato Salsa (page 93)

A classic of Neapolitan cuisine, PIZZAIOLA is a rich and highly flavored tomato sauce used with meat and pasta.

KOFTA, or meatballs, are ubiquitous in Arab cooking, although they vary widely from place to place in their exact ingredients. They may even be shaped into fingers or flat cakes, like hamburgers. For the right texture the meat must be ground two or three times, or pulsed in a food processor until smooth.

NEAPOLITAN STEAKS WITH PIZZAIOLA SAUCE

SERVES 4

2 tbsp olive oil
4 thick boneless sirloin steaks
salt and freshly ground black pepper
FOR THE PIZZAIOLA SAUCE
2 tbsp olive oil
2 onions, minced
4 garlic cloves, minced
1 small red sweet pepper, seeded and minced
1½ lb very ripe tomatoes, chopped
⅛ teaspoon dried oregano
3 tbsp coarsely chopped fresh flat-leaf parsley
dash of hot pepper sauce

First make the sauce: heat the oil in a saucepan and sauté the onions until lightly colored, 2 or 3 minutes. Add the garlic and minced red pepper and cook 1 minute more.

Add the tomatoes, oregano, and most of the parsley. Season with salt and pepper and hot pepper sauce. Cover and simmer over low heat about 15 minutes, stirring from time to time. The tomatoes should not become too pulpy.

Towards the end of this time, over medium-high heat, heat the oil in a large sauté pan that has a lid. Season the steaks and brown them rapidly on both sides.

Once the steaks are browned on both sides, reduce the heat to very low and pour the sauce over them. Cover and cook 3-7 minutes, depending on how well done you want the steaks to be. Adjust the seasoning if necessary.

Serve the steaks with the sauce poured over them and sprinkled with the reserved parsley.

NOTE: try adding some chopped mushrooms to the sauce for extra flavor.

FRUIT AND NUT KOFTA

SERVES 4

2 tbsp butter
2 onions, minced
2 garlic cloves, minced
⅔ cup pine nuts
2¼ lb finely ground lean steak or lamb, or a mixture
3 or 4 dried apricots, minced
⅓ cup raisins
2 eggs, lightly beaten
pinch of ground allspice
salt and freshly ground black pepper
2 tbsp flour
2 tbsp freshly grated Parmesan cheese
2 tbsp olive oil
chopped fresh flat-leaf parsley, for garnish
lemon slices, for serving

Melt the butter in a large sauté pan over medium heat and sauté the onion, garlic, and pine nuts until just beginning to color.

Transfer these to a large bowl and knead together with the meat, fruit, eggs, allspice, salt, and pepper. Form into walnut-sized meatballs.

In a shallow plate, mix the flour and cheese and season well. Roll the meatballs in the mixture.

Heat the oil in the pan and sauté the meatballs over low heat until golden brown and cooked through.

Arrange in concentric circles on a warmed serving plate, garnish with parsley, and serve with lemon slices.

These meatballs are delicious served hot with a lemony yogurt or spicy tomato sauce and accompanied by rice or potatoes. They are equally good cold with salad, as part of a buffet or picnic.

SPICY LAMB MEATBALLS ON SKEWERS

MAKES 16

¾ lb ground lamb
⅔ cup fresh white bread crumbs
½ small onion, minced or grated
1 tbsp minced fresh parsley
⅓ cup pine nuts
3 tsp chopped raisins
½ tsp ground cinnamon
1 egg, lightly beaten
salt and pepper
FOR SERVING
1 small mild onion, sliced and separated into rings
¼ cup thick plain yogurt

In a bowl, combine all the ingredients thoroughly (easiest in a food processor) and season well. With wet hands, form the mixture into 16 walnut-sized balls. Chill 2-3 hours, or up to 24, to firm them up.

If using wooden skewers, soak 4 of them in water for 1 hour beforehand to prevent them from burning during cooking. Preheat the barbecue until the coals are quite hot.

Thread the meatballs carefully on 4 skewers and grill, turning them occasionally (handle them carefully as they are quite fragile), until the outsides are crisp and brown, 15-20 minutes. The exact time will depend on the heat of the charcoal.

Serve immediately, accompanied by the onion rings and yogurt.

PROVENÇAL LAMB BROCHETTES

SERVES 4

3 garlic cloves, minced
juice of 1 lemon
2 tbsp extra virgin olive oil
1 tbsp herbes de Provence
salt and pepper
2 lb lean boneless leg of lamb, cut into about 1-inch cubes
2 onions, cut into about 1-inch chunks

Mix the garlic, lemon juice, oil, herbs, and seasoning in a bowl. Add the lamb cubes and mix thoroughly. Cover with plastic wrap and let the meat marinate, stirring occasionally, at least 1 hour at room temperature, or up to 12 in the refrigerator.

If using wooden skewers, soak 8 of them in water for 1 hour beforehand to prevent their burning during cooking. Preheat the barbecue coals or the grill until quite hot.

Thread the meat on 8 skewers, alternating the pieces with chunks of onion.

Cook on the barbecue, or under the broiler, about 4-5 minutes on each side, until cooked through.

YOGURT MOUSSAKA

SERVES 6-8

2 eggplants, thinly sliced
about ½ cup olive oil
¾ lb ground lean steak or lamb
4 large onions, thinly sliced
3 large garlic cloves, minced
3 tbsp minced fresh flat-leaf parsley
2 cups canned plum tomatoes, drained and chopped
⅓ cup tomato paste
2 eggs
2 cups thick plain yogurt
2 tbsp lemon juice
pinch of freshly grated nutmeg
½ cup freshly grated Parmesan cheese
salt and freshly ground black pepper

The Greeks claim MOUSSAKA *as their own dish, although the Turks adopted it and spread it throughout the Islamic world. This version uses yogurt and eggs instead of the more usual white sauce.*

Put the eggplant slices in a colander and sprinkle them generously with salt. Let drain about 30 minutes and then rinse thoroughly. Pat dry.

Heat 2 tablespoons of the oil in a large frying pan over medium heat and brown the eggplant slices in batches, draining them on paper towels as they are ready and adding more oil to the pan as needed.

Add 1 or 2 more tablespoons of the oil to the pan, increase the heat to high, and brown the meat: spread it out into a flat cake and cook rapidly, undisturbed, until the underside is well colored. Then break up the cake, stir the meat well, and form it into a flat cake again. Cook in the same way. Repeat this process until the meat is a uniform color. Transfer to a bowl.

Heat 1 or 2 more tablespoons of the oil in the pan over medium heat and cook the onions until soft, 2-3 minutes. Add the garlic and parsley and cook for 1 minute or so longer. Add the tomatoes, browned meat, and tomato paste and simmer about 30 minutes. Season well.

Preheat the oven to 350°F and grease a deep baking dish generously with 1 tablespoon of the remaining oil.

Put a layer of one-third of the eggplant slices in the bottom of the prepared dish. Spoon over half the meat mixture and then repeat the layers, finishing with a layer of eggplant slices.

Mix the eggs into the yogurt and season with salt, pepper, lemon juice, and nutmeg. Pour this over the contents of the dish. Sprinkle Parmesan over the top and bake until golden brown, about 45 minutes.

NOTE: try adding layers of sautéed mushrooms or zucchini, par-boiled potatoes or spinach, or slices of Gruyère cheese for extra interest. (You can then even omit the meat to make a vegetarian moussaka.) Add some red wine or 1 or 2 spoonfuls of brandy to the onions for extra flavor.

HONEYED LAMB KEBABS

SERVES 4

2 lb boned leg of lamb, cut into 1-inch cubes
4 onions, quartered
4 tomatoes, quartered
2 red sweet peppers, quartered and seeded
2 green sweet peppers, quartered and seeded
8 bay leaves
chopped fresh oregano or flat-leaf parsley, for garnish
lemon wedges, for serving
FOR THE HONEY MARINADE
1 washed lemon
¼ cup honey
6 tbsp olive oil
2 garlic cloves, minced
2 tbsp chopped fresh oregano
2 tsp crushed black peppercorns

First make the honey marinade: finely grate 1 teaspoon of lemon zest and extract the lemon juice. Mix these with the remaining ingredients in a bowl. Add the pieces of lamb and onion quarters and stir well to coat them thoroughly. Cover and let marinate 2-3 hours in a cool place, stirring occasionally.

Preheat a hot grill, broiler or barbecue. Drain the lamb and onion well and thread on skewers, interleaved with pieces of tomato, pepper, and bay leaves. Grill until well browned on all sides, basting with the marinade from time to time.

Garnish with chopped oregano and serve with lemon wedges. A green, or tomato and onion salad makes an excellent accompaniment.

NOTE: add rolled bacon slices or quartered mushrooms to the kebabs for extra interest. Try replacing the oregano with mint, rosemary, or basil.

Clockwise from the top: Fruit and Nut Kofta (page 74) with a lemon-yogurt sauce, Honeyed Lamb Kebabs with a spicy tomato sauce, and Chicken Drumsticks with Garlic and Lime (page 90)

LEG OF LAMB WITH WHOLE ROAST GARLIC

SERVES 4-6

1 lamb center-leg roast, weighing about 3½ lb
salt and freshly ground black pepper
1 tsp dried English mustard
3 large fresh rosemary sprigs
3 whole heads of garlic
1 tbsp olive oil
¾ cup port wine
¼ cup red currant jelly
1 tsp cornstarch
rosemary sprigs, for garnish (optional)
red currant sprigs, for garnish (optional)

Preheat the oven to 450°F. Sprinkle the lamb with salt, pepper, and mustard and rub in well.

Cut 2 of the rosemary sprigs into 1½-inch pieces. Using a pointed knife, make incisions deep in the lamb and insert the rosemary pieces into them.

Place the remaining rosemary sprig in a roasting pan and place the lamb on top. Roast 20 minutes, then lower the oven temperature to 350°F and continue roasting 1½ hours longer. The lamb should still be a little pink inside.

About 40 minutes before the end of the roasting time, brush the heads of garlic with the olive oil and add them to the roasting pan.

Transfer the cooked lamb and garlic to a warmed serving platter and let rest 12-15 minutes before carving the lamb and serving.

Meanwhile, prepare the sauce: pour off any excess fat from the roasting pan. Add the port to the pan together with ½ cup of water. Bring to a boil and cook over medium-high heat 2 minutes, stirring and scraping up the browned bits with a wooden spoon.

Add the red currant jelly and stir until melted. Simmer 1 minute. Blend the cornstarch with 2 tablespoons of cold water and add to the sauce. Stir until thickened.

Season the sauce to taste and serve with the lamb, garnished with rosemary and red currants if using, and the roast garlic.

IRISH HOTCHPOTCH

SERVES 4

8-12 lamb blade or shoulder chops
2 onions, thinly sliced
½ lb carrots, thickly sliced
1½ lb potatoes, thinly sliced
1 tbsp fresh rosemary leaves (optional)
salt and freshly ground black pepper
1¼ cups well-flavored beef or lamb stock
2 tbsp butter
chopped fresh parsley, for garnish

Preheat the oven to 325°F.

Trim any excess fat from the chops and layer them in a large casserole dish with the onions, carrots, potatoes, and rosemary, if using. Season each layer with salt and pepper and finish with a layer of overlapping slices of potato.

Bring the stock to a boil and pour it into the casserole. Dot the butter over the surface. Cover tightly with a lid or foil and bake 2 hours.

Remove the lid from the casserole and increase the oven temperature to 425°F. Continue baking until the potatoes are browned, 15-20 minutes longer.

Serve the hotchpotch in soup plates, sprinkled with chopped parsley.

Left: Leg of Lamb with Whole Roast Garlic; right: Gratin Dauphinois (page 162)

NUT OILS, *such as those made by pressing walnuts and hazelnuts, have fine nutty flavors. Excellent in moderation in salad dressings, they are available from specialty stores and many supermarkets. Buy them in small quantities because a little goes a long way and they turn rancid quickly.*

HERBED LEG OF LAMB WITH TOMATO SAUCE

SERVES 6-8

1 boned lamb center-leg roast, weighing about 3 lb
3 small sprigs of fresh rosemary
½ tsp each snipped fresh basil, thyme, and oregano
sea salt and freshly ground black pepper
FOR THE SAUCE
1 tsp olive oil
2 onions, coarsely chopped
2 garlic cloves, minced
1 green sweet pepper, seeded and thinly sliced
1 red sweet pepper, seeded and thinly sliced
2 cups canned peeled tomatoes, drained
1 tbsp tomato paste
¼ lb oyster mushrooms, coarsely chopped
⅔ cup dry white wine

Preheat the oven to 450°F.

Lay the meat out flat and sprinkle it with the herbs and seasoning. Roll up as tightly as possible, then tie with string.

Place in a roasting pan and roast 25 minutes. Reduce the temperature to 425°F and roast 45-50 minutes longer. Transfer to a warmed serving platter and keep warm.

Make the sauce: put the olive oil in a heavy pan over medium heat, add the onions and garlic, and sauté until translucent, 3-5 minutes.

Add the peppers and combine thoroughly with the onions. Cook 2 minutes, then add the tomatoes, tomato paste, and mushrooms. Stir well and cook 2 minutes longer.

Season and add the wine. Increase the heat and bring to a boil, stirring constantly. Continue to boil to reduce a little, then serve with the lamb.

SAUTÉED LAMB WITH FENNEL SAUCE

SERVES 6

2 tbsp walnut oil
2 lb boneless lamb loin or sirloin, cut into small pieces ½-inch thick
¼ tsp salt
freshly ground black pepper
FOR THE FENNEL SAUCE
⅔ cup vegetable stock
2 fennel bulbs, thinly sliced, with the feathery leaves reserved for garnish
2 tbsp butter
1 tbsp flour
1¼ cups light cream
salt and freshly ground black pepper

First make the sauce: put the stock in a pan with the fennel. Cover, bring to a boil, and simmer 25 minutes over medium heat. Remove from the heat and let cool.

When cool, purée the mixture in a blender or food processor and then push through a fine strainer.

Melt the butter in a pan over medium heat, add the flour, and cook, stirring constantly, for 3 minutes.

Remove from the heat and stir in the fennel purée. Return to the heat and stir constantly for 5 minutes. Gradually add the cream and then season to taste.

Heat the walnut oil in a frying pan over medium heat and add the lamb slices. Sprinkle with salt and pepper, increase the heat, and sauté the lamb 3 minutes, stirring constantly.

Transfer the lamb to a warmed serving dish, cover with the fennel sauce and garnish with the reserved fennel fronds.

BEEF AND LAMB WITH ALMONDS

SERVES 4

3 tbsp olive oil
⅓ cup blanched almonds
¾ lb chuck steak, cubed
¾ lb boneless lamb, cubed
1 onion, chopped
2 garlic cloves, chopped
2 tsp coriander seeds, lightly crushed
¼ tsp ground allspice
1¼ cups beef stock
salt and freshly ground black pepper
4 oz plump dried apricots, halved
chopped fresh cilantro, for garnish

Preheat the oven to 350°F.

Heat 1 tablespoon of the olive oil in a large heavy saucepan over medium heat. Add the almonds and cook, stirring, until golden brown, 2-3 minutes. Transfer to a plate and set aside.

Add the remaining oil to the pan, increase the heat slightly, and cook the meat, in batches if necessary, until well browned on all sides. Using a slotted spoon, transfer the meat to a large casserole dish.

Add the onion, garlic, and spices to the pan and cook over medium heat 5 minutes, stirring frequently. Pour in the stock and bring to a boil. Add the contents of the pan to the casserole. Season with salt and pepper. Cover and transfer to the oven. Cook 1 hour.

At the end of this time, add the apricots and browned almonds to the casserole and mix well. Cover again and return to the oven to cook until the meat is tender, 45-60 minutes longer.

Adjust the seasoning, if necessary. Serve sprinkled with chopped fresh cilantro and accompanied by basmati rice.

NAVARIN OF LAMB

SERVES 4

4 tbsp olive oil
1½ lb boneless lamb shoulder, diced
12 baby onions
8-12 baby carrots
6 small baby turnips
2 garlic cloves, minced
1 tbsp flour
2½ cups well-flavored stock
1¼ cups red wine
bouquet garni
salt and freshly ground black pepper
8 small new potatoes
chopped fresh parsley, for garnish
FOR THE CROUTES
4 large slices of white bread, crusts removed
3 tbsp light olive oil

Heat 2 tablespoons of the oil in a Dutch oven over high heat. Add the meat and cook, stirring, until the pieces are browned on all sides. Using a slotted spoon, transfer the meat to a plate.

Put the remaining oil in the pot. Add the onions, carrots, and turnips and cook for 5 minutes, stirring, over medium-high heat. Using a slotted spoon, transfer the vegetables to a plate and reserve.

Add the garlic to the pot and cook 1 minute. Stir in the flour and cook, stirring, for 2 minutes. Gradually stir in the stock and wine. Bring to a boil, then return the meat to the pot. Add the bouquet garni and season. Bring back to a boil. Lower the heat, cover, and simmer 45 minutes, stirring occasionally.

Add the reserved vegetables and the potatoes to the pot. Cover and continue to simmer 30 minutes. Then remove the lid and cook uncovered 10-15 minutes longer to let the sauce reduce slightly.

While the sauce is reducing, make the croûtes: cut the slices of bread into triangles or use a cookie cutter

NAVARIN OF LAMB *is a traditional French lamb stew and derives its name from* navet, *the French word for the turnip. When made this way with spring vegetables, the dish is also known as "Navarin printanier."*

The region of
NORMANDY
produces most of
France's apple crop
and for this reason it
is a center of the
manufacture of cider
and Calvados, the
apple brandy. It is
also the province
most associated with
dairy products.
Hence, dishes with
apples, cider,
Calvados, or lots of
butter and cream
characterize the
cooking of
Normandy.

to cut out rounds or other shapes. Heat the oil in a frying pan over medium-high heat. When the oil is really hot, add the bread, a few pieces at a time, and cook until golden and crisp, 30-45 seconds on each side. Drain on paper towels.

Adjust the seasoning of the navarin, sprinkle with parsley and serve with the croûtes.

PORK WITH JUNIPER, CELERY, AND PRUNES

SERVES 4

3 tbsp vegetable oil
1½ lb pork tenderloin, cut into 1½-inch pieces
2 shallots, minced
2 celery stalks, cut into matchstick strips
2 tsp juniper berries, lightly crushed
1 cup dry white wine
3 tbsp sherry wine
1 bay leaf
4 fresh sage leaves, shredded
12 plump prunes
salt and freshly ground black pepper
fresh sage leaves, for garnish

Heat the oil in a Dutch oven over high heat. Add the pork and brown on all sides. Using a slotted spoon, transfer to a plate and set aside.

Add the shallots to the pot and cook over medium heat until soft, 4-5 minutes. Add the celery and juniper and cook 2 minutes longer. Add the wine, sherry, and herbs and bring to a boil. Return the meat to the pot, cover, and simmer 20 minutes.

Add the prunes and continue cooking, uncovered,

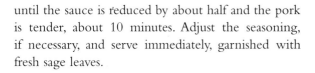

until the sauce is reduced by about half and the pork is tender, about 10 minutes. Adjust the seasoning, if necessary, and serve immediately, garnished with fresh sage leaves.

NORMANDY PORK CHOPS

SERVES 4

3 tbsp vegetable oil
4 pork or veal chops, about 1-inch thick
¼ cup brandy, preferably Calvados
salt and freshly ground black pepper
FOR THE SAUCE
1¼ cups whipping cream
2 tbsp butter
1 tbsp chopped fresh parsley
FOR THE GLAZED APPLES
2 apples
1 tbsp lemon juice
2 tbsp butter
1 tsp sugar

Heat the oil in a large heavy frying pan over high heat. Add the chops and brown them on both sides. Add the brandy to the pan and carefully set it aflame. Let the flames subside, then season.

Lower the heat and cook the chops until done, 3-4 minutes on each side. Transfer the chops to a warmed serving plate and keep warm.

Make the sauce: add the cream and butter to the pan, stirring well to scrape up all the browned bits. Stir in the parsley and simmer until the sauce begins to thicken, 3-4 minutes. Season and keep warm.

Make the glazed apples: peel and core the apples. Cut into thick wedges and toss in the lemon juice. Melt the butter in a frying pan over medium heat and add the apples. Sprinkle with the sugar and fry until golden brown, 2-3 minutes.

Serve the chops accompanied by the glazed apples and the sauce.

PAPRIKA AND CARAWAY ROAST PORK WITH APPLESAUCE

SERVES 6-8

1 pork shoulder butt roast, weighing about 4 lb,
trimmed of fat and neatly tied
2 tbsp olive oil
salt and pepper
2 tsp paprika
2 tsp caraway seeds
2 large tart apples, peeled, cored, and cut into uniform
pieces
1 tbsp flour
2-2½ cups chicken stock or water from
cooking potatoes or vegetables

Preheat the oven to 350°F.

Place the pork on a rack set in a roasting pan. Drizzle the oil over it and season it generously with salt and pepper. Roast 3 hours, basting occasionally. After 2 hours, baste thoroughly and sprinkle with the paprika and caraway seeds.

Toward the end of the cooking time, make the applesauce: put the apples and 2 tablespoons of water in a saucepan that has a tight-fitting lid. Cook over medium heat, shaking the pan occasionally, until the apples dissolve into a light mush. The exact cooking time will depend on the apples. Watch them carefully to ensure that they do not burn. Stir in a pinch of salt to bring out the flavor and then keep the applesauce warm.

When the meat is done, transfer it to a warmed serving plate and let it rest while making the gravy. Remove the fat from the roasting pan, leaving about 1 tablespoon (there might not be much more than that if the meat was really lean), and place the roasting pan over medium heat. Stir in the flour and mix it well into the fat, stirring up the browned bits on the bottom of the pan (a wire balloon whisk is useful for this job).

Pour in about 2 cups of stock or vegetable water and bring to a boil, whisking all the time to make sure no lumps form. Simmer 2-3 minutes. Adjust the seasoning and add more stock if necessary to give a good pouring consistency. (The gravy should not be too thick.) Strain into a warmed gravy boat.

To serve: slice the meat as thinly as possible and serve with the gravy and the applesauce.

Previous page, left: Paprika and Caraway Roast Pork with
Applesauce; bottom right: Provençal Gratin of Zucchini (page
165)

SPICED CHICKEN TART★

SERVES 6

6 oz frozen puff pastry, thawed
FOR THE FILLING
2 tbsp butter or margarine
1 leek, thinly sliced
1 garlic clove, minced
½ tsp ground turmeric
2 tsp ground cumin
2 tsp garam masala
½ lb chicken breast meat, diced
1 potato, peeled, diced, and cooked
1 tbsp chopped fresh cilantro
grated zest and juice of 1 washed lime
½ tsp salt and ¼ tsp freshly ground black pepper
1 tbsp mango chutney
⅔ cup light cream
2 eggs★
(★see page 2 for advice on eggs)
FOR GARNISH
sprigs of fresh cilantro

Roll the pastry out thinly on a lightly floured surface and use it to line a 9-inch round tart or pie pan. Flute the edges and chill 30 minutes.

Preheat the oven to 400°F.

Bake the pastry shell "blind" until lightly browned at the edges, 10-15 minutes.

While the shell is baking make the filling: melt the butter or margarine in a saucepan over medium heat. Add the leek and garlic and cook quickly for 1 minute. Stir in the spices, chicken, and potato. Cook, stirring frequently, until the chicken has turned white. Add the cilantro, lime zest, juice, salt, pepper, and chutney. Remove from the heat.

Beat together the cream and eggs and stir into the chicken mixture. Pour into the pastry shell and bake until the filling has set, 15-20 minutes.

Serve hot or cold, garnished with cilantro.

CHICKEN BREASTS WITH COCONUT-TARRAGON CREAM

SERVES 4

3 tbsp butter
1 tbsp hazelnut oil
2 tbsp chopped fresh tarragon
4 large boneless chicken breast halves
2 tbsp canned unsweetened coconut cream
salt and freshly ground black pepper

Melt the butter with the oil in a heavy pan over medium heat. Add half the tarragon, followed by the chicken breasts. Cover and cook about 5 minutes.

Remove the lid and turn the chicken breasts over. Season, increase the heat a little, and cook 5 minutes longer.

Reduce the heat to medium and add the coconut cream. Baste the chicken and adjust the seasoning, if necessary.

Increase the heat again, turn the breasts once more, and cook 2 minutes longer.

Transfer the chicken and its sauce to a warmed serving platter and garnish with the remaining tarragon.

NOTE: this dish works equally well with more economical pieces of chicken such as drumsticks, thighs, or wings.

GARAM MASALA, *meaning "hot spice mixture," is an intensely aromatic blend of ground spices used in some Indian recipes. It is available commercially but it is possible to grind your own garam masala. There are many different blends, but most use coriander, cumin, cardamom, ginger, cloves, and black pepper.*

OLD-FASHIONED POULTRY PIE

SERVES 6

FOR THE FILLING

1½ lb boneless chicken or turkey, cut into thin strips
½ lb chicken or turkey livers, chopped
½ lb slab bacon, chopped
1 tbsp green peppercorns in brine, drained
2 garlic cloves, minced
3 tbsp sherry wine
salt and freshly ground black pepper

FOR THE HOT-WATER-CRUST PASTRY

5 oz (10 tbsp) lard, diced, plus more for greasing
3 cups flour
1 tsp salt
1 egg, beaten
milk, for glazing

Mix all the filling ingredients and set aside.

Preheat the oven to 400°F. Grease a hinged pâté-en-croûte mold or a 6-inch springform cake pan with some lard.

Make the pastry: sift the flour and salt into a large bowl. In a small saucepan, heat the lard and ½ cup of water until melted. Bring to a boil, then pour over the flour. Mix thoroughly to a soft dough.

Turn onto a lightly floured surface and knead until just smooth. While still warm, roll out three-quarters and use to line the prepared mold or pan.

Spoon in the filling. Roll out the remaining dough to make a lid. Crimp the edges to seal and make a few steam holes in the crust. Use pastry trimmings to decorate the crust. Mix the beaten egg and some milk and brush the crust with this glaze.

Bake 30 minutes, then lower the temperature to 350°F and bake another 1¼ hours longer. Cool in the mold and serve cold.

CHICKEN WITH GARLIC AND OLIVES

SERVES 4

8 small chicken pieces (preferably drumsticks and thighs), skinned
salt and freshly ground black pepper
sprig of fresh thyme
sprig of fresh rosemary
1 bay leaf
3 tbsp olive oil
1 large onion, thinly sliced
5 garlic cloves, halved
1 cup dry white wine
12 pitted black olives
12 pitted green olives, sliced
chopped fresh parsley, for garnish

Rinse the chicken pieces, pat them dry, and season. Tie the herbs into a bundle with string.

Heat the oil in a large heavy saucepan over medium-high heat. Add the chicken pieces and brown them on all sides.

Add the herbs, onion, and garlic and cook 5 minutes longer. Stir in the wine and bring to a boil. Then lower the heat, cover, and cook 30 minutes.

Using a slotted spoon, transfer the chicken to a warmed serving platter. Stir the juices in the pan thoroughly to blend the garlic.

Add the olives to the pan and simmer, uncovered, about 5 minutes to reduce the sauce by about one-third. Discard the herbs, adjust the seasoning to taste, and pour the sauce over the chicken.

Serve sprinkled with chopped fresh parsley.

Left: Old-fashioned Poultry Pie; right:Celery Root and Rutabaga Purée and Carrot and Parsnip Purée from the Trio of Vegetable Purées (page 162)

MOROCCAN LEMON CHICKEN

SERVES 4

4 washed lemons
1 free-range chicken, weighing about 3½ lb,
giblets retained
2 onions
1 bay leaf
1 tsp black peppercorns
3 tbsp minced fresh flat-leaf parsley
1 tbsp olive oil
1 tsp minced fresh gingerroot
pinch of ground cinnamon
salt and freshly ground black pepper
3 tbsp minced fresh cilantro

Preheat the oven to 425°F.

Grate 1 tablespoon of zest from the lemons and pare off 2 or 3 thin strips of zest. Quarter 2 of the other lemons.

Trim the giblets, removing any dark bits, and put in a small pan with 1 of the onions, the bay leaf, peppercorns, the strips of lemon zest, and any stems from the parsley. Cover with water, bring to a boil, and simmer gently about 1 hour. Strain and reserve.

Finely chop the remaining onion. Heat the oil in a sauté pan over medium heat and sauté the onion, together with the grated lemon zest, ginger, cinnamon, and seasoning until soft.

Transfer to a bowl and mix in most of the minced parsley and cilantro. Stuff the chicken with this mixture and the lemon quarters, squashing them lightly as you insert them.

Place the chicken in a roasting pan, breast down. Add just enough water to cover the bottom of the pan and roast for about 50-60 minutes, turning over halfway through and basting regularly, until well browned all over and the juices run clear when the thickest part of the thigh is pierced.

Transfer the chicken to a warmed serving platter, tipping it so that any liquid inside the bird drains back into the pan. Garnish with one of the remaining lemons, cut into wedges, and the remaining herbs.

Deglaze the roasting pan with the juice from the last of the lemons, scraping up any browned bits with a wooden spoon, and boil briefly to reduce to a sticky liquid. Add the giblet stock and boil to reduce to a sauce-like consistency. Adjust the seasoning and serve this sauce separately, adding any juices that run from the chicken during carving.

In North Africa this dish would be made using lemons that have been dried or preserved in oil, giving a much more pungent flavor.

The ancient Persian Faisinjan *sauce of pomegranates and walnuts was used mostly for wild duck and other game birds, but suits chicken and domestic duck. If fresh pomegranates are unavailable, use 2 or 3 tablespoons of pomegranate syrup mixed with 1¼ cups of water instead of the strained juice, but do not add sugar.*

CHICKEN DRUMSTICKS WITH GARLIC AND LIME

SERVES 4

3 garlic cloves, minced
2 tbsp olive oil
4 limes
salt and freshly ground black pepper
12 chicken drumsticks, preferably from free-range birds
cayenne pepper, for garnish

Mix together the garlic, olive oil, and the juice of 3 of the limes in a large bowl and season well. Add the chicken pieces and mix them in so that they are well coated. Cover and let marinate in the refrigerator for several hours, turning from time to time.

Preheat the oven to 400°F.

Drain the drumsticks and arrange in a baking dish. Bake until browned and the juices run clear when the thickest part is pierced, about 30 minutes.

While the chicken is cooking, pour the marinade into a saucepan and boil it until reduced to a sticky sauce-like consistency. Adjust the seasoning (according to preference, the tartness may also be cut slightly with a little sugar).

Serve the drumsticks dusted lightly with cayenne, with the remaining lime cut into wedges and the sauce in a bowl for dipping.

DUCK BREAST FAISINJAN

SERVES 4

4 pomegranates
juice of 1 large lemon
1 tbsp light brown sugar or honey
salt and freshly ground black pepper
4 boned duck breast halves
1 tbsp olive oil
1 onion, minced
¾ cup chopped walnuts

Halve the pomegranates and scoop the seeds into a food processor, reserving 2 or 3 tablespoons. Blend briefly and then press through a strainer.

Put this juice into a pan and add half its volume of water, the lemon juice, sugar, and season. Bring to a boil and simmer gently about 20 minutes. Cool.

Prepare the duck breasts by making several diagonal cuts through the fat to the meat.

Put the duck breasts in a bowl and pour over the cooled pomegranate mixture. Stir well, cover, and let marinate 2-3 hours.

Preheat the broiler. Drain the duck breasts, reserving the marinade. Pat them dry and broil skin-side up until well browned, 5-8 minutes. Turn and cook the other side in the same way. (Duck is best served fairly pink; if you prefer it well done, reduce the heat and cook another 10 minutes or so.)

While the duck is cooking, heat the oil in a saucepan over medium heat and add the onion and walnuts. Cook until the onion is soft, 2-3 minutes. Add the pomegranate mixture to the saucepan, bring to a boil, and simmer about 5 minutes. Adjust the seasoning and the sweet-and-sour balance with more lemon juice or sugar.

Serve the duck thickly sliced, sprinkled with the reserved seeds. Pass the sauce separately.

Duck Breast Faisinjan garnished with watercress

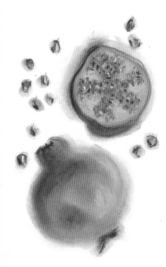

PESTO SAUCE *is
sold by specialty
stores and good
supermarkets.
However, you can
easily make your
own by crushing a
handful of fresh basil
leaves with 1 garlic
clove, 1 heaped
tablespoon of pine
nuts, and 2
tablespoons of freshly
grated Parmesan in
a mortar. Then work
in enough olive oil
to produce a thick
paste. Use the rest as
a pasta sauce.*

CHICKEN BAKED WITH SAVORY AND ORANGE

SERVES 4

1 tbsp freshly grated peeled gingerroot
½ tsp ground cloves
¾ tsp coarse salt
1 tsp coarsely ground black pepper
½ tsp ground coriander seeds
8 sprigs of fresh winter savory
3 tbsp butter, softened
1 large chicken, cut into quarters
1½ tbsp orange juice
thinly pared zest from 1 washed orange, cut into julienne strips
¾ cup dry white wine

Preheat the oven to 400°F.

Place the ginger, cloves, salt, black pepper, coriander seeds, and 2 sprigs of winter savory in a blender or food processor and process until fine. In a bowl, blend the mixture into the softened butter.

Lift the skin gently from the chicken quarters and make several incisions in the meat. Fill the incisions with the butter mixture, then replace the skin, securing with wooden toothpicks.

Line a baking dish with foil and place the remaining winter savory sprigs in the dish. Put the chicken on top of the savory and pour over the orange juice.

Bake until tender and the juices run clear when a skewer is inserted in the thickest part of the thigh, 40-50 minutes. Transfer the chicken to a warmed serving platter and keep warm.

Place the orange zest strips in a small pan and add the wine. Cover and simmer 3 minutes. Add the juices and the savory from the baking dish and bring to a boil. Boil 2 minutes to reduce slightly.

Strain the sauce into a warmed gravy boat and serve with the chicken.

BRIE AND BASIL CHICKEN

SERVES 4

1 chicken, weighing about 3-4 lb, with giblets
4 oz Brie cheese, mashed
1 tbsp pesto sauce
1 tbsp extra virgin olive oil
salt and pepper
FOR THE STOCK
1 onion, chopped
1 bay leaf
sliver of zest from a washed lemon
2-3 parsley sprigs

First make the stock by putting all the ingredients for the stock in a small pan together with the chicken giblets and 2 cups of water. Bring to a boil and then simmer gently 1 hour. Strain and discard the solids. There should be about 1¼ cups of stock left. Make that quantity with additional water, if necessary.

Preheat the oven to 400°F.

Prepare the chicken: starting at the end with the large cavity, carefully ease a hand under the skin to release it from the flesh. The skin will stay attached at the breastbone. Now ease the fingers under the skin of the drumsticks to loosen this too. (This is easier than it sounds and takes only a second or two.)

Mix the mashed cheese with the pesto and, using the fingers, work this paste all over the breast and legs under the skin. Pull the skin back to cover the flesh and secure with skewers, if necessary.

Place the prepared chicken in a small roasting pan or shallow ovenproof dish. Brush it all over with the oil and season with salt and pepper. Pour the stock around the chicken and roast 1½ hours, basting every 20 minutes or so. If the stock dries up before the bird is cooked, add a little water. At the end of cooking there should just be a few spoonfuls of flavorsome juice in the pan.

Carve the chicken and serve with these pan juices and plainly cooked fresh vegetables.

RABBIT WITH PRUNES, OLIVES, AND BACON

SERVES 4

1 large rabbit, cut into pieces
¼ lb pitted prunes, halved
2 tbsp oil
1 tbsp flour
1¼ cups red wine
1¼ cups chicken stock
2 garlic cloves, minced
1 bouquet garni
salt and fresh ground black pepper
5 oz bacon, cut into strips
½ cup pitted black olives, halved
FOR THE MARINADE
1¼ cups red wine
2 tbsp oil
1 large onion, coarsely chopped
1 large carrot, coarsely chopped
12 black peppercorns
1 bay leaf

Mix the marinade ingredients in a bowl and add the rabbit and prunes. Stir well, cover, and let marinate in a cool place 2-3 hours, stirring occasionally.

Remove the rabbit, prunes, and vegetables from the marinade and pat dry. Heat the oil in a Dutch oven over medium heat and brown the rabbit in it. Remove the rabbit and brown the vegetables. Sprinkle over the flour and sauté about 1 minute.

Stir in the marinade, wine, and stock together with the garlic, bouquet garni, and seasoning. Return the rabbit pieces to the pot. Bring to a boil, cover, and simmer gently about 30 minutes.

Toward the end of this time, fry the bacon until brown. Add it, the olives, and prunes to the pot and cook 15 minutes more. Transfer rabbit, prunes, olives, and bacon to a serving dish. Boil the juices rapidly to reduce to a sauce.

BUTTERFLIED QUAILS WITH TOMATO SALSA

SERVES 4

4 tbsp extra virgin olive oil
4 quails
salt and pepper
FOR THE SALSA
½ lb tomatoes, minced
1 small mild onion, minced
1 garlic clove, minced
3 tbsp minced fresh parsley
grated zest and juice of ½ washed lemon
2 tsp sugar

If using wooden skewers, soak 8 of them in water for 1 hour beforehand to prevent them from burning during cooking.

First make the salsa: combine all the ingredients in a bowl together with 1 tablespoon of the olive oil and chill 30-60 minutes to let the flavors develop. Preheat the barbecue until coals are quite hot.

Place the quails, breast-side down, on a work surface. Using a sharp knife or a pair of kitchen scissors, cut along either side of the backbone and remove it. (This is much easier than it sounds and only takes a few seconds.) Flatten each bird by turning it over, placing the palm of the hand on the breast, and pressing down firmly. (Again, easier than it sounds.)

Thread 2 skewers diagonally through each bird, each from one wing to the opposite leg. This will hold them flat and neat for cooking. Brush all over with some of the remaining olive oil and season.

Grill 25-30 minutes, turning occasionally and brushing with a little more oil as necessary. Make sure the birds are cooked through (pierce the thickest part of the thigh with a knife or skewer; the juices should run clear).

Serve immediately, with the cold salsa.

BUTTERFLYING *is a means of preparing any bird for the rapid process of grilling, flattening the bird while leaving it whole and on the bone.*

ROAST DUCK WITH BABY TURNIPS

SERVES 4

1 duckling, weighing about 4 lb
salt and freshly ground black pepper
3 tbsp butter
1½ lb small baby turnips
2-3 tsp light brown sugar
sprigs of fresh herbs, for garnish
FOR THE SAUCE
2 shallots, minced
1 tsp grated zest from a washed lemon
⅔ cup dry white wine
⅔ cup chicken stock
⅓ cup Marsala wine
2 tsp cornstarch

Preheat the oven to 400°F. Using a needle or skewer, prick the skin of the duck all over to let the fat run. Season the duck well with salt and pepper, rubbing it well into the skin. Place the bird on a rack in a roasting pan and cover loosely with foil.

Roast 1-1¼ hours, removing the foil halfway through cooking to let the skin brown and crisp. When the foil is removed, take 3 tablespoons of duck fat from the roasting pan and reserve.

Make the sauce: heat the reserved duck fat in a small heavy saucepan over low heat. Add the shallots and cook gently until soft and just beginning to brown, 5-7 minutes.

Stir in the lemon zest, wine, and stock. Bring to a boil, cover, and simmer 10 minutes. Stir in the Marsala. Blend the cornstarch with 2 tablespoons of cold water, add this to the sauce, and stir until thickened. Season to taste, then cover and set aside.

Melt the butter in a large heavy pan. Add the turnips and cook, stirring, over medium heat for 2 minutes. Add ⅔ cup of water to the pan together with the sugar, salt, and pepper. Bring to a boil. Cook,

If BABY TURNIPS *are unavailable, glaze some baby onions in the same way and serve the duck garnished with these and some fresh green peas.*

uncovered and stirring frequently, until the turnips are just tender and the liquid has evaporated to a caramelized glaze, about 15 minutes.

Serve the duck on a warmed platter, surrounded by the glazed baby turnips and garnished with sprigs of herbs. Gently reheat the sauce to accompany it.

GAME PIE

SERVES 6

2-4 game birds, depending on size (about 3 lb)
6 black peppercorns
1 bouquet garni
2 onions
4 tbsp butter
½ lb small mushrooms, thickly sliced
¼ lb slab bacon, chopped
1 tbsp flour
3 hard-cooked eggs, shelled and quartered
1 tbsp chopped fresh parsley
salt and freshly ground black pepper
FOR THE QUICK PUFF PASTRY
(makes about 1 lb)
1⅔ cups flour
1½ sticks (12 tbsp) chilled butter, cut into small dice
1 tsp lemon juice
about ⅔ cup ice water
1 egg, beaten
milk, for glazing

Make the pastry: sift the flour with a pinch of salt into a mixing bowl. Stir in the butter, add the lemon juice, and mix in sufficient ice water to form a firm dough. Do not break up the butter pieces. Turn the dough onto a floured surface and form into a brick shape. Wrap and chill 10 minutes.

On a well-floured surface, lightly roll out the dough to a long rectangle about ¼-inch thick. It should be about three times longer than it is wide.

Fold the bottom third up and the top third down. Press the edges lightly with the rolling pin. Cover and chill 10 minutes.

Return the dough to the floured surface, giving it a quarter turn clockwise. Roll out to a rectangle again, and fold and chill as before. Repeat this turning, rolling, and chilling process twice more. Wrap and chill at least 30 minutes.

While the dough is chilling put the birds, peppercorns, and bouquet garni in a large pan. Quarter one of the onions and slice the other. Add the quartered onion to the pan. Add just enough water to cover and bring to a boil. Lower the heat, cover, and simmer until the meat is easily separated from the bone, 45-60 minutes. Transfer the birds to a plate and let them cool. Strain the stock.

Preheat the oven to 425°F. When the birds are cool enough to handle, pull the meat from the carcasses, keeping it in fairly large pieces. Arrange these in the bottom of a deep baking dish.

Melt the butter in a heavy saucepan over medium heat. Add the sliced onion, the mushrooms, and bacon and cook, stirring, for 5 minutes. Stir in the flour and cook 1 minute longer. Gradually stir in 1¼ cups of the reserved stock and bring to a boil. Simmer gently 5 minutes to give a rich sauce.

Add the egg quarters to the baking dish, piling them slightly in the center. Sprinkle with the parsley and season. Cover with the sauce.

Roll out the pastry dough to a round large enough to cover the dish generously. Dampen the rim of the dish with water and cut a long strip of dough to fit it. Once in place, dampen this and use the remaining dough to cover the pie. Crimp the edges. Brush the crust with egg and milk to glaze. Lightly mark a lattice pattern in the crust.

Bake until the pastry is well risen and golden brown, about 30 minutes. Serve hot.

Roast Duck with Baby Turnips

RABBIT CASSEROLE WITH MUSTARD AND MARJORAM

SERVES 6

½ cup vegetable oil
1 rabbit, weighing about 2¼-3 lb, cut into pieces
2 tbsp Dijon-style mustard
¼ cup flour
2 tbsp tomato paste
3 bay leaves
1 tsp dried marjoram
1¼ cups vegetable stock
1¼ cups red wine
2 garlic cloves, minced
salt and freshly ground black pepper
½ lb thin slices of bacon
4 slices of whole wheat bread, for garnish

Preheat the oven to 350°F.

Heat half the oil in a deep sauté pan over medium heat and brown the pieces of rabbit on all sides.

Using a slotted spoon, transfer the browned rabbit pieces to a large casserole dish. Using a spatula, spread them with the mustard.

Add the flour and tomato paste to the oil in the sauté pan and cook 2 minutes, stirring constantly. Add the herbs, stock, and wine, followed by the garlic.

Season with the 1 teaspoon of salt and some pepper. Bring to a boil and simmer 2 minutes.

Pour the sauce over the rabbit, cover the casserole, and cook in the oven for 2½ hours.

Roll up the bacon slices, then halve these rolls. Skewer them with wooden toothpicks and fry them until well browned. Add them to the casserole 30 minutes before the end of the cooking time.

About 10 minutes before the end of the cooking time, cut each slice of bread into 4 triangles. Heat the remaining oil in a frying pan until very hot and fry the bread triangles until golden brown. Drain.

Adjust the seasoning of the casserole, if necessary, and serve garnished with the bread croûtes.

VENISON AND SAGE PATTIES WITH PEARS

SERVES 6

1½ lb ground venison
1 tbsp grated zest and 3 tbsp juice from 1 washed lemon
½ tbsp minced fresh sage
1 bay leaf, minced
½ tbsp chopped fresh parsley
salt and freshly ground black pepper
12 thin slices of bacon
6 fresh pears, peeled, sliced, and warmed

Mix the venison, lemon zest and juice, sage, bay leaf, and parsley in a bowl. Cover and let marinate 24 hours.

Preheat the broiler or a charcoal grill.

Season the marinated mixture and form it into 6 patties. Wrap 2 slices of bacon around each one and secure with wooden toothpicks. Broil or grill 6 minutes on each side.

Place on a warmed serving platter and arrange the warmed pear slices decoratively on top before serving.

ROAST PHEASANT WITH THYME-BRANDY CREAM

SERVES 4-6

2 large young pheasants
2 washed oranges, quartered
2 washed lemons, quartered
5 tbsp butter
6 thin slices of bacon
1 tbsp hazelnut oil
4 onions, chopped
4 bay leaves
2 large sprigs of fresh thyme
2 tbsp brandy
1¼ cups whipping cream
salt and freshly ground black pepper
large bunch of watercress, for garnish

Preheat the oven to 450°F.

Wipe the pheasants thoroughly inside and out and stuff the cavities with alternating orange and lemon quarters.

Place the pheasants in a roasting pan and smooth 2 tablespoons of the butter over each bird, using a spatula. Cover the breasts with the bacon. Season and pour ⅔ cup of water into the pan.

Place on the middle shelf of the oven and roast 45 minutes, basting frequently with the pan juices.

Toward the end of this time, melt the remaining butter with the hazelnut oil in a saucepan over medium heat. Add the onions and sauté gently until translucent. Add the bay leaves and sprinkle the thyme into the onions. Cover and simmer 5 minutes.

When the pheasants are cooked, use a spoon to squash the oranges and lemons into the birds' cavities, then drain the juice into the pan. Remove and discard the citrus quarters, place the pheasants on a warmed serving platter and keep hot.

Add the roasting pan juices to the onion mixture and increase the heat. Warm the brandy in a small pan over very low heat and add it to the sauce. Then gently stir in the cream, taking care that it does not boil. Adjust the seasoning, if necessary, and transfer to a warmed gravy boat.

Serve the carved birds garnished with watercress, accompanied by the sauce.

PORK CHOPS WITH APPLE AND JUNIPER

SERVES 4

4 or 8 large center-cut pork chops
2½ cups buttermilk
8 juniper berries, crushed
salt and freshly ground black pepper
6 crab apples or tart red apples, unpeeled, cored, and sliced
½ tbsp cornstarch

In a shallow dish, marinate the chops in the buttermilk for 36 hours.

Preheat a broiler. Remove the chops and reserve the buttermilk. Pat the meat dry. Mix the juniper berries with salt and pepper and press this mixture on both sides of the pieces of meat. Broil for 5-10 minutes on each side, until cooked as desired.

While the chops are broiling, put the buttermilk in a heavy saucepan and add the apple slices. Bring to a boil and then simmer gently for 5 minutes.

In a small bowl, add 2 tablespoons of the buttermilk with the cornstarch and mix thoroughly. Add this to the buttermilk and apple mixture and bring to a boil, stirring constantly. Reduce the heat and simmer gently for 3 minutes, still stirring. Season. Serve this sauce immediately to accompany the pork chops.

GUINEA FOWL *can be substituted for pheasant. Its slightly game-like flavor is enhanced by the rich sauce.*

FISH AND SHELLFISH

Nowadays shellfish like scallops, mussels, and oysters – even some fish – are thought of as rather sophisticated ingredients that are the preserve of grand restaurants. In the old days, of course, their abundance made them poor men's food. This is reflected in the traditional ways in which they were cooked – unadorned by rich creamy sauces flavored with brandy and truffles. Instead their delicate flavor was brought out by plain cooking or the addition of readily obtained ingredients like herbs, cheese, nuts, and fruit.

Even dishes like the classic Bouillabaisse of France started as a means whereby the local fishermen made the best use of what they hadn't managed to sell.

In our new health-conscious mood we are turning more to fish dishes, especially those involving the nutritious and health-giving oily fish like mackerel, sardines, and tuna.

In this chapter you will also find interesting new slants on old favorites, like Baked Cod in Cheese Sauce, Fragrant Kedgeree with Coriander Seeds, and Salmon Cakes with Dill and Egg Sauce.

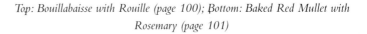

Top: Bouillabaisse with Rouille (page 100); Bottom: Baked Red Mullet with Rosemary (page 101)

Conger eel, gurnard, and the Mediterranean rascasse, or scorpion fish, are essential for an authentic version of the Provençal fish soup, BOUILLABAISSE, but any good selection of white and firm-fleshed fish will do. The soup must boil vigorously to emulsify the oil.

The spicy mayonnaise, ROUILLE, accompanies many fish dishes, especially soups. Traditionally, slices of bread are spread with a little rouille, placed in the bottom of deep bowls, and the broth ladled over.

BOUILLABAISSE WITH ROUILLE⋆

SERVES 6-8

2¼ lb mixed whole white fish, such as whiting, bass, haddock, cod, red mullet, monkfish, and red snapper
1½ lb whole rich fish, such as striped bass, mackerel and eel
½ lb mussels
3 onions
3 leeks
3 celery stalks
2 pinches of saffron
2 cups canned chopped plum tomatoes
4 garlic cloves, minced
1 bouquet garni
½ small fennel bulb, minced
thin strip of orange zest
bunch of fresh flat-leaf parsley
¾ cup olive oil
salt and freshly ground black pepper
1 bay leaf
juice of ½ lemon
1 tbsp tomato paste
thick slices of country bread, toasted, for serving

FOR THE ROUILLE
4 garlic cloves, minced
2 egg yolks⋆
(⋆see page 2 for advice on eggs)
1 tsp cayenne pepper
6 tbsp olive oil
1 or 2 tbsp tomato paste

Make sure that the fish have been cleaned and scaled, if necessary. Cut all the fish into large chunks, reserving the heads and tails. Place the chunks in a large bowl, keeping the white and rich fishes separate. Scrub the mussel shells well, and discard any that do not close on being tapped.

Cut one each of the onions, leeks, and celery stalks into large pieces; chop the remainder.

Soak the saffron in a few spoonfuls of warm water. Add half of it to the bowl of fish along with the chopped onions, leeks, and celery, the tomatoes, garlic, bouquet garni, fennel, orange zest, and two-thirds of the parsley, minced. Pour over the oil and season well. Cover and let marinate 1-2 hours in a cool place.

Meanwhile, place the fish heads and tails in a large pan. Add the vegetables that have been cut into large pieces, most of the remaining bunch of parsley, the bay leaf, and lemon juice and just cover with water. Season and bring to a simmer. Simmer 20 minutes and then strain.

Remove the pieces of fish from the marinade and set aside. Tip the marinade into a large saucepan. Add the strained fish stock and the remaining saffron and its water. Bring to a boil and simmer about 30 minutes.

While this cooks, make the rouille: put the garlic and egg yolks in a food processor and add the cayenne and a tiny pinch of salt. Blend to a thick paste. With the machine running, add the oil in a thin steady stream as if making mayonnaise. The finished sauce should have a thick, creamy consistency. Color it with tomato paste and season with more salt and cayenne as necessary (it should be quite spicy).

Bring the simmering liquid to a rapid boil and add the chunks of rich fish and the prepared mussels. Continue to boil vigorously about 6 minutes and then add the white fish chunks. Continue to boil until the flesh of the white fish flakes readily, about 5 minutes longer.

Transfer the fish and shellfish to a warmed serving dish, discarding any mussels that have failed to open. Remove the bouquet garni and orange zest from the broth and pour it into a warmed tureen. Add just enough tomato paste to give a good color and adjust the seasoning. Snip the remaining parsley over fish and broth for garnish.

BAKED RED MULLET WITH ROSEMARY

SERVES 4

4 tbsp olive oil
6 tbsp minced shallots
2 garlic cloves, minced
6 sprigs of fresh rosemary
1 cup dry white wine
4 small red mullet, cleaned, but with their livers retained
salt and freshly ground black pepper
juice of 1 lemon
2 tbsp minced fresh flat-leaf parsley
lemon wedges, for serving

Preheat the oven to 450°F and grease a baking dish with some of the oil.

Put the shallots and garlic in a saucepan with 2 rosemary sprigs, cut in half. Add all but 6 tablespoons of the wine and boil until reduced by about three-quarters, to leave the softened shallots and a sticky liquid. Discard the rosemary.

With a sharp knife, make some shallow cuts on both sides of the fish to allow the heat to penetrate. Slip a rosemary sprig into the cavity of each fish and season.

Spread the shallot mixture in the bottom of the baking dish, season, and arrange the fish on top, alternating heads and tails. Drizzle over the remaining oil and wine and bake 15 minutes, basting from time to time.

Sprinkle with the lemon juice and parsley to serve, accompanied by lemon wedges.

MARINATED SARDINES

SERVES 4

8 fresh sardines, cleaned and filleted
1¼ cups olive oil
1 large onion, thinly sliced
3 garlic cloves, minced
strip of washed orange zest
2-3 sprigs of fresh thyme
2-3 sprigs of fresh rosemary
1 bay leaf
juice of 2 lemons
salt and freshly ground black pepper
cayenne pepper
2 tbsp minced fresh flat-leaf parsley, for garnish
lemon wedges, for serving

Put the sardine fillets in a large sauté pan and add half the oil. Heat to a gentle simmer and cook until golden. Turn and cook the other sides in the same way. Transfer the sardines to a deep dish.

Mix the onion, garlic, orange zest, herbs, and lemon juice into the oil in the pan together with the remaining oil and 3 tablespoons of water. Season with salt, pepper, and a large pinch of cayenne.

Bring to a boil and simmer about 15 minutes. Let cool slightly, then pour the cooled mixture over the sardines. Let marinate overnight.

Garnish with the chopped parsley and serve with lemon wedges, crusty bread, and a green salad.

RED MULLET *is a popular fish all around the Mediterranean. It isn't a true mullet, but is a member of the goatfish family. Red mullet is rarely available in the USA, except on the Gulf Coast, but you can prepare other fish with firm, lean flesh, such as red snapper, in the same way.*

BACCALÀ IN GOLDEN BREAD CROÛTES

1 lb salt coa
4 thick slices from a square white loaf of bread
3 tbsp butter, melted
2 garlic cloves
⅞ cup olive oil
about ⅔ cup light cream, warmed
2 tsp walnut oil
1 tbsp lemon juice
pinch of grated nutmeg
salt and freshly ground black pepper
1 tbsp minced fresh flat-leaf parsley, for garnish
lemon wedges, for serving

Soak the salt cod 1 or 2 days, ideally under cold running water, to remove excess saltiness.

Drain the fish and put it in a large pan with cold water to cover. Cover, bring to a boil, and simmer very gently until just tender, 6-7 minutes.

Drain and let cool until it can be safely handled. Remove and discard all skin and bones and flake the flesh into a large bowl.

Preheat the oven to 350°F.

Trim out a deep hollow on one side of each slice of bread, taking care not to tear all the way through. Using a pastry brush, paint the pieces of hollowed-out bread all over with melted butter.

Bake the croûtes until a uniform golden color, 15-20 minutes. Remove from the oven and, while still warm, carefully rub them all over with one of the garlic cloves. Keep warm.

While the croûtes are baking, warm ⅔ cup of the oil in a heavy pan. When very hot, reduce the heat and add the fish. Using a wooden spoon, beat in the fish over very low heat.

When the mixture begins to be really mushy, mince the remaining garlic and stir it in. Transfer to a large mortar or food processor. Start adding the

remaining oil and the warmed cream in alternating small amounts, pounding or blending in each addition thoroughly before adding any more. Do not over-process or the mixture will lose its texture.

The resulting purée should be smooth and stiff enough to hold a shape. Stir in the walnut oil, lemon juice, and nutmeg and season to taste.

Spoon the mixture into and around the croûtes. Sprinkle with the parsley and serve, accompanied by lemon wedges and a tomato salad.

BROILED SOLE WITH LEMON AND PARMESAN

SERVES 4

2 washed lemons
8 Dover sole fillets, skinned
salt and freshly ground black pepper
3 tbsp butter, melted
3 tbsp freshly grated Parmesan cheese
lemon wedges, for serving

Finely grate 1 tablespoon of zest from 1 of the lemons and squeeze the juice from both.

Rinse the sole fillets, pat them dry, and lay them in a shallow baking dish. Mix the lemon zest into the juice and season with a little salt and some pepper. Pour this over the fish and let marinate about 30 minutes, turning the fillets occasionally.

Preheat the broiler.

Remove the fish from the marinade. Arrange the fillets in the broiler pan and brush the tops with some butter. Broil 3-4 inches from the heat, about 5 minutes. Turn the fillets, brush the other sides with butter, and sprinkle with Parmesan. Broil until the cheese is melted and golden, 5-7 minutes longer.

Serve the sole immediately with the pan juices poured over them and with lemon wedges.

BACCALÀ, or salt cod, is popular in the cooking of many Mediterranean countries, from Spain and Portugal to Greece. The French have their own celebrated version of the fish, puréed with oil and milk, known as brandade de morue. Thorough soaking of the fish to remove excess saltiness is essential.

FRAGRANT KEDGEREE WITH CORIANDER SEEDS

SERVES 4

1⅓ cups basmati rice
1 lb smoked fish fillet, preferably finnan haddie
2 bay leaves
1 small onion, halved
1 tbsp coriander seeds, lightly crushed
½ tsp turmeric
1¼ cups milk
2 tbsp butter
3 hard-cooked eggs, shelled
freshly ground black pepper
chopped fresh parsley, for garnish (optional)
lemon wedges, for garnish

Cook the rice in 2½ cups of simmering salted water in a covered pan until all the water is absorbed, 8–10 minutes. Set aside and keep hot.

Put the fish in a large shallow pan together with the bay leaves, onion, and spices. Pour over the milk, bring to a boil and poach gently 5 minutes.

Remove and discard the onion. Lift out the fish and transfer it to a plate. When it is cool enough to handle, skin and flake the fish, removing any bones. Add the fish to the rice.

Add the butter to the contents of the pan, bring to a boil, and cook rapidly for 3 minutes to reduce slightly.

Coarsely chop 2 of the hard-cooked eggs and add these to the pan. Warm through a minute or so, then add to the rice and fish mixture. Toss lightly to mix.

Season with pepper and serve immediately, sprinkled with chopped fresh parsley, if using, and garnished with lemon wedges and the remaining hard-cooked egg, cut in slices or quarters.

SKATE WITH CAPERS AND BLACK BUTTER

SERVES 4

4 pieces of skate, each weighing 8–10 oz, skinned
1 small onion, sliced
1 bay leaf
1 tbsp chopped fresh parsley + a few parsley stems
1¼ cups dry white wine (optional)
1½ tbsp capers
salt
4 tbsp butter
1 tsp black peppercorns, lightly crushed
2 tbsp white wine vinegar

Place the skate in a large pan with the onion, bay leaf, and parsley stems. Pour over the wine, if using, or water to cover. Bring to a boil, lower the heat and simmer until the fish is just cooked, 12–15 minutes.

Using a slotted spatula, transfer the fish to a large warmed dish. Sprinkle with the chopped parsley and capers and season with salt. Cover loosely with foil and keep hot.

Melt the butter in a pan with the peppercorns, letting the butter foam and brown slightly.

Pour this mixture over the fish. Add the vinegar to the pan and bring to a boil, swirling it around.

Pour the contents of the pan over the fish and serve at once.

Skate is related to rays and sharks. The fish is so large that only skinned pieces of the "wings" are seen in markets. Thicker pieces give the best value, as the proportion of flesh to skeleton is higher. Skate is the only fish that is better for being a day or two out of the water.

Kedgeree originated in British India and quickly became a favorite breakfast dish back home. The original Indian dish consisted simply of rice with onions and eggs; the British added fish.

BAKED COD IN CHEESE SAUCE

SERVES 4

2 tbsp butter
4 cod steaks, each about 1-inch thick
juice of ½ lemon
salt and freshly ground black pepper
⅓ cup fresh white bread crumbs
FOR THE CHEESE SAUCE
2 cups milk
1 bay leaf
1 small onion, quartered
2 whole cloves (optional)
3 tbsp butter
3 tbsp flour
1 tsp Dijon-style mustard
¾ cup shredded sharp Cheddar cheese
3 tbsp whipping cream
⅛ tsp freshly grated nutmeg

Preheat the oven to 350°F and use a little of the butter to grease a shallow baking dish large enough to hold the cod steaks in one layer.

Arrange the fish in the dish and sprinkle with the lemon juice, salt, and pepper. Dot with the remaining butter. Cover loosely with foil and bake about 30 minutes, removing the foil after 20 minutes.

Meanwhile, prepare the cheese sauce: put the milk in a small pan with the bay leaf, onion, and cloves, if using. Bring to a boil, cover, remove from the heat, and let infuse 15-20 minutes. Strain.

Melt the butter in another small heavy saucepan. Stir in the flour and cook, stirring, 1-2 minutes. Stir in the mustard. Gradually add the strained milk, stirring constantly. Bring to a boil, still stirring, and cook until thick and smooth.

Left: one of the Salmon Cakes with Dill and Egg Sauce (page 107); right: Baked Cod in Cheese Sauce

Add two-thirds of the cheese to the sauce and stir until smooth again. Stir in the cream and season with nutmeg, salt, and pepper.

Pour the hot sauce over and around the cod steaks. Sprinkle with the bread crumbs and the remaining cheese. Return to the oven and bake until browned, 8-10 minutes longer.

TROUT WITH ALMONDS

SERVES 4

4 whole trout, cleaned
salt and freshly ground black pepper
2 tbsp light olive oil
1 shallot, minced
1 garlic clove, minced
½ cup sliced almonds
6 tbsp butter
grated zest and juice of ½ washed lemon
1 tbsp chopped fresh parsley
lemon wedges, for garnish
parsley sprigs, for garnish

Preheat the broiler. Using a sharp knife, make 2 or 3 diagonal slits in the flesh of each side of the fish. Season inside and out with salt and pepper.

Cook the fish under the broiler until the flesh flakes easily from the bone, about 3 minutes on each side. Do not overcook or it will be dry.

Meanwhile, heat the oil in a frying pan over medium heat. Add the shallot and garlic and cook until soft, 2-3 minutes. Stir in the almonds and cook until they are pale golden in color.

Add the butter and let it sizzle, but take care that it does not burn. Stir in the lemon zest and juice and the chopped parsley. Season to taste.

Transfer the cooked fish to warmed serving plates and spoon over the almond-butter mixture. Serve at once, garnished with lemon and parsley.

TROUT WITH ALMONDS *can be made with any type of trout. Farmed rainbow trout are easily obtainable and economical, but wild brook trout or speckled trout — when available — are much tastier.*

The simple old-fashioned SALMON MOLD *recipe is perfect for picnics as it can be transported in the mold and then unmolded on a serving plate at the picnic. It can be made with fresh salmon, but canned salmon actually gives a better flavor.*

NANTUCKET TURNOVERS

SERVES 4

⅔ cup finely diced cucumber
butter for greasing
3 oz cream cheese
2 tbsp whipping cream
1 tbsp minced fresh dill or parsley
salt and pepper
10 oz puff pastry, thawed if frozen
¼ lb cooked fresh salmon, skin and bones removed
1 egg yolk
2-3 tbsp milk

Sprinkle the cucumber with a little salt and let it drain in a colander 1 hour. Rinse well and dry thoroughly on a clean dish towel.

Preheat the oven to 425°F and grease a baking sheet with butter. Thoroughly mix the cheese with the cream and the herbs. Season.

Roll out the pastry thinly. Using the top of a suitable bowl as a guide, cut out 4 rounds with a diameter of about 7 inches. Leaving a clear border around their edges, divide the cheese mixture between the rounds. Then pile the flaked salmon and cucumber on top to make neat mounds.

Dampen the pastry borders lightly with water. Fold each round in half over the filling to make half-moons. Seal the edges well with a fork, pressing in a little ridge all the way to make a decorative seam.

Now turn the semi-circles so that there is a flat part underneath and the seams are standing up. Flute these seams to give a decorative finish.

Mix the egg yolk and milk and brush the turnovers with this glaze. Arrange on the baking sheet and bake until evenly browned, 15-20 minutes. After about 7-8 minutes baking, prick each turnover in a couple of places to let any steam escape.

Once they are cooked, remove them from the oven and let cool.

SALMON MOLD WITH DILL AND MUSTARD SAUCE

SERVES 4-6

1 lb canned red salmon, drained
1 cup fresh bread crumbs, preferably white
juice of ½ lemon
⅓ cup milk
2 eggs, beaten
scrape of nutmeg
salt and pepper
FOR THE SAUCE
2 tbsp sugar
2 tbsp white wine vinegar
2 tbsp chopped fresh dill
2 tbsp Dijon-style mustard
1 tsp salt
⅔ cup canola oil, plus more for greasing

Preheat the oven to 400°F and grease an ovenproof bowl or mold with oil.

Either mash the salmon and mix it well with all the other ingredients, or process them all in a food processor.

Season the mixture generously, pack it into the prepared bowl or mold, and cover tightly with foil.

Place in a water bath, or roasting pan half-filled with boiling water, and bake until firm, about 45 minutes. Remove from the oven and let cool completely.

Make the sauce: mix together the sugar, vinegar, dill, mustard, and salt. Whisking all the time, pour in the oil in a thin steady stream until the mixture emulsifies.

Unmold the salmon and serve cut in slices accompanied by the sauce.

SALMON CAKES WITH DILL AND EGG SAUCE★

SERVES 4

1 lb piece of salmon (tail piece)
⅔ cup milk
6 black peppercorns
1 bay leaf
½ lb potatoes, peeled
2 tbsp butter
1 egg yolk★
(★see page 2 for advice on eggs)
1 tsp finely grated zest from a washed lemon
1 tbsp minced fresh parsley
salt and freshly ground black pepper
flour, for dusting
vegetable oil, for frying
FOR THE DILL AND EGG SAUCE
2 tbsp butter
⅔ cup light cream
2 hard-cooked eggs, shelled and chopped
2 tbsp chopped fresh dill
2 tsp lemon juice

Put the salmon, milk, peppercorns, and bay leaf in a pan. Bring to a boil, cover, and simmer gently 15 minutes. Transfer the fish to a plate, reserving the liquid. When cool enough to handle, remove and discard the skin. Flake the flesh into a large bowl, removing any bones. Mash lightly with a fork.

While the fish is cooking, cut the potatoes into 1½-inch chunks and cook them in boiling salted water until soft, 12-15 minutes. Drain well and return to the heat for a few seconds to dry. Add the butter and 1 tablespoon of the reserved cooking liquid from the fish. Mash until smooth.

Add the potato to the fish together with the egg yolk, lemon zest, and parsley. Season with salt and pepper. Mix together lightly, then divide the mixture into 4 equal portions and shape these into flat cakes on a floured surface. Chill until required.

Meanwhile, prepare the sauce: melt the butter in a small pan. Add the cream, hard-cooked eggs, and dill and bring to a boil. Cook, stirring, until creamy, 2-3 minutes. Stir in the lemon juice, season, and keep warm while cooking the fish cakes.

Heat the oil in a frying pan over medium heat. When the oil is quite hot, cook the fish cakes until golden brown, 6-8 minutes, turning once or twice.

Serve the fish cakes with the sauce.

GRILLED SALMON WITH PICKLE BERRY SAUCE

SERVES 4

4 salmon steaks
2 tbsp extra virgin olive oil
salt and pepper
FOR THE SAUCE
1 lb mixed soft fruits, such as strawberries (sliced if large),
raspberries, blackberries, blueberries, red currants, etc.
2 tbsp sugar
½ tsp salt
1 tbsp wine vinegar, preferably balsamic
1 small garlic clove, minced
1-2 fresh green or red hot chili peppers, seeded and minced
2 tbsp chopped fresh cilantro leaves

Preheat the barbecue until coals are quite hot.

First make the sauce by putting all the ingredients except the cilantro in a saucepan. Bring to a boil, cover, and simmer over the lowest possible heat for 5 minutes. Stir in the cilantro and keep warm if serving hot (see below).

Brush the salmon with olive oil and season with salt and pepper on both sides. Grill about 5-10 minutes on each side until cooked, brushing occasionally with extra oil. The exact time will vary very much depending on the thickness of the steaks, the type of barbecue, and the heat of the charcoal. Keep testing to see when the fish is cooked to your liking. Do not overcook.

Serve immediately, with a little of the sauce, which may be served hot or cold. This recipe makes more sauce than will probably be needed, but it is not worth making a smaller quantity. However, any leftover sauce will keep for several days in the refrigerator and is excellent with plainly roasted duck or other poultry or grilled meat.

The Tuna and Corn Cakes can be made with white potatoes and can also be simply fried in a little oil.

TUNA AND CORN CAKES

MAKES 8

1 large sweet potato
7 oz canned tuna, drained and mashed
½ cup canned or frozen corn, drained or thawed
1⅓ cups fresh white bread crumbs
1 egg, lightly beaten
1 tbsp melted butter
¼ tsp hot chili powder
salt and pepper
flour, for coating
dill pickles, to serve

Preheat the oven to 400°F.

Bake the sweet potato until tender, 30-40 minutes. Let cool slightly and then scoop out 1 cup of the flesh, firmly packed.

In a bowl, thoroughly mix together the measured sweet potato with all the other ingredients, seasoning well. Form this mixture into 8 flat round patties about ½-inch thick.

Coat the patties in flour and shake off the excess, then chill at least 1 hour (or up to 12) to let them firm up.

Preheat the barbecue until coals are quite hot.

Cook the fish cakes on the hot barbecue until crispy and brown, 5-10 minutes on each side.

Serve immediately, with dill pickles.

TUNA ROULADE WITH DILL AND CAPERS

SERVES 4-8

7 oz canned tuna in oil
4 eggs, separated
salt and freshly ground black pepper
2 tbsp freshly grated Parmesan cheese
FOR THE FILLING
1¼ cups milk
1 onion, quartered
2 large sprigs of parsley, minced
1 bay leaf
2 tbsp butter
3 tbsp flour
4 hard-cooked eggs, shelled and coarsely chopped
1 tsp grated zest and 1 tsp juice from a lemon
2 tbsp minced fresh dill
1 tsp capers

Preheat the oven to 400°F and line a 13- x 9-inch jelly roll pan with wax paper.

Prepare the filling: pour the milk into a small pan and add the onion, parsley, and bay leaf. Bring quickly to a boil. Cover and let infuse off the heat at least 20 minutes.

Meanwhile, in a mixing bowl, mash the tuna with its oil to a purée using a hand blender or fork.

Beat the egg yolks lightly, then beat them into the tuna purée. Season. Beat the egg whites to stiff peaks and gently fold them into the tuna mixture.

Pour the mixture into the prepared pan and level with a spatula. Bake on the top shelf of the oven until well risen, firm and lightly golden in color, 10-15 minutes. Let cool in the pan.

Finish the filling: melt the butter in a saucepan over medium heat. Add the flour and stir 2 minutes. Add the strained milk, stirring constantly, and gently bring to a boil. Reduce the heat and simmer 3 minutes. Add the eggs, lemon zest and juice, dill, and capers. Season.

Sprinkle a piece of wax paper slightly larger than the jelly roll pan with the Parmesan cheese. Turn the cooled roulade out on the paper and peel off the lining paper from the base.

Reheat the filling, if necessary, and spread it over the roulade with a spatula, leaving a 1-inch clear border all the way around.

Lift one short end of the paper, roll up the roulade like a jelly roll. Transfer to a serving dish, sprinkle any remaining Parmesan on the top, and serve immediately, cut in thick slices.

ROULADE is the French term for rolled and stuffed items, especially used for meats and omelette mixtures, as with this TUNA ROULADE. Canned salmon makes a good alternative to tuna.

These two recipes are good examples of how oily fish such as mackerel, herrings, and sardines – even salmon – suit sharp dressings that offset their oiliness.

SOUSED HERRINGS

SERVES 6

12 fresh herrings, cleaned
salt and freshly ground black pepper
blade of mace
1 bay leaf
6 black peppercorns
2 whole cloves
1 onion, sliced
½ cup white wine vinegar

Preheat the oven to 400°F.

Remove and discard the heads of the herrings. Cut open the fish along the opening made from cleaning them, down to the tail. Lay them skin-side up and press firmly along the backbones to loosen them. Turn them over and lift away the bones.

Season the filleted fish with salt and pepper and roll them up to the tail. Secure each rolled herring with a wooden toothpick.

Arrange the rolled herrings in a baking dish or roasting pan and add the mace, bay leaf, peppercorns, and cloves. Scatter the onion slices over and around the fish. Mix the vinegar with ½ cup of water and pour this over the fish.

Cover the dish with foil and bake about 40 minutes, removing the foil for the last 15 minutes of cooking.

Serve hot with buttered new potatoes, or let cool in the baking dish and serve cold with salad and rye bread.

BAKED MACKEREL WITH GOOSEBERRY SAUCE

SERVES 4

1 tbsp butter
4 whole mackerel, cleaned
4 sprigs of fresh rosemary
salt and freshly ground black pepper
1 large onion, thinly sliced
½ cup dry white wine
FOR THE GOOSEBERRY SAUCE
2 tbsp butter
1 shallot, minced
1 lb (about 3 cups) gooseberries, halved
2 tbsp caster sugar

Preheat the oven to 400°F and use the butter to grease a shallow baking dish large enough to hold the fish in one layer.

Cut the heads from the mackerel, if preferred. Using a sharp knife, make 2 or 3 deep slits in the flesh on each side. Tuck a rosemary sprig into the cavity of each fish and season them inside and out with salt and pepper.

Arrange the onion slices in the base of the dish and place the mackerel on top. Pour over the wine and bake until the fish is tender and the flesh flakes easily from the bone, about 30 minutes.

Meanwhile, prepare the gooseberry sauce: melt the butter in a small heavy pan over medium heat. Add the shallot and cook until soft but not colored, 4-5 minutes. Add the gooseberries, sugar, and 2 tablespoons of water. Season. Cover and cook, stirring frequently, until soft, about 10 minutes.

Purée the sauce in a blender or food processor and then press it through a strainer. Return the gooseberry purée to the pan.

When the mackerel is cooked, add 2-3 tablespoons of the cooking liquid to the sauce and warm it through. Adjust the seasoning and serve.

GRILLED MACKEREL WITH HORSERADISH AND YOGURT SAUCE

SERVES 4

2 large mackerel, each weighing about 2 lb (or 4 small mackerel), cleaned
1 lemon, thinly sliced
salt and pepper
FOR THE SAUCE
⅔ cup low-fat plain yogurt
2 scallions, minced
1 tbsp minced fresh parsley
2 tbsp prepared horseradish

Preheat the barbecue coals until quite hot.

First make the sauce: combine the ingredients in a bowl and chill 30-60 minutes to let the flavors develop.

Season the cavities of the fish with salt and pepper and fill them with the lemon slices.

Put the fish on the barbecue and cook them 6-7 minutes on each side, or until cooked through. (Smaller fish will take only 4-5 minutes on each side.)

Serve the fish immediately with the chilled sauce and garnished with more lemon slices and sprigs of herbs, if desired.

NOTE: this piquant sauce works well with most oily and smoked fish, such as herring or smoked trout. Try replacing the parsley with dill.

GRILLED JUMBO SHRIMP WITH PASSION FRUIT VINAIGRETTE

SERVES 4

3 tbsp extra virgin olive oil
2 garlic cloves, minced
16-20 raw jumbo shrimp in shells
FOR THE DRESSING
seeds and pulp from 2 passion fruit
1 tbsp lemon juice
2 tbsp sunflower or corn oil
2 tsp sugar
salt and pepper

Mix the oil and garlic in a bowl. Add the shrimp and toss until each one is well coated. Cover the bowl with plastic wrap and let marinate at room temperature 30 minutes.

Preheat the barbecue until the coals are quite hot.

Meanwhile, make the dressing by combining the ingredients, seasoning well. Transfer to a serving bowl or small pitcher.

Remove the shrimp from the marinade and grill them on the barbecue until they have turned pink and are cooked through, 2-3 minutes on each side. Brush them with any remaining marinade when turning them over. Do not overcook the shrimp or they will become tough.

Serve immediately, with the vinaigrette as a dipping sauce. As these shrimp have to be eaten with the fingers, provide plenty of napkins.

For GRILLED JUMBO SHRIMP WITH PASSION FRUIT VINAIGRETTE, *it is imperative that you use raw shrimp in their shells. These are available fresh and frozen from some supermarkets, fish stores, and Asian stores (there they may be called "Tiger" prawns).*

SEAFOOD IN HERB AND SAFFRON SAUCE

SERVES 4

3 tbsp olive oil
1 onion, chopped
1 red sweet pepper, seeded and sliced
1 green sweet pepper, seeded and sliced
2 large garlic cloves, minced
2 tsp paprika
¼ lb prepared squid, coarsely chopped
4 tomatoes, peeled and coarsely chopped
½ tsp ground saffron
2 bay leaves
1 cup sliced almonds
¾ cup dry white wine
grated zest and juice of 1 washed lime
1¼ cups fish stock
salt and freshly ground black pepper
¼ lb shelled and deveined medium or large shrimp
¼ lb shucked small hardshell clams
¼ lb sea scallops, halved if large
3 tbsp brandy
1 tbsp chopped fresh dill
½ cup light cream
fresh flat-leaf parsley, for garnish
hot crusty bread, for serving

SAFFRON, *the dried stamens of a type of crocus, is one of the most ancient and valued of spices. As well as imparting a wonderful golden color, it also gives a subtly strong flavor that works particularly well with fish and seafood, rice, and some pastries.*

Heat the oil in a large heavy pot over medium heat. Add the onion, peppers, garlic, paprika, and squid and sauté gently for 10 minutes.

Stir in the tomatoes, saffron, bay leaves, almonds, wine, lime zest and juice, and stock. Bring to a boil and simmer 3 minutes. Season.

Reduce the heat and add the shrimp, clams, and scallops. Mix thoroughly, cover, and simmer 5 minutes. Add the brandy and dill and simmer 3 minutes more. Stir in the cream and adjust the seasoning, if necessary. Garnish with parsley just before serving, with hot crusty bread.

SWEDISH FISH SOUFFLÉ WITH DILL

SERVES 4-6

7 tbsp butter, plus more for greasing
2 tbsp dry bread crumbs
4 eggs, separated
⅔ cup flour
2½ cups milk
½ lb cooked finnan haddie, flaked
1 tbsp minced fresh dill
salt and freshly ground black pepper

Preheat the oven to 425°F and grease a 7-inch soufflé dish carefully with butter, making sure that the rim is also well coated. Then dust this layer of butter with the bread crumbs, shaking out any excess.

Beat the egg whites to stiff peaks.

Melt the butter in a large heavy saucepan over medium heat. Stir in the flour and cook gently 2 minutes. Slowly add the milk, stirring constantly. Reduce the heat and cook 5 minutes longer.

Remove from the heat and add the egg yolks, one at a time, followed by the fish. Stir a spoonful of the egg whites into this mixture to loosen it and then carefully fold in the remaining egg whites together with the dill and seasoning to taste.

Fill the prepared dish with the soufflé mixture and tap the dish on a work surface to help the mixture settle with a level top and no air pockets.

Set the dish in a roasting pan and pour boiling water into this to about halfway up the sides of the soufflé dish.

Bake until the soufflé is well risen and golden brown, 30-40 minutes. Serve immediately.

Left: Tuna Roulade with Dill and Capers (page 109); right: Seafood in Herb and Saffron Sauce

FISH AND SHELLFISH STEW

SERVES 6

*2 lb assorted cleaned whole fish, such as eel, monkfish,
mullet, mackerel, porgy, cod, or whiting*
¾ lb fresh mussels in their shells
2 crab claws, shells cracked
½ lb raw crayfish or jumbo shrmp in their shells
¼ cup olive oil
1 onion, chopped
1 large leek, sliced
3 garlic cloves, chopped
1 small fennel bulb, sliced
1 lb ripe tomatoes, peeled and chopped
1 bay leaf
bouquet garni
large pinch of saffron strands
2 strips of zest from a washed orange
1¼ cups dry white wine
salt and freshly ground black pepper
toasted slices of French bread, for serving
chopped fresh parsley, for garnish

Remove the heads and bones from the fish (or ask your fishmonger to do it). Set aside the fish and put the trimmings into a large saucepan. Add water to cover and bring to a boil. Then lower the heat, cover, and simmer 15 minutes. Strain and reserve the stock.

Cut the fish into pieces. Scrub the mussels and remove any "beards." Discard any open mussels that do not close on being tapped. Rinse the crab claws and the crayfish or shrimp.

Heat the oil in a large saucepan over medium heat. Add the onion, leek, garlic, and fennel and cook gently about 10 minutes, stirring frequently.

Add the tomatoes, herbs, saffron, orange zest, and wine to the pan. Pour in the strained fish stock and bring to a boil. Season. Boil 10 minutes, then lower the heat to a gentle simmer.

Add the fish, starting with firm-fleshed types, such

as eel and monkfish, which will need up to 10 minutes cooking, followed by the flaky white fish, such as cod and whiting. Finally add the shellfish, which will require only 2 or 3 minutes cooking. Discard any mussels which do not open.

First serve the broth, ladled into soup bowls over the toasted slices of French bread. Serve the seafood as a separate course, sprinkled with chopped fresh parsley for garnish.

SHRIMP AND SCALLOP PIE

SERVES 4

1½ lb potatoes, peeled and quartered
4 tbsp butter
6 tbsp light cream
⅛ tsp freshly grated nutmeg
salt and freshly ground black pepper
white parts of 4 scallions, chopped
2 tomatoes, peeled, seeded, and quartered
6 oz oyster mushrooms
1 lb sea scallops, halved if large
3 tbsp flour
1¼ cups dry white wine
1¼ cups fish or chicken stock
½ lb peeled cooked bay or small shrimp
2 tbsp chopped fresh herbs, such as parsley, tarragon, or dill
juice of ½ lemon

Preheat the oven to 400°F.

Cook the potatoes in boiling salted water until soft, 12-15 minutes. Drain well and return to the pan briefly to dry them. Mash with half the butter and half the cream until smooth. Season with the nutmeg, and salt and pepper to taste.

Melt the remaining butter in a large heavy saucepan over medium heat. Add the scallions and cook until they are soft but not brown, 4-5 minutes. Stir in the tomatoes, mushrooms, and scallops and cook 3 minutes. Sprinkle over the flour and cook 1 minute longer, then remove from the heat and gradually stir in the wine and stock. Cook, stirring, until thickened. Simmer 1 minute.

Stir in the remaining cream, the shrimp, herbs, and lemon juice. Season.

Transfer to a 5-cup (1½-quart) baking dish. Either spoon or pipe the potato mixture on top. Bake until the top is browned and the filling is piping hot, 25-30 minutes.

SEAFOOD LASAGNE

SERVES 6

1 lb fresh mussels
⅔ cup dry white wine
2 garlic cloves, thinly sliced
½ lb peeled cooked bay or small shrimp
½ lb sea scallops, sliced
½ lb skinless fillets of firm white fish, such as cod or
whiting, diced
3 tbsp olive oil
1 onion, sliced
1 small green or red sweet pepper, seeded and chopped
1 lb tomatoes, seeded and chopped
salt and freshly ground black pepper
1 tbsp chopped fresh parsley
1 tbsp chopped fresh dill
2 tbsp brandy
butter, for greasing
8 sheets fresh or dried green lasagne noodles
5 tbsp freshly grated Parmesan cheese
FOR THE BECHAMEL SAUCE
3 tbsp butter
3 tbsp flour
3 cups milk
1 bay leaf
⅛ tsp freshly grated nutmeg

Scrub the mussels and remove any "beards." Discard any open mussels that do not close when tapped.

Put the wine and garlic in a large saucepan and bring to a boil. Add the mussels, cover, and cook over high heat until almost all of the mussel shells have opened, about 3 minutes. Drain, reserving the cooking liquor. Discard any unopened mussels. Reserve a few good-looking open whole mussels for garnish and shell the rest. Set aside with the shrimp, scallops, and fish.

Heat the oil in a large shallow pan over medium heat. Add the onion and sweet pepper and cook until they have just softened, 4-5 minutes.

Stir in the tomatoes and the strained mussel cooking liquor. Season with salt and pepper. Bring to a boil. Then lower the heat, cover, and simmer 10 minutes. Stir in the scallops, fish, herbs, and brandy and cook 2 minutes longer. Add the shrimp and shelled mussels and remove from the heat.

Preheat the oven to 375°F and lightly grease a shallow baking dish with butter.

Cook the lasagne in a large pan of rapidly boiling salted water until just tender. Drain well.

Make the bechamel sauce: melt the butter in a small heavy saucepan. Add the flour and cook, stirring constantly, 1-2 minutes. Gradually add the milk, stirring constantly. Still stirring, cook until smooth and thickened.

Add the bay leaf and season with nutmeg, salt, and pepper. Cook over very low heat about 5 minutes, then remove the bay leaf.

Fill the prepared dish with alternating layers of seafood mixture, pasta, and sauce, finishing with a layer of sauce. Sprinkle with grated Parmesan and bake until the top has browned, 30-35 minutes, .

Serve hot, garnished with the reserved open mussels still in their shells.

For a more economical version of SEAFOOD LASAGNE, *omit the scallops and use less shrimp. Add a layer of chopped mixed vegetables, such as celery, zucchini, broccoli, and mushrooms that have been lightly sautéed in butter.*

Small hardshell CLAMS *can be used instead of mussels, if you prefer.*

To be absolutely sure of the cleanliness of MUSSELS and to remove lingering grittiness, it is a good idea to soak them in salted water for a couple of hours before further preparation. Adding some fine oatmeal or flour to the water can make the mussels plumper and tastier.

MUSSELS WITH CREAM AND BACON

SERVES 4-6

3 lb fresh mussels
1 tbsp butter
1 tbsp olive oil
1 onion, chopped
2 garlic cloves, minced
¼ lb slab bacon, chopped
1 bay leaf
2 tbsp coarsely chopped fresh oregano
¾ lb tomatoes, peeled, seeded, and quartered
1¼ cups dry white wine
½ cup whipping cream
salt and freshly ground black pepper
sprigs of flat-leaf parsley, for garnish

Scrub the mussels and remove any "beards." Discard any open mussels that do not close when tapped.

Melt the butter with the olive oil in a large saucepan over medium heat. Add the onion, garlic, and bacon and cook, until just beginning to color, about 5 minutes. Pour off excess fat.

Stir in the bay leaf, oregano, tomatoes, and wine. Bring to a boil. Add the mussels, cover, and cook until almost all of the shells open, 4-5 minutes. Using a slotted spoon, transfer the mussels to a plate, discarding any that do not open. Set aside.

Boil the sauce over high heat 5 minutes to reduce by about one-third. Meanwhile, remove about half the mussels from their shells. Discard these shells.

Stir the cream and all the mussels into the sauce and season with salt and pepper.

Garnish with the sprigs of parsley before serving, accompanied by warm crusty bread or pasta.

Left: Mussels with Cream and Bacon; right: Shrimp and Scallop Pie (page 114)

ASIAN DELIGHTS

The Asian style of eating is quite different from our traditional Western concept of main courses. Instead, an Asian meal will usually consist of a central dish of rice or noodles accompanied by a variety of "made" dishes. These might be only a couple of stir-fries for a simple family meal, or there could be a succession of countless elaborate recipes for a banquet or special occasion. Whatever the type of meal, however, the balance of ingredients will invariably tip heavily towards fresh vegetables, grains, and fruit, with meat, poultry, and fish appearing in much smaller quantities than is generally the case in the West. For this reason alone, the Asian diet is a very healthy one.

Many of the dishes in this chapter can be served as Western-style main courses with accompanying rice and vegetables.

Dover Sole with Mushrooms and Pork (page 132) served with steamed white rice

STUFFED BEAN CURD

MAKES 8

block of firm tofu, weighing about 1½ lb
1 tsp cornstarch, mixed with a little water, plus more
for dusting
3 tbsp vegetable oil
1 cup chicken stock
½ tsp salt
4 tsp Chinese oyster sauce
2 thinly sliced scallions, for garnish
FOR THE STUFFING
¼ lb ground chicken
1 tbsp minced onion
2 tbsp light soy sauce
1½ tsp cornstarch

First make the stuffing by mixing together the ingredients in a bowl.

Cut the tofu into 4 equal portions; they will be about 4-inches square and 1¼-inches thick. Now cut these diagonally across to make triangular wedges. Using a sharp knife, cut a slit into the long side of each wedge and scoop out a little of the tofu to make a pocket to take the stuffing. Be careful not to cut too deeply, and work very carefully as the tofu is very fragile.

Dust the inside of each pocket with a little cornstarch and carefully fill with the stuffing.

Heat the oil in a pan wide enough to take the pieces of tofu in one layer (a sauté pan or frying pan is ideal) over very low heat. Place the tofu in the pan, stuffed-side down and cook until the stuffing is golden brown, about 5 minutes.

Pour in the stock, cover the pan, and simmer 3 minutes. Remove the tofu and keep warm.

Add the salt, oyster sauce, and cornstarch mixture to the pan and simmer until thickened, stirring.

Arrange the tofu on a warmed serving plate, pour over the sauce, and garnish with scallions.

SPICED BEEF

SERVES 4-6

2 tbsp vegetable oil
2 lb boneless beef rump roast or fresh brisket
2 tbsp soy sauce
¼ cup dry sherry
2 garlic cloves, minced
3 star anise
1 tbsp sugar
salt and freshly ground black pepper
3 carrots, thinly sliced
2 tbsp butter
1 tsp Asian sesame oil
2 tsp lemon juice
1 tsp black mustard seeds

Heat the vegetable oil in a saucepan that has a tight-fitting lid and is just large enough to hold the piece of meat snugly. Brown the meat on all sides.

Add the soy sauce, sherry, garlic, and star anise. Cover the pan tightly and cook over very low heat. undisturbed, about 1 hour.

Add the sugar and a good grinding of black pepper, replace the lid, and continue cooking 1 more hour.

Lift the meat out of the pan and let it rest 10 minutes. Meanwhile, boil the liquid in the pan rapidly to reduce it to a sticky sauce.

At the same time, steam the carrots until just tender. Melt the butter with the sesame oil in a saucepan over medium heat and add the lemon juice, mustard seeds, and a pinch of salt. Toss the steamed carrots in this to coat thoroughly.

Cut the meat into slices and arrange them on a warmed serving platter. Drizzle the sauce over and surround the meat with the carrots. Serve accompanied by steamed white rice.

BREADED GINGER STEAKS

SERVES 4

2 boneless steaks, each weighing about 6 oz
1 tbsp soy sauce
1 tbsp dry sherry or white wine
1 garlic clove, minced
1-inch cube of peeled fresh gingerroot, crushed through a garlic press
flour, for coating
1 egg, beaten
1⅓ cup fine fresh white bread crumbs
3 tbsp vegetable oil
chopped scallions, for garnish

Cut each steak in half to make 4 equal pieces in all. Place these between 2 sheets of plastic wrap, and flatten them with a rolling pin until they are as thin as possible. They should at least double in size.

Mix together the soy sauce, sherry or wine, garlic, and ginger in a wide bowl and then put the flattened steaks into it. Mix well so that all surfaces of the meat are coated. Cover and let marinate in the refrigerator at least 6 hours or up to 24.

Drain the marinated steaks well and pat them dry with paper towels.

Put some flour, the beaten egg, and the bread crumbs in 3 separate shallow dishes. Dip the pieces of steak first in the flour, then shake off any excess. Then dip them in the beaten egg and finally the bread crumbs.

Heat the oil in a frying pan (not a wok) over medium-high heat and fry the pieces of steak, in batches if necessary, until the coating is crisp and golden, 1-2 minutes on each side.

Serve Western-style, with plain rice or potatoes and vegetables, or slice the steaks into strips and serve as part of an Asian-style meal. Either way, garnish with chopped scallions.

STIR-FRIED BEEF WITH CELERY

SERVES 4

3 tbsp soy sauce
2 garlic cloves, minced
2 tsp cornstarch
1 tsp sugar
1 lb boneless sirloin steak, cut into thin bite-sized strips
3 tbsp vegetable oil
½ lb celery, cut across at an angle into thin slices
1½-inch cube of peeled fresh gingerroot, thinly sliced

Combine the soy sauce, garlic, cornstarch, and sugar in a small bowl. Add the beef strips and mix well until each piece is coated. Let marinate 20-30 minutes.

Heat the oil in a wok or frying pan over medium heat and add the meat mixture. Stir-fry 3-4 minutes.

Add the slices of celery and ginger and continue to stir-fry 4 minutes more. Serve immediately.

Based on a traditional Japanese dish, BREADED GINGER STEAKS is a simple and unusual way to cook steak. It also allows a little expensive meat to go a long way, so it is worth buying the best-quality beef.

SWEET-AND-SOUR SPARERIBS

SERVES 4

3 lb pork spareribs
2 tbsp soy sauce
3 tbsp tomato ketchup
6 tbsp orange juice
2 tbsp white or red wine vinegar
2 tbsp brown sugar
1 tsp salt
2 garlic cloves, minced
1-inch cube of peeled fresh gingerroot, minced
¼ tsp chili powder
freshly ground black pepper

Separate the ribs by cutting down between the bones and put the pieces in a wide baking dish or roasting pan.

Combine the remaining ingredients, season well with pepper, and pour over the ribs. Mix well so that each rib is coated. Cover and let marinate at least 6 hours, or up to 24 in the refrigerator.

Preheat the oven to 350°F.

Bake the ribs, uncovered, for 1½ hours, basting them every 15-20 minutes. Increase the oven to 425°F and cook the ribs 30 minutes longer, turning them over after 15 minutes. The liquid will have almost entirely evaporated, leaving the ribs a deep mahogany brown and covered in a delicious sticky glaze.

These ribs are best eaten with the fingers, so supply lots of napkins and finger-bowls.

Left to right: Stir-fried Beef with Celery (page 121), Stuffed Bean Curd (page 120), and Sweet-and-Sour Spare Ribs

PORK WITH NOODLES, MUSHROOMS, AND SPINACH

SERVES 4

¼ lb Chinese noodles
3 tbsp vegetable oil
½ small onion, minced
1-inch cube of peeled fresh gingerroot, minced
2 garlic cloves, minced
2 hot red or green chili peppers, seeded and minced, plus extra for garnish (optional)
1 lb lean boneless pork, cut into thin bite-sized strips
6 oz firm mushrooms, thinly sliced
salt and freshly ground black pepper
¼ cup white wine or light stock
¾ lb spinach, torn into small shreds

There is a wide variety of very different types of CHINESE NOODLE, *which require varying degrees of cooking. Always check the package for cooking times.*

First cook the noodles according to the directions on the package. Drain them well and then toss them in 1 tablespoon of the oil to prevent them from sticking together. Set aside.

Heat the remaining oil in a wok or large saucepan over high heat and stir-fry the onion 1 minute. Add the ginger, garlic, and chili peppers and stir-fry 1 more minute.

Add the pork strips and mushrooms and continue to stir-fry until the meat is cooked and the mushrooms are beginning to soften, 3-4 minutes.

Season with salt and pepper, pour in the wine or stock, and add the spinach. Stir-fry just until the spinach begins to wilt. Do not over-cook: each piece of spinach should still retain some shape and stay separate rather than sticking together.

Add the noodles to the mixture and continue to stir-fry 1-2 minutes longer, until the ingredients are well mixed and the noodles are really hot.

Serve immediately in 4 warmed bowls and garnish with extra chopped chili peppers, if using.

NOTE: if good fresh spinach is not available, use collard greens or romaine lettuce.

BALINESE PORK

SERVES 4

2 tbsp vegetable oil
1 lb pork tenderloin, cut into ¾-inch cubes
1 onion, minced
3 garlic cloves, minced
1 hot chili pepper or more to taste, seeded and finely chopped
1 tsp ground coriander seed
1 tsp turmeric
1 tsp cornstarch
1¼ cups canned coconut cream
1 tsp salt

Heat half the oil in a wok or frying pan that has a tight-fitting lid over medium heat. Stir-fry the pork until the meat is colored all over, 3-4 minutes. Using a slotted spoon, remove the pork from the wok and set aside.

Add the remaining oil to the wok and stir-fry the onion until softened, 3-4 minutes. Add the garlic, chili, coriander, and turmeric and continue to stir-fry 2-3 minutes longer. Return the pork to the wok.

Mix the cornstarch with 1 tablespoon of water and stir this into the coconut cream. Add to the wok and bring to a boil. Add the salt and simmer, covered, over the lowest possible heat until the meat is tender, about 1 hour.

Transfer to a warmed dish to serve.

Pork with Noodles, Mushrooms, and Spinach

CRISPY DUCK WITH PANCAKES

SERVES 4-6

1 duck, weighing 4-4 ½ lb, giblets removed
salt
24 small Chinese pancakes (Beijing doilies)
hoisin sauce, for serving
4 scallions, cut into small shreds, for serving
¼ English cucumber, cut into small sticks, for serving

At least 6 hours ahead, pour a large kettle of boiling water over the duck. This will tighten the skin. Then dry the bird thoroughly inside and out, place it on a rack, and let dry in an airy place at least 6 hours, but preferably up to 12.

Preheat the oven to 350°F.

Prick the skin of the duck all over with a skewer to let the fat escape during cooking, then rub the skin all over with salt.

Place the bird on a rack in a roasting pan and roast 2 hours. The meat will become very tender and the skin very crisp.

To serve: pull the meat off the carcass and shred this and the skin by pulling it apart with two forks. Arrange the meat and skin on a warmed serving platter and keep warm.

Warm the pancakes for a couple of minutes in a steamer and then serve these on a warmed serving plate. Serve the sauce, scallions, and cucumber in separate bowls.

Each pancake is spread with a little sauce. A few pieces of scallion and cucumber are then arranged on top of this, followed by some of the duck meat and some of the crispy skin. The pancake is then rolled up and eaten with the fingers. Be sure to provide plenty of napkins and finger-bowls.

CHINESE PANCAKES *for this well-loved dish are available in packages from Asian markets.*

The recipe for BALINESE-STYLE DUCK was given to me by a dance teacher in whose house I stayed on Bali. I have had to adapt it slightly, as not all the spices used are available in the West.

BALINESE-STYLE DUCK

SERVES 6

1 duck, weighing 4-4 ½ lb, with giblets
1½ tsp salt
½ tsp chili powder
½ tsp ground cumin
½ tsp ground coriander
6 hard-cooked eggs, quartered, for serving
deep-fried onion rings, for garnish (optional)

FOR THE SAUCE

1 tbsp vegetable oil
1 small onion, chopped
1 garlic clove, minced
1-inch cube of peeled fresh gingerroot, crushed through a garlic press or minced
1 hot chili pepper, seeded and chopped
grated zest and juice of 1 washed lemon
2 tsp brown sugar
1¼ cups canned coconut cream
2 tsp soy sauce

At least 6 hours ahead, remove the giblets from the duck and set them aside. Pour a large kettle of boiling water over the duck. This will tighten the skin. Then dry the bird thoroughly inside and out, place it on a rack and let dry in an airy place at least 6 hours, but preferably up to 12.

Put the giblets in a small pan, add just enough water to cover and bring to a boil, skimming off any scum that rises to the surface. Cover and simmer 1 hour. Discard the giblets and boil the stock hard until reduced to about 2 tablespoons. Set aside.

Preheat the oven to 350°F.

Prick the skin of the duck all over with a skewer to let the fat escape during cooking. Mix 1 teaspoon of the salt with the chili powder, cumin, and coriander and rub this all over the skin. Place the bird on a rack in a roasting pan and roast 2 hours. The skin will become crisp and golden.

Towards the end of this time, make the sauce. Heat the oil in a pan over medium heat and cook the onion until translucent. Add the reduced stock with the garlic, ginger, chili, lemon zest and juice, sugar, coconut cream, soy sauce, and remaining salt. Bring to a boil, cover, and simmer 30 minutes.

When the duck is cooked, remove from the oven and let it rest 10 minutes. Remove all the skin, cut it into bite-sized pieces, and set aside.

Remove the meat and cut into bite-sized pieces. Toss in the sauce to coat thoroughly.

Transfer to a warmed serving dish, surround with the egg quarters, sprinkle over the crispy skin pieces, and garnish with the fried onion rings, if using. Serve with steamed white rice.

JAPANESE DEEP-FRIED CHICKEN

SERVES 4

1 lb skinless boneless chicken breast, cut in 1¼-inch cubes
cornstarch, for dusting
vegetable oil, for deep-frying
1 green sweet pepper, seeded and cut into strips, for garnish

FOR THE MARINADE

2 tbsp soy sauce
1 tbsp sake, dry sherry, or white wine
1 garlic clove, minced
juice from a 1¼-inch cube of peeled fresh gingerroot, crushed through a garlic press

Make the marinade: mix the ingredients in a bowl. Add the chicken cubes, mix well, and let marinate 1 hour, stirring occasionally.

Drain the chicken thoroughly, discarding the marinade. Toss the pieces of chicken in cornstarch and shake off any excess. Deep-fry them, in batches, in hot oil in a wok until golden brown and crispy, 3-4 minutes. Drain on paper towels and keep each batch warm while cooking the rest.

When all the chicken is cooked, arrange on a warmed serving plate, surround with the pepper strips, and serve immediately.

LEMON CHICKEN

SERVES 4

1 egg white, lightly beaten
3 tsp cornstarch
10 oz skinless boneless chicken breast, cut across into ½-inch strips
vegetable oil, for deep-frying
6 tbsp chicken stock
juice of 1 lemon
2 tsp sugar
2 tsp light soy sauce
2 tsp dry sherry
1 garlic clove, minced
pinch of chili powder
½ small green sweet pepper, seeded and cut into equal bite-sized pieces

Mix the egg white thoroughly with 2 teaspoons of the cornstarch in a bowl. Then mix in the chicken strips, making sure they are all well coated. Cover and chill 30 minutes.

Deep-fry the chicken in hot oil in a wok for 1 minute, then drain on paper towels. Keep warm.

In a bowl, mix together the stock, lemon juice, sugar, soy sauce, sherry, garlic, and chili powder.

Pour all but 1 tablespoon of oil from the wok and stir-fry the pepper 2 minutes over medium heat. Stir in the stock mixture and simmer 1 minute.

Mix the remaining cornstarch with 1 tablespoon of water, add this to the pan, and simmer 1 more minute, stirring. Return the chicken to the pan and stir-fry about 30 seconds. Serve immediately.

STICKY CHICKEN

SERVES 4

8 chicken wing portions
3 garlic cloves, minced
1½-inch cube of peeled fresh gingerroot, crushed through a garlic press or minced
juice of 1 lemon
2 tbsp soy sauce
2 tbsp honey
½ tsp chili powder

Divide each chicken wing into pieces by cutting through the joints. Discard the wing tips or use for stock. There should be 16 pieces left.

Combine all the remaining ingredients in a shallow baking dish large enough to accommodate the chicken pieces snugly in 1 layer. Add the chicken and mix to coat thoroughly.

Cover and marinate at least 2 hours in a cool place or up to 24 in the refrigerator.

Preheat the oven to 425°F.

Uncover the dish, turn the chicken pieces once more in the marinade, and put the dish in the oven. Bake 20 minutes, turning and basting halfway through. The chicken will be coated with a delicious sticky glaze.

These pieces of chicken wing are best eaten with the fingers, so supply plenty of napkins and finger-bowls.

SAKE is the rice wine of Japan and is much used in Japanese cooking. Dry sherry makes a good substitute.

Chicken drumsticks or thighs also work well in the STICKY CHICKEN recipe. Increase the cooking time if using these.

CHICKEN WITH STRAW MUSHROOM CURRY

SERVES 4

4 skinless chicken breast halves
2 tbsp vegetable oil
salt and freshly ground black pepper
FOR THE SAUCE
2 tbsp vegetable oil
1 onion, chopped
1 garlic clove, minced
1 stalk of lemongrass, minced
1 hot chili pepper, seeded and chopped
¼ tsp ground cinnamon
½ tsp ground cardamom
1 heaping tsp curry powder
1¼ cups canned coconut cream
15 oz canned straw mushrooms, drained
juice of ½ lemon

If you can't find lemongrass for CHICKEN WITH STRAW MUSHROOM CURRY, *substitute the grated zest of ½ a lemon or lime. Small egg-shaped* STRAW MUSHROOMS *are rarely seen fresh in the West, but are readily available canned from Asian markets.*

First make the sauce: heat the oil in a saucepan over medium heat and cook the onion with the garlic and lemongrass, stirring occasionally, until the onion has softened, 4-5 minutes.

Add the chili, dry spices, and curry powder. Stir-fry 1 minute. Add the coconut cream and simmer 5 minutes.

Purée the sauce in a blender or food processor and return it to the pan. Add the mushrooms and simmer until they are warmed through, 2-3 minutes. Stir in the lemon juice and a pinch of salt.

Meanwhile, season the chicken lightly. Heat the oil in a frying pan over medium heat and fry the breast halves gently until golden brown and cooked through, 3-4 minutes on each side.

Arrange the cooked chicken on a warmed serving platter and spoon over the sauce. If serving as part of a meal to be eaten with chopsticks, slice the chicken across into bite-sized pieces.

CHICKEN WITH CASHEW NUTS

SERVES 4

6 oz skinless boneless chicken breast, cut into bite-sized pieces
⅓ cup sliced carrot
2 tbsp vegetable oil
⅓ cup unsalted cashew nuts
3 tbsp sliced canned bamboo shoots
1 tbsp frozen peas
FOR THE MARINADE
2 tbsp cornstarch
1 tsp vegetable oil
FOR THE SAUCE
1 tsp soy sauce
1 tsp dry sherry
½ tsp cornstarch
pinch of salt

First make the marinade: in a small bowl, mix together the cornstarch and oil with 2 tablespoons of water. Add the chicken, mix well, and let marinate 10 minutes.

Blanch the carrot slices in boiling salted water for 2 minutes. Drain.

Heat a wok until it is very hot, then add the oil and stir-fry the chicken until cooked through, 3-4 minutes.

Add the carrot, nuts, bamboo shoots, and peas and stir-fry another minute.

Mix the sauce ingredients together with ¼ cup of water. Add this to the pan and cook another minute or so, until the sauce has thickened. Serve immediately.

Top: Chicken with Straw Mushroom Curry served with cooked noodles; bottom: Chicken with Cashew Nuts

Nuts such as almonds or walnuts can be used instead of cashews in the recipe for CHICKEN WITH CASHEW NUTS.

SESAME-CRUSTED SALMON WITH GINGER CREAM

SERVES 4

⅓ cup sesame seeds
1 egg, beaten
flour, for coating
4 skinless pieces of salmon fillet, each weighing 4-5 oz
salt and freshly ground black pepper
3 tbsp vegetable oil
FOR THE SAUCE
1¼ cups light cream
1½-inch cube of peeled fresh gingerroot, crushed through a garlic press
1 tbsp light soy sauce or more to taste

Toast the sesame seeds in a frying pan over low to medium heat until lightly colored and aromatic. Put the toasted sesame seeds, beaten egg, and some flour in 3 separate shallow dishes.

Season the fish fillets on both sides with salt and pepper. Dip them first in the flour, shaking off the excess, then dip them in the egg, and finally in the toasted sesame seeds.

Heat the oil in a frying pan over medium-low heat and fry the coated fish until crisp and golden and cooked through, 2-3 minutes on each side.

Meanwhile, make the sauce: combine the cream, ginger, and soy sauce in a small pan and simmer 2-3 minutes. Add a little more soy sauce to taste.

Serve accompanied by steamed white rice or noodles and fresh steamed or boiled vegetables.

DOVER SOLE WITH MUSHROOMS AND PORK

SERVES 4

1½ oz dried Chinese black mushrooms
1 whole Dover sole, weighing about 1 lb 2 oz, skinned
1 tsp cornstarch
2 tsp dry sherry
½ tsp Asian sesame oil, plus more for greasing
¼ tsp soy sauce
1 tsp oyster sauce
1½ oz lean boneless pork, shredded
1 slice of bacon, cut crosswise into thin strips
½-inch cube of peeled fresh gingerroot, cut into fine matchsticks
1 small scallion, thinly sliced, for garnish
chopped fresh cilantro, for garnish

Soak the mushrooms in warm water for 30 minutes. Drain them thoroughly, cut off and discard the stems, and thinly slice the caps.

Arrange the fish in a steamer. (First put 2 strips of lightly oiled foil in a cross shape in the bottom of the pan; this will make it easier to remove the fish when it is cooked.)

Blend the cornstarch with a little of the sherry, then mix this thoroughly with the remaining sherry, the sesame oil, soy and oyster sauces, pork, bacon, and ginger.

Spoon this mixture on top of the fish and steam it over boiling water until the flesh flakes readily, 10-15 minutes.

Transfer the fish to a warmed serving plate and garnish with the scallion and cilantro.

CHILI SHRIMP IN PINEAPPLES

SERVES 4

2 small ripe pineapples
1 tbsp vegetable oil
1 onion, chopped
1 garlic clove, minced
1 large or 2 small celery stalks, coarsely chopped
2 tbsp chopped sweet pepper (preferably red)
1 tsp chili powder or more to taste
salt and freshly ground black pepper
1 cup chicken stock
2 heaping tsp arrowroot, mixed with a little water
¾ lb peeled cooked small or medium shrimp
1 cup small seedless grapes (any color or mixed)
½ cup blanched split almonds, toasted, for garnish
4 large or 8 cooked medium shrimp in their shells, for garnish

Cut the pineapples in half lengthwise, including the crown of green leaves. Being careful not to cut through the skin, cut out all the flesh and set the shells aside in a warm place. Cut the flesh into bite-sized pieces, discarding any hard core, and set the flesh aside.

Heat the oil in a large saucepan and cook the onion until translucent. Add the garlic, celery, sweet pepper, and chili powder with salt and pepper to taste. Stir-fry until the vegetables are softened, 2-3 minutes.

Stir in the stock, bring to a boil, and simmer 15 minutes. Add the arrowroot mixture and stir well until the mixture has thickened.

Add the peeled shrimp, grapes, and pineapple pieces and continue to cook gently until these are just heated through. (The shrimp will toughen if cooked too long.)

Pile the cooked shrimp mixture into the reserved pineapple half shells and garnish with toasted almonds and the shrimp in shells.

For a striking buffet party dish, serve the CHILI SHRIMP IN PINEAPPLE *in one or two half shells from a large pineapple. A wide variety of seafood suits this treatment: try using scallops or crab meat.*

For the CRISPY SESAME SHRIMP, *it is important to keep the tails attached to the shrimp when peeling them. They then look much more attractive when cooked and are easier to dip in the sauce and eat.*

CRISPY SESAME SHRIMP

SERVES 4

½ lb large raw shrimp, peeled and deveined
vegetable oil, for deep-frying
Asian sweet chili sauce or other dipping sauce, for serving
FOR THE BATTER
⅔ cup flour
3 tbsp cornstarch
1 tsp baking powder
¼ tsp chili powder
½ tsp salt
1 tbsp vegetable oil
2 tbsp sesame seeds

At least 1 hour ahead, make the batter. Thoroughly mix the flour, cornstarch, baking powder, and chili powder with ¾ cup water in a bowl. Let the batter rest at least 1 hour.

Just before using, beat the salt and oil into the batter until well incorporated and then stir in the sesame seeds.

Dip the shrimp in the batter and deep-fry them, a few at a time, in hot oil in a wok. Drain on paper towels and keep warm while the rest are being cooked.

Serve as soon as all the shrimp are cooked, accompanied by a dipping sauce, such as sweet chili sauce or a mixture of equal parts light soy sauce and rice or white wine vinegar.

INDONESIAN SQUID

SERVES 4

1 tbsp vegetable oil
1 small onion, chopped
2 garlic cloves, minced
1-inch cube of peeled fresh gingerroot, minced
½ tsp chili powder
grated zest and juice of 1 washed lime
1 tbsp brown sugar
1¼ cups thick canned coconut milk
12 small prepared squid, sacs sliced into thin rings
salt
chopped fresh cilantro, for garnish

Heat the oil in a saucepan or wok over medium heat and fry the onion, garlic, and ginger 2–3 minutes.

Add the chili powder, lime zest and juice, the sugar, and salt to taste. Stir to mix well, then add the coconut milk. Simmer 10 minutes.

Add the squid tentacles and slices and simmer 10 minutes. Do not overcook or it will become tough and rubbery. Serve sprinkled with chopped cilantro.

Prepared SQUID *are available fresh from better fish stores and frozen from Asian markets.*

Top: Sesame-crusted Salmon with Ginger Cream (page 132); bottom: Crispy Sesame Shrimp

SPICED CRAB CLAWS

SERVES 4

2 tbsp vegetable oil
8 large or 12 medium shelled crab claws, thawed if frozen
1 small onion, minced
2 garlic cloves, minced
2 hot chili peppers, minced
1½-inch cube of peeled fresh gingerroot, minced
½ tsp ground coriander seeds
1 tsp sugar
1 tbsp soy sauce
2 tsp tomato paste
salt
juice of ½ lime

Shelled crab claws can be bought frozen from Asian markets.

MALAYSIAN MILD CURRY PASTE is sold in many specialty markets. If unavailable, substitute another strong curry paste or a mild Malaysian curry powder.

In a frying pan or wok, heat the oil over medium heat and fry the crab claws until cooked through, 3-4 minutes. Remove with a slotted spoon and keep warm.

In the oil remaining in the pan, fry the onion, garlic, and chili 3 minutes. Add the ginger, coriander, sugar, soy sauce, tomato paste, and salt to taste with 3 tablespoons of water and simmer 3 minutes.

Return the crab claws to the pan. Add the lime juice, stir to coat thoroughly, and simmer 1-2 minutes, stirring until piping hot.

MUSSELS WITH CURRIED COCONUT NOODLES

SERVES 4

2¼ lb cleaned and debearded mussels in their shells
1¼ cups canned coconut cream
7 oz jar Malaysian mild curry paste
½ lb Chinese noodles
curls of fresh coconut, peeled with a swivel-bladed vegetable peeler, for garnish
chopped fresh cilantro, for garnish (optional)

Soak the mussels in cold water at least 1 hour to remove any traces of dirt or sand, changing the water at least 3 times. Drain the mussels and give any that remain open a sharp tap. Those that do not close again are dead and must be thrown away.

Put the coconut cream and the curry paste in a large saucepan that has a tight-fitting lid and place over medium heat, stirring gently. Add the mussels, cover the pan, and cook about 5 minutes, shaking the pan occasionally, until all the shells have opened. (Those few that do not should also be discarded.) Do not overcook or the mussels will become tough and rubbery.

Meanwhile, cook the noodles in boiling water, according to the package directions, and then drain them thoroughly.

To serve: divide the noodles among 6 warmed bowls or dishes and pour the mussels and sauce over them. Sprinkle with coconut curls and chopped cilantro, if using, and serve immediately.

Top: Mussels with Curried Coconut Noodles; bottom: Spiced Crab Claws

VEGETARIAN MAIN COURSES

*F*ortunately, the old concept of meat being an essential part of a meal is now dying away. As well as the pressure of more and more families now having to accommodate at least one vegetarian in their ranks, greater foreign travel - with a resulting awareness of other cuisines - and the extraordinary range of fresh vegetables, leaves, herbs, and fruit now available in our shops have caused even the most conventional cooks to broaden their horizons. Cultures which have traditionally made more of vegetables - or perhaps just used meat and fish more as flavoring ingredients - include the Mediterranean peoples, the Indians, Chinese, Japanese, and Latin Americans. Looking towards their heritage gives us myriad wonderful ways of preparing sustaining main-course salads and other dishes based mainly on vegetables.

Top: Bean Stew with Herb Dumplings (page 141); bottom: Vegetable Gratin (page 162)

CURLY ENDIVE LOAF WITH CAPER SAUCE

SERVES 4

5 heads of curly endive
5 tbsp butter
¼ cup flour
1 cup cream
4 eggs, beaten
salt and freshly ground black pepper
FOR THE CAPER SAUCE
2 tbsp butter
2 tbsp olive oil
2 onions, sliced
¾ lb tomatoes, peeled, seeded, and coarsely chopped
1½ tbsp capers

Preheat the oven to 350°F.

Put 3½ quarts of water in a large pan and bring it to a boil. Carefully place the endive heads in the water, bring it back to a boil and cook, uncovered, 15 minutes. Drain and let cool. Then squeeze out all remaining liquid and chop the endive coarsely.

Make a béchamel sauce (see page 12), using 4 tablespoons of the butter, the flour, and cream. Add the beaten eggs and then the chopped endive. Season.

Grease a 1-quart charlotte mold with the remaining butter. Fill with the mixture, tapping the mold sharply from time to time to remove air pockets. Let settle.

Place the mold in 2 inches of hot water in a deep roasting pan. Put this in the oven and bake until the surface of the loaf is golden brown, about 1 hour. The water should not boil at any time during the baking.

While the loaf is cooking, make the caper sauce: melt the butter with the oil in a heavy pan over medium heat. Add the onions and sauté until translucent. Then add the tomatoes and cook until tender, about 5-7 minutes. Season and let cool slightly. Then purée in a blender or food processor and stir in the capers.

Remove the loaf from the oven. Insert a knife to the bottom of the mold: if it comes out clean the loaf is cooked through; if sticky, return it to the oven for a further 10-15 minutes.

Let cool out of the oven 3 minutes and then unmold on a warmed serving dish and serve with the caper sauce.

LEEK, MOZZARELLA, AND PESTO GRATIN

SERVES 4

8 large leeks, trimmed but leaving as much green as possible
½ cup low-fat cream cheese
2 tbsp pesto sauce
¼ cup pine nuts
¼ lb mozzarella cheese, thinly sliced
salt and freshly ground black pepper

Preheat the oven to 400°F.

Cut each of the leeks into 4 equal lengths. Then place them in a pan of boiling salted water and cook 5-7 minutes. Remove, refresh under cold running water, and place in colander to drain.

Place the drained leeks in an ovenproof dish. Mix the cream cheese and pesto together and season. Using a spatula, smooth the mixture over the leeks. Sprinkle over the pine nuts and arrange the mozzarella slices over the top.

Bake in the oven until the mozzarella has turned golden brown, 20-30 minutes.

BEAN STEW WITH HERB DUMPLINGS

SERVES 4

3 tbsp olive oil
1 onion, chopped
1-2 garlic cloves, minced
2 celery stalks, chopped
2 carrots, sliced
1 cup dried white kidney beans or black-eyed peas, soaked
overnight in cold water and drained
bouquet garni
1 lb tomatoes, peeled and chopped
3½ cups well-flavored chicken or vegetable stock
salt and freshly ground black pepper
FOR THE HERB DUMPLINGS
2 oz shredded vegetable suet
1⅓ cups fresh white bread crumbs
6½ tbsp self-rising flour
3 tbsp chopped fresh mixed herbs

Heat the oil in a large pan over medium heat. Add the onion and garlic and sauté for 4 minutes. Stir in the celery and carrots and cook 2 minutes longer.

Add the remaining ingredients and bring to a boil. Season. Lower the heat, cover, and simmer 45 minutes, stirring occasionally.

Toward the end of this time make the dumplings: mix all the ingredients together with seasoning and about 5 tablespoons of cold water to a firm dough. Shape into 12 balls.

Arrange on top of the stew. Cover and continue simmering until the dumplings are light and fluffy, about 20 minutes. Serve at once.

PUMPKIN STEW WITH NAVY BEANS OR BARLEY

SERVES 4-6

¾ cup dried navy beans or pearl barley, soaked overnight in
cold water
2 tbsp butter
2 tbsp olive oil
1 onion, cut into wedges
1 garlic clove, minced
¾ lb piece of pumpkin, peeled and diced
2 carrots, sliced
1 small fennel bulb, sliced
1 tsp ground turmeric
1 tsp ground coriander seeds
½ tsp ground cinnamon
4 tomatoes, peeled and quartered
1 tbsp chopped fresh mint
1 tbsp chopped fresh cilantro
½ lb green beans
¼ lb small button mushrooms
3½ cups vegetable stock
salt and freshly ground black pepper
garlic bread, for serving

Drain the navy beans or barley and put them in a saucepan. Cover with water and bring to a boil. Cook 25 minutes for navy beans or 15 minutes for barley. Drain and set aside.

Melt the butter with the oil in a large heavy saucepan over medium heat. Add the onion and garlic and cook 3 minutes. Stir in the pumpkin, carrots, fennel, and spices and continue cooking 10 minutes, stirring frequently.

Add the beans or barley and all the remaining ingredients to the pan. Season with salt and pepper. Bring to a boil, cover, and simmer 20-25 minutes.

Serve hot with garlic bread.

SPICED WINTER VEGETABLE CASSEROLE

SERVES 6

2 tbsp butter
1 onion, chopped
10 garlic cloves
½ lb small turnips, halved
½ lb kohlrabi, cut into 1-inch cubes
½ lb carrots, cut into matchsticks
¼ lb Jerusalem artichokes, diced
½ cinnamon stick
4 whole cloves
large sprig of fresh thyme
1¼ cups red wine
⅔ cup well-flavored vegetable stock
salt and freshly ground black pepper
2 tsp cornstarch

Preheat the oven to 400°F.

Melt the butter in a large heavy saucepan over medium heat. Add the onion and garlic cloves and cook, stirring, until they begin to brown, about 5 minutes - but do not let them burn.

Stir in all the vegetables and continue cooking 3 minutes. Transfer to a casserole dish and add the spices and thyme. Pour in the wine and stock and season. Cover and bake until all the vegetables are tender, about 1¼ hours.

Blend the cornstarch with 2 tablespoons of cold water and stir this into the stew. Return to the oven, uncovered, and cook until the juices thicken, about 10 minutes. Remove the cinnamon and adjust the seasoning before serving.

STUFFED SQUASH

SERVES 6

5 tbsp olive oil
2 garlic cloves, minced
1 shallot, minced
2 sprigs of fresh sage or oregano
1 ½ lb fresh fava beans, shelled
¾ lb ripe tomatoes, peeled and chopped
salt and freshly ground black pepper
2 tbsp chopped fresh parsley
1 summer squash, weighing 2¼-3 lb
¼ cup freshly grated Parmesan cheese

Preheat the oven to 375°F.

First prepare the filling: heat 3 tablespoons of the oil in a heavy saucepan over medium heat. Add the garlic, shallots, and herb sprigs and cook, 5 minutes, stirring frequently.

Stir in the beans and tomatoes and season with salt and pepper. Cover and cook 15 minutes, stirring frequently. Remove the herb sprigs and stir in the chopped parsley.

While the filling is cooking, slice the squash into six disks. Scoop out the seeds in the center of each disc together with a little of the inner flesh and arrange the rings that remain in an oiled baking dish.

Brush the squash flesh with the remaining olive oil. Divide the prepared filling among the squash rings, cover with foil, and bake until the squash is tender, about 35 minutes.

Serve hot, sprinkled with the freshly grated Parmesan cheese.

Top: Red Cabbage with Cloves and Chestnuts (page 163); bottom: Stuffed Squash

DAIKON, *a Japanese radish is said to aid digestion and is generally served raw and thinly sliced in salads and fish dishes. It also cooks a little like turnip and is used in stews.*

RED LENTILS WITH CINNAMON AND COCONUT

SERVES 6

1¼ cups split red lentils
3½ cups spring water
3 tbsp extra virgin olive oil
2 large purple garlic cloves, sliced
2 large onions, diced
2 carrots, sliced
2 leeks, cut into 1-inch slices
1 daikon radish, weighing about ¼ lb, diced
½ tsp ground cinnamon
½ tsp mustard seeds
½ tsp ground or crushed cumin seeds
1 tbsp shredded coconut
½ oz fresh gingerroot, peeled and grated
salt and freshly ground black pepper

Thoroughly wash the lentils in cold water. Drain.

Bring the spring water to a boil and add the lentils. Bring back to a boil, stirring constantly. Season, cover, and simmer until the lentils are cooked, about 45 minutes. Drain.

Toward the end of the lentil cooking time, place a large heavy pan over medium heat. Pour in the olive oil, then add the garlic and sauté it briefly. Add all the vegetables and sauté them 5 minutes. Add the cinnamon, mustard seeds, cumin, coconut, and fresh ginger. Stir 2 minutes.

Gently stir the vegetable and spice mixture into the drained lentils. Adjust the seasoning, heat through, thoroughly and serve.

STUFFED EGGPLANT

SERVES 6

6 large eggplants
4 tbsp extra virgin olive oil
1 large purple garlic clove, minced
6 anchovy fillets
1 tsp herbes de Provence
¼ lb tomatoes, peeled, seeded, and coarsely chopped
⅔ cup diced onions
½ cup minced Greek olives (Kalamata)
4 cups fresh whole wheat bread crumbs
salt and freshly ground black pepper

Preheat the oven to 400°F and line a baking sheet with foil.

Cut the eggplants in half lengthwise. Using a small teaspoon, scoop out the eggplant flesh, leaving about ¼ inch of flesh under the skin and taking care not to break the skin at any point.

Spread the scooped-out flesh on the prepared baking sheet and bake 30 minutes.

Meanwhile, brush the flesh left in the eggplant shells with some of the olive oil and then sprinkle with salt. Place the shells in a baking dish and bake for the last 15 minutes with the scooped-out flesh.

Toward the end of this time, heat the remaining oil in a sauté pan over medium heat and add the garlic, anchovies, herbs, tomatoes, and onions. Sauté lightly 3-5 minutes.

Blend these to a smooth purée, then mix this well with the chopped olives and baked eggplant flesh. Season this mixture and use it to stuff the shells. Sprinkle the tops with the bread crumbs.

Bake the stuffedeggplant halves 10-15 minutes and then serve immediately.

Left: Red Lentils with Cinnamon and Coconut;
right: Stuffed Eggplant

Tofu, *or bean curd,
is made from
soybeans and is rich
in proteins. Rather
like fresh cheese in
appearance and
texture, its gentle
flavor lends its use
with a variety of
vegetables, herbs, and
spices. It is
particularly tasty
when smoked.*

PUMPKIN STUFFED WITH LEEKS AND SMOKED TOFU

SERVES 2

*1 pumpkin, weighing 2-3 lb
1½ tbsp light soy sauce
2 tsp Asian sesame oil
½ lb smoked tofu, mashed
2 young leeks, thinly sliced or shredded
½ tsp freshly grated nutmeg*

Preheat the oven to 400°F.

Cut off the top of the pumpkin and reserve. Scoop out and discard all the seeds and fibers.

Mix the soy sauce and oil into the tofu with the leeks and nutmeg. Pack the mixture into the pumpkin and place the top back on. Wrap in foil and bake 1-1½ hours, depending on size.

Remove the top and halve the pumpkin to serve.

CAULIFLOWER CHEESE CASSEROLE WITH NUTS AND OATS

SERVES 4-6

*1 large head of cauliflower
4 tbsp unsalted butter
2 onions, minced
1¼ cups milk
¾ cup shredded Swiss cheese
salt and freshly ground black pepper
5 eggs, beaten
2 cups fresh whole wheat bread crumbs
3 tbsp almonds, toasted
3 tbsp hazelnuts, toasted
1 cup rolled oats*

Preheat the oven to 350°F.

Remove all large outer leaves surrounding the cauliflower, but leave the young green ones. Cut the cauliflower lengthwise into 6 parts, complete with core.

Place the cauliflower in a large pan of lightly salted water. Bring to a boil, then reduce the heat and simmer 5 minutes. Drain thoroughly and place in a 2 quart ovenproof dish.

Melt half the butter in a sauté pan over medium heat and sauté the onions until soft.

Bring the milk to a boil in a saucepan and stir in the Swiss cheese and the remaining butter. Season with salt and pepper and stir in the onions. Remove from the heat, then blend in the eggs and one-third of the bread crumbs.

Cover the drained cauliflower with this sauce and bake on the middle shelf of the oven for 20 minutes.

Remove the baking dish from the oven and sprinkle with the nuts, oats, and remaining bread crumbs. Return to the oven, turn the heat up to 400°F and bake until the oats are golden, 10-15 minutes.

VEGETARIAN TORTA WITH SAGE HOLLANDAISE★

SERVES 6

3 tbsp hazelnut oil, plus more for greasing
2 onions, coarsely chopped
3 Roma tomatoes, coarsely chopped
¼ lb oyster mushrooms, coarsely chopped
1 tsp herbes de Provence
1 tbsp light soy sauce
nearly ½ cup buckwheat groats
2½ tbsp brown rice
1 egg, beaten
⅔ cup vegetable stock
freshly ground black pepper
1 tbsp crushed hazelnuts
2 large fresh sage leaves, for garnish
FOR THE GOLDEN SAGE HOLLANDAISE SAUCE
1 tbsp finely snipped golden sage
2 tbsp lemon juice
1 tbsp white wine vinegar
14 tbsp unsalted butter
3 egg yolks★
(★see page 2 for advice on eggs)
1 tbsp dry white wine
salt and freshly ground black pepper

Preheat the oven to 375°F and lightly grease a 7-inch shallow loaf pan with a little hazelnut oil.

Heat the hazelnut oil in a pan over medium heat. Add the onions, tomatoes, and mushrooms, toss gently to coat evenly, and cook 3 minutes. Add the herbs and the soy sauce and cook 2 minutes longer. Add the buckwheat and rice and cook 2 minutes more. Then stir in the egg.

Add the vegetable stock and bring to a boil, stirring constantly. Reduce the heat, cover, and simmer until all the liquid has been absorbed, 20-25 minutes. Season with pepper and add the hazelnuts.

Transfer the mixture to the prepared pan and bake 45 minutes.

Meanwhile, make the hollandaise sauce: mix the chopped sage with 1 tablespoon of the lemon juice, the vinegar, and 1 tablespoon of water in a small pan and bring to a boil. Drain the sage in a strainer and set aside. Melt 12 tablespoons of the butter in the top pan of a double boiler over very low heat. Transfer to a warmed measuring jug.

Place the egg yolks in the double boiler and beat them quickly with a whisk. Add half the remaining lemon juice and all the wine together with a pinch of salt. Beat again. Add half the remaining unmelted butter and place the pan over the bottom pan of the double boiler.

Whisking steadily, cook gently until the egg yolks are creamy and beginning to thicken. Immediately remove the pan from the heat and stir in the remaining unmelted butter until evenly blended.

Drizzle the melted butter into the yolk mixture, whisking fast. Add the butter more rapidly as the sauce thickens. When the sauce is the consistency of whipping cream, add the remaining lemon juice with the reserved sage and adjust the seasoning.

Serve the sauce with the hot vegetarian torta, garnished with the whole sage leaves.

The SAGE HOLLANDAISE sauce also goes very well with chicken and veal and with rice, cheese, and tomato dishes.

ZUCCHINI, TOMATO, AND GARLIC FLAN

SERVES 4

butter or margarine, for greasing
pie pastry made with 1 cup flour, 6 tbsp shortening,
and 2 tbsp ice water
¼ lb zucchini
2 eggs, beaten
⅔ cup milk
⅔ cup whipping cream
2 garlic cloves, minced
1 tsp tomato paste
1 tsp Worcestershire sauce
¼ tsp freshly grated nutmeg
salt and freshly ground black pepper
¼ lb tomatoes, sliced

Preheat the oven to 400°F and grease a 7-inch loose-bottomed tart or quiche pan with some butter.

Roll out the pastry and use it to line the pan. Line with wax paper and weight with some dried beans. Bake 15 minutes. Let cool and then remove the beans and lining paper.

Grate the zucchini and blanch the shreds 30 seconds only in boiling salted water. Drain, refresh under cold running water, and set aside.

In a bowl, thoroughly mix the eggs, milk, cream, garlic, tomato paste, Worcestershire sauce, nutmeg, and seasoning. Add the well-drained zucchini and spread this mixture evenly in the pastry shell. Arrange the tomatoes decoratively on the top.

Bake until set and golden in colour, 30-40 minutes.

ASPARAGUS AND DILL TART★

SERVES 6

FOR THE PASTRY
1¼ cups flour
½ tsp salt and ¼ tsp freshly ground black pepper
¼ tsp dried English mustard
6 tbsp butter or margarine, cut into small pieces
½ cup finely grated Cheddar cheese
1 egg yolk
FOR THE FILLING
6 oz asparagus tips
1 egg + 1 extra yolk★
(★see page 2 for advice on eggs)
1¼ cups light cream
½ tsp salt and ¼ tsp finely ground black pepper
3 tbsp chopped fresh dill
2 tsp Dijon-style mustard

To make the pastry: sift the flour, salt, pepper, and dried mustard into a bowl, add the butter or margarine and rub it in finely with the fingertips. Stir in the cheese, egg yolk, and 1-2 tablespoons of cold water and mix together to a firm dough.

Knead the dough on a lightly floured surface until smooth. Roll it out thinly and use to line a 14- x 4-

inch rectangular loose-bottomed tart pan or form set on a baking sheet. Chill 30 minutes.

Preheat the oven to 400°F.

Bake the pastry shell "blind" until lightly browned at the edges and cooked on the bottom, 10-15 minutes. Reduce the oven temperature to 350°F.

While the shell is baking make the filling: cook the asparagus in boiling water 1 minute, then drain well. In a bowl beat together the egg and egg yolk, cream, salt, pepper, dill, and mustard until well blended. Pour this filling into the pastry shell and arrange the asparagus tips on top.

Return to the cooler oven and bake until the filling has just set, 20-25 minutes.

Let cool in the pan, then remove carefully and serve warm or cold.

SPINACH AND RAISIN TART★

SERVES 4-6

FOR THE PASTRY
¾ cup flour
½ tsp salt
4 tbsp butter or margarine, cut into small pieces
1 tbsp lemon juice
FOR THE FILLING
½ lb fresh spinach leaves
2 eggs★
(★see page 2 for advice on eggs)
¾ cup thick plain yogurt
½ tsp salt and ¼ tsp finely ground black pepper
1 tsp freshly grated nutmeg
⅓ cup raisins

To make the pastry: sift the flour and salt into a bowl, add the butter or margarine and rub it in finely with the fingertips. Stir in the lemon juice and 2-3 tablespoons of cold water and mix together with a fork to form a firm dough.

Knead on a lightly floured surface until smooth. Roll it out thinly and use to line an 8-inch round loose-bottomed fluted tart pan. Chill 30 minutes.

Preheat the oven to 400°F.

Bake the pastry shell "blind" until lightly browned at the edge and cooked on the bottom, 10-15 minutes. Remove from the oven, and reduce the oven temperature to 350°F.

While the shell is baking, make the filling: plunge the spinach in boiling water for 1 minute. Drain well and chop finely.

Place the eggs, yogurt, salt, pepper, and nutmeg in a bowl and beat them together until well blended. Stir in the spinach and raisins and pour the mixture into the pastry shell. Return the tart to the cooler oven until the filling has set, 20-25 minutes.

Let cool in the pan, then remove it carefully. Serve warm or cold.

ASPARAGUS *is in season from February through June. When buying asparagus, look for tightly closed "buds" or tips and fresh green, unwrinkled stalks. Nowadays, ready-trimmed tips are available from supermarkets, but you can use the stalks for soups and sauces.*

FRESH HERB AND GARLIC TART★

SERVES 4

FOR THE PASTRY
¾ cup flour
1 tbsp freshly grated Parmesan cheese
¼ tsp dried English mustard
½ tsp salt and ¼ tsp freshly ground black pepper
4 tbsp butter or margarine, cut into small pieces

FOR THE FILLING
2 garlic cloves, minced
¼ cup chopped mixed fresh herbs, including parsley,
rosemary, oregano, and basil
½ cup ricotta or cream cheese
¼ cup thick plain yogurt
2 eggs, beaten★
(★see page 2 for advice on eggs)
½ tsp salt and ¼ tsp freshly ground black pepper

To make the pastry: sift the flour, Parmesan, mustard, salt, and pepper into a bowl. Add the butter or margarine and rub it in finely with your fingertips. Stir in 2-3 tablespoons of cold water and

mix together with a fork to form a firm dough.

Knead on a lightly floured surface until smooth. Roll out thinly and use to line an 8-inch round loose-bottomed tart pan. Chill 30 minutes.

Preheat the oven to 400°F.

Bake the shell "blind" until lightly browned at the edge and cooked on the bottom, 10-15 minutes. Reduce the oven temperature to 350°F.

While the shell is baking make the filling: mix the garlic, herbs, and soft cheese in a bowl until well blended. Stir in the yogurt, eggs, salt, and pepper and mix well.

Pour the mixture into the pastry shell and return it to the cooler oven until the filling has set, 20-25 minutes. Serve warm or cold.

ONION AND SAGE TART★

SERVES 6

FOR THE PASTRY
1¼ cups flour
½ tsp salt
¼ cup shortening, cut into small pieces
4 tbsp butter or margarine, cut into small pieces

FOR THE FILLING
¾ lb pearl or other tiny onions, unpeeled
2 tbsp butter
15 cherry tomatoes
2 tbsp chopped fresh sage
1 tbsp flour
⅔ cup vegetable stock
½ cup light cream
2 eggs, beaten★
(★see page 2 for advice on eggs)
½ tsp salt and ¼ tsp freshly ground black pepper

FOR THE TOPPING
1 tbsp freshly grated Parmesan cheese
1 tbsp chopped fresh sage

To make the pastry: sift the flour and salt into a bowl, add the shortening and butter or margarine, and rub them in finely with the fingertips. Stir in 2 tablespoons of cold water and mix together with a fork to form a firm dough.

Knead the dough on a lightly floured surface until smooth. Roll it out thinly and use to line a 9-inch round loose-bottomed tart pan. Chill 30 minutes.

Preheat the oven to 400°F.

Bake the pastry shell "blind" until lightly browned at the edge and cooked on the bottom, 10-15 minutes.

While the shell is baking make the filling: place the onions in a saucepan and cover with cold water. Bring to a boil, cover, and cook for 10 minutes, until tender. Drain and cover with cold water. Drain again and then peel off the onion skins.

Melt the butter in a saucepan over medium-high heat. Add the peeled onions, the tomatoes, and sage and cook quickly for 1-2 minutes, shaking the saucepan constantly. Using a slotted spoon, transfer the tomatoes and onions to a plate. Let cool slightly then cut them in half. Arrange them in the pastry shell.

Add the flour to the juices in the saucepan and stir well. Add the vegetable stock, bring to a boil, and cook 1 minute. Remove the saucepan from the heat, stir in the cream, eggs, salt, and pepper.

Pour the mixture into the pastry shell and return it to the oven to bake 15 minutes. Remove from the oven and give the tart its topping: sprinkle the top with Parmesan cheese and sage. Continue baking until the filling has set and is golden brown, 10-15 minutes. Serve hot or cold.

Left: Fresh Herb and Garlic Tart; right: Onion and Sage Tart

POTATOES WITH WINTER VEGETABLE TRICOLOR

SERVES 4

1 lb thin-skinned potatoes, washed but not peeled
½ tbsp coarse salt
1 large head of celery root, peeled and cut into chunks
1½ lb spinach, stems removed
3 large carrots, thinly sliced
salt and freshly ground black pepper
½ tsp celery salt
1 tbsp light cream
¼ tsp freshly grated nutmeg

Put the potatoes and coarse salt in a pan of water and place over medium heat. Bring to a boil, reduce the heat, and cook the potatoes until tender. Drain and place them on a warm plate. The salt should dry on the potato skins.

When cool enough to handle, cut the potatoes into thick slices. Keep warm.

Preheat the oven to 450°F.

Cook the celery root in unsalted boiling water until tender, 15-20 minutes. Steam the spinach until tender, 10-15 minutes. Cook the carrots in the celery root water until tender, 15-20 minutes.

Blend each vegetable individually to a purée. Season the purées and add the celery salt to the celery root, the cream to the spinach, and the nutmeg to the carrots.

Spoon the purées decoratively over the potatoes. Place them in the oven and heat through 5 minutes. Serve immediately.

SWISS CHARD AND PINE NUT TART

SERVES 4

2 tbsp butter
1 tbsp olive oil
1 onion, minced
2 large garlic cloves, minced
10 oz Swiss chard leaves
6 tbsp minced fresh flat-leaf parsley
juice of ½ lemon
salt and freshly ground black pepper
½ lb frozen pie pastry, thawed
2 eggs, beaten
½ cup pine nuts
⅔ cup crème fraîche or whipping cream
6 tbsp milk
pinch of freshly grated nutmeg
sun-dried tomatoes in oil, for garnish (optional)

Preheat the oven to 350°F.

Melt the butter with the oil in a large sauté pan over medium heat. Sauté the onion and garlic until translucent and then add the Swiss chard, parsley, lemon juice, and some seasoning.

Sauté briefly over medium-high heat until the chard is softened. Set aside.

Roll out the pastry on a lightly floured surface and use it to line a 10-inch tart or quiche pan. Cover the bottom with foil and weight with dried beans.

Bake about 10 minutes and then remove the beans and foil. Return to the oven and bake until the pastry is firm but not yet brown, about 10 minutes longer. Brush with a little of the beaten egg and bake 5 minutes more.

While the tart shell is baking, toast all but 1 tablespoon of the pine nuts on a baking sheet until golden brown, 5-10 minutes.

In a bowl, mix the cream, milk, eggs, and nutmeg. Season and stir in the chard mixture. At the last minute, stir in the toasted pine nuts.

Pour into the pastry shell, scatter over the remaining pine nuts, and bake 20 minutes.

Garnish with chopped sun-dried tomatoes in oil, if desired.

NOTES: Spinach can be used instead of the Swiss chard. Some chopped bacon or ham can be cooked with the chard for extra flavor.

Alternatively, for a delicious and unusual sweet tart, replace the onion, garlic, parsley, and seasoning with golden raisins, honey, and a pinch of ground allspice.

VEGETABLES AND SALADS

*E*ven the most adventurous of cooks is quite likely to serve plain boiled, steamed, or baked vegetables as side dishes to accompany main meals. Although there is nothing wrong with this no-nonsense approach, there are also many wonderfully easy ways to make vegetable accompaniments little feasts on their own without really spending much more time, money, or effort. It may be as simple as tossing in some chopped fresh herbs or a few toasted nuts with the knob of butter just before serving, or an unusual and attractive means of presentation, such as the String Bean Bouquets, or perhaps a novel way of cooking a traditional favorite, like Deep fried Eggplant with Black Bean Sauce. Many of the recipes which follow, as well as being capable of enlivening the plainest of main courses, are also colorful and interesting enough to be used as appetizers, snacks or light meals in their own right.

Left to right: Braised Red Onions (page 166); Herbed Carrots Tossed in Lemon Mayonnaise (page 167); Stir-Fried Zucchini (page 166)

BABY BRUSSELS SPROUTS WITH PINE NUTS

SERVES 4

1 lb baby Brussels sprouts
½ tbsp hazelnut oil
⅔ cup pine nuts
salt and freshly ground black pepper

Steam the sprouts 3 minutes over boiling water, without removing the lid. Remove from the heat.

Put the hazelnut oil in the bottom of a warmed serving dish. Add the pine nuts and salt and pepper, followed by the sprouts.

Toss gently until thoroughly coated with oil and then serve immediately.

CABBAGE WITH CARAWAY SEEDS AND SESAME OIL

SERVES 4

2 tbsp butter
2 tbsp roasted sesame oil
1 tsp caraway seeds
¾ lb head of white cabbage, thinly sliced
salt and freshly ground black pepper

Melt the butter with the oil in a pan over medium heat. Add the caraway seeds and toss gently 1 minute. Add the cabbage and toss to coat thoroughly with the butter and oil.

Place the lid on the pan and increase the heat. Cook 2-3 minutes only, shaking the pan constantly. Season and transfer to a warmed serving dish. Serve immediately.

CABBAGE WITH CARAWAY SEEDS AND SESAME OIL *lends itself to many variations. Try replacing the caraway seeds with poppy seeds, fennel seeds, or crushed coriander seeds mixed with blanched strips of zest from a washed orange.*

Left: Cabbage with Caraway Seeds and Sesame Oil; right: Baby Brussels Sprouts with Pine Nuts

BROCCOLI AND CAULIFLOWER WITH FIVE-HERB BUTTER

SERVES 4-6

½ lb broccoli florets
½ lb cauliflower florets
salt
FOR THE HERB BUTTER
1 stick (8 tbsp) butter
½ tsp each minced fresh marjoram, mint, chives, and
tarragon
1 tsp minced fresh parsley
1 tbsp lemon juice

Several hours before, make the herb butter: cream the butter in a bowl until light. Gently work in the herbs and lemon juice. Leave at room temperature about 2 hours to let the herbs to release their flavors and then chill 1-2 hours.

Blanch the broccoli and cauliflower florets in boiling salted water 3-5 minutes, depending on the desired degree of crunchiness.

Using a wire skimmer or slotted spoon, transfer the vegetables to a colander and refresh under cold water. Then return the florets to the boiling water for 1 minute only to reheat.

Transfer to a warmed serving dish, dot with herb butter, and serve immediately.

RATATOUILLE

SERVES 4

6 zucchini
6 eggplants
2 green sweet peppers
2 red sweet peppers
2¼ cups extra virgin olive oil
4 large onions, each cut into 6 pieces
6 tomatoes, peeled, seeded, and coarsely chopped
4 purple garlic cloves, minced
large sprig of fresh oregano
juice of ½ large lemon
salt and freshly ground black pepper

Cut the zucchini and eggplants into slices about ¾-inch thick. Arrange these on a wire rack and sprinkle generously with salt. Let drain 30 minutes, then rinse and pat dry with paper towel.

While these drain, skin the peppers by piercing them with a fork and holding them over a flame or under the broiler. Turn them so that the skin blisters uniformly. Let cool slightly; the blackened skin will come off with ease. Cut the peppers in half, remove the seeds, and slice the flesh in thick strips.

Pour 7 tablespoons of the oil into a large frying pan over medium heat, then add the zucchini. Raise the heat and cook until the slices are browned on both sides. Using a slotted spoon, transfer the zucchini to a large flameproof casserole. Repeat this process with the eggplant, onions, and peppers, adding more oil as necessary.

Add tomatoes, garlic, oregano, and rest of the oil to the casserole. Add lemon juice and season with pepper but no salt. Place over medium heat and cover. Bring to a boil, then lower heat and simmer gently 50-60 minutes, stirring once or twice.

Season with salt. (If there is surplus liquid, drain it off into a pan and boil rapidly to reduce it, then return it to the dish.) Serve hot, warm, or cold.

DEEP-FRIED EGGPLANT WITH BLACK BEAN SAUCE

SERVES 4

6 small to medium eggplants
2 eggs, beaten
3 tbsp flour
salt and freshly ground black pepper
2 tbsp black bean sauce
vegetable or peanut oil, for deep-frying

Cut the eggplants across into disks about ¾-inch thick. Lay these flat, sprinkle with salt, and let drain 30 minutes. Rinse and pat dry.

Put the egg in a small bowl and put the flour on a shallow plate. Season the flour.

Spread both sides of each eggplant slice with a thin coating of black bean sauce. Dip both sides of each slice into the beaten egg, then in the flour. Shake off any excess flour.

Place a batch of eggplant slices in a single layer in the wire basket of a deep-fryer. Heat the oil in the deep-fryer to 360°F (a small cube of dry bread browns in 60 seconds). Fry the eggplant, until well browned, 2-3 minutes.

Drain on paper towels, then place on a warmed serving dish. Serve as soon as all the slices are fried.

Bottled or canned BLACK BEAN SAUCE *is now readily available in Asian stores and supermarkets. It will give an authentic Cantonese flavor to many foods, especially stir-fry dishes.*

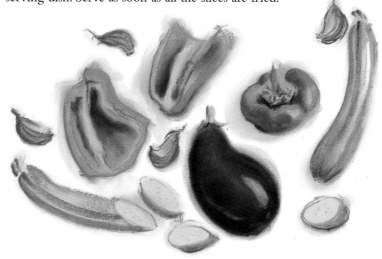

A bit like a quiche without the pastry, the traditional Italian FRITTATA is a sort of cross between an omelet and a pancake. A frittata makes ideal picnic food as it can be transported in the pan in which it was made.

MINTED NEW POTATO AND SUMMER VEGETABLE FRITTATA

SERVES 4

1 lb new red potatoes
¼ lb zucchini, sliced
1 cup shelled fresh fava beans or green peas
1 tbsp chopped fresh mint
¼ cup freshly grated Parmesan cheese
5 eggs, lightly beaten
salt and pepper
2 tbsp butter

Preheat the oven to 350°F.

In separate pans, steam or boil the vegetables in lightly salted water until just tender but still firm. Drain, refresh in cold running water, and then drain well again. Dice the potatoes.

In a bowl mix the vegetables with the mint and Parmesan. Stir in eggs and season with a little salt (remember the cheese will be salty) and pepper.

Melt the butter in a suitable metal quiche pan that can go both over a direct heat and in the oven. Add the egg mixture and cook over the lowest possible heat, undisturbed, for 5 minutes. Transfer to the oven and bake 10 minutes.

Let cool. Transport the frittata to the picnic in the pan and serve it cut in wedges.

GRILLED FENNEL AND EGGPLANT

SERVES 4

1 eggplant, weighing about ¾ lb, cut across into
½-inch slices
2 small fennel bulbs, cut lengthwise into quarters
¼ cup olive oil
salt and pepper
lemon wedges, for serving

Sprinkle the eggplant slices with salt and let drain 30 minutes in a colander to remove the bitter juices. Rinse thoroughly and pat dry with paper towels.

Preheat the barbecue until coals are quite hot.

Brush the eggplant slices and the pieces of fennel on all sides with olive oil. Season with salt and pepper and arrange in a single layer on the barbecue. Cook until done: it is impossible to give exact cooking times, as these will depend on the size of the vegetable pieces, the type of barbecue, and the heat of the coals. Simply keep turning the pieces of vegetable, brushing them with a little more oil, if necessary, and wait until they begin to take on a slightly charred look.

Serve immediately, with lemon wedges to squeeze over them.

Many firm-textured vegetables – such as zucchini, sweet peppers, plum tomatoes, and onions – can be grilled in this manner. Just keep turning the pieces and brushing them with olive oil until suitably charred in appearance.

Minted New Potato and Summer Vegetable Frittata

One of the classics of French cuisine, GRATIN DAUPHINOIS turns ordinary potatoes into a luxurious treat. It can also be enriched by the addition of one or two eggs.

GRATIN DAUPHINOIS

SERVES 4-6

2 tbsp butter
2 lb potatoes, very thinly sliced
1 garlic clove, chopped
⅛ tsp freshly grated nutmeg
salt and freshly ground black pepper
1¼ cups whipping cream
½ cup shredded Gruyère or Swiss cheese

Preheat the oven to 375°F. Use half of the butter to grease a shallow 5-cup (1½-quart) baking dish.

Layer the potatoes in the dish, dotting the layers with the remaining butter and the garlic and seasoning with nutmeg, salt, and pepper.

Pour the cream over the top and bake 1¼ hours. Sprinkle with the cheese, return to the oven, and bake 15-20 minutes longer. Serve hot.

VEGETABLE GRATIN

SERVES 4

1 small head of cauliflower, broken into florets
½ lb broccoli, broken into florets
white parts of 4 scallions, halved
3 tbsp butter
3 tbsp flour
1 tsp Dijon-style mustard
2 cups milk
1 cup shredded sharp Cheddar cheese
½ cup shredded Gruyère or Swiss cheese
¼ cup roughly chopped hazelnuts
salt and freshly ground black pepper

Cook the cauliflower, broccoli, and scallions in boiling salted water for 4 minutes. Drain thoroughly and arrange in a gratin dish. Keep warm.

Melt the butter in a small heavy saucepan, stir in

the flour, and cook, stirring, 1-2 minutes. Stir in the mustard and milk and bring to a boil, stirring constantly until thickened and smooth. Stir in the Cheddar and season with salt and pepper.

Preheat the broiler. Pour the sauce over the vegetables and sprinkle with the Gruyère and hazelnuts. Cook under the broiler until golden brown. Serve hot.

TRIO OF VEGETABLE PURÉES

SERVES 6

FOR THE JERUSALEM ARTICHOKE PURÉE
10 oz Jerusalem artichokes (sunchokes), diced
6 oz potato, diced
1 tbsp butter
2 tbsp light cream
⅛ tsp freshly grated nutmeg
FOR THE CARROT AND PARSNIP PURÉE
6 oz carrots, sliced
6 oz parsnips, sliced
1 tbsp butter
½ garlic clove, minced
FOR THE CELERY ROOT AND RUTABAGA PURÉE
½ lb celery root
¼ lb rutabaga
1 tbsp butter
squeeze of lemon juice
1 tbsp chopped fresh parsley
salt and freshly ground black pepper

In 3 separate saucepans, cook the vegetables for each purée in boiling water until soft, 8-10 minutes. Drain the three vegetable mixtures and return them to their saucepans.

Add the butter to each and season with their respective flavorings, salt, and pepper. Using a potato masher or ricer, mash each until smooth. Serve hot.

RED CABBAGE WITH CLOVES AND CHESTNUTS

SERVES 6

1½ lb red cabbage, finely shredded
2 small apples, peeled, cored, and sliced
2 tsp juniper berries, crushed
1 tbsp fresh rosemary leaves
salt and freshly ground black pepper
2 tbsp butter
1 tbsp olive oil
1 onion, minced
½ tsp ground cinnamon
4 whole cloves
2 tbsp red currant jelly
2 tbsp red wine vinegar
⅔ cup port wine
½ lb cooked whole chestnuts
chopped fresh parsley, to garnish

Preheat the oven to 300°F.

Arrange the cabbage and apples in layers in a large casserole dish, seasoning each layer with juniper, rosemary, salt, and pepper.

Melt the butter with the oil in a heavy saucepan over medium heat. Add the onion and cook 4-5 minutes. Stir in the cinnamon, cloves, red currant jelly, vinegar, and port. Bring to a boil, stirring until the jelly has melted.

Pour this over the cabbage and cover the casserole tightly with foil and a lid. Bake 2 hours. Check from time to time to see if all the liquid has evaporated, adding a little more port or water as necessary.

Add the chestnuts to the casserole, cover again, and return to the oven. Bake 15-20 minutes longer to warm them through. Serve sprinkled with chopped parsley.

GRANDMOTHER'S POTATO PANCAKES

SERVES 4

1½ lb freshly cooked potatoes
1 tbsp butter
1 egg yolk
2 tbsp whipping cream
1 tsp salt
½ tsp freshly grated nutmeg
freshly ground black pepper
6 tbsp whole wheat bread crumbs
2 tbsp corn oil

Mash the potatoes well, then mix in the butter, egg yolk, cream, salt, nutmeg, and pepper to taste.

Divide the mixture into 8 equal portions and shape into fat cakes. Then roll the cakes in bread crumbs to coat the outsides evenly.

Put the oil in a frying pan over medium heat and fry the cakes until golden brown on both sides.

Drain briefly on paper towels and serve with apple sauce if desired.

For good results with the PROVENÇAL GRATIN OF ZUCCHINI, *it is essential to dry the zucchini thoroughly after blanching them; otherwise any residual moisture will thin down the sauce. A preheated oven is also a key to success.*

ASPARAGUS WITH LIME ZEST BUTTER

SERVES 4

1-2 lb asparagus (depending on appetite)
salt and pepper
FOR THE LIME BUTTER
grated zest of ½ washed lime
1 stick (8 tbsp) butter, softened

First make the lime butter: mix the grated lime zest with the softened butter and put this on a small piece of plastic wrap. Wrap tightly, forming the butter into a small fat log shape, and chill until needed (30 minutes in the freezer will do).

Either steam the asparagus or boil in lightly salted water until cooked to taste and drain well.

While the asparagus is cooking, unwrap the butter and cut the cylinder across into 4 round pats.

Divide the asparagus among 4 warmed plates, season it with salt and pepper, and place a pat of lime butter on each serving. Garnish with some strips of lime zest, if desired.

SAUTÉ OF SWEET POTATO AND BACON

SERVES 4

1 lb orange-fleshed sweet potatoes
6 slices of bacon
2 tbsp butter
salt and pepper
1 tbsp chopped fresh parsley or chives, for garnish

Preheat the oven to 350°F.

Bake the sweet potatoes in their skins for 45 minutes. Remove from the oven and let cool slightly. When cool enough to handle, peel off the skins and discard them. Cut the flesh into 1-inch cubes.

Meanwhile heat a frying pan over medium heat and cook the bacon until really crisp. Using a slotted spoon, remove the bacon from the pan, drain it on paper towels, and roughly crumble.

Add the butter to the fat in the frying pan and stir-fry the sweet potato cubes, until crisp and golden, 5-10 minutes.

Season with salt and pepper and mix in the bacon pieces. Transfer to a warmed serving dish and sprinkle with chopped herbs.

SCALLOPED POTATOES AND MUSHROOMS

SERVES 4

2 lb potatoes, peeled and thinly sliced
6 oz mushrooms, thinly sliced
salt and pepper
1¼ cups light cream
1 garlic clove, minced
butter, for greasing

Preheat the oven to 375°F and grease an ovenproof dish with some butter.

Arrange the slices of potato and mushroom in alternating layers in the dish, seasoning each layer and finishing with a layer of potatoes.

In a small pan, heat the cream with the garlic until almost boiling. Pour this over the potatoes.

Bake until cooked through and golden brown on top, about 1½ hours.

PROVENÇAL GRATIN OF ZUCCHINI

SERVES 4

4 tbsp butter, plus more for greasing
6½ tbsp flour
2½ cups milk
1 cup grated Gruyère cheese
¼ tsp grated nutmeg
1 lb zucchini, thinly sliced
1 egg, lightly beaten
1 cup fresh white bread crumbs
salt and pepper

Preheat the oven to 475°F and grease an ovenproof dish with some butter.

In a heavy saucepan, melt the butter and add the flour. Cook over medium heat 2–3 minutes, stirring constantly. Add the milk and simmer 2–3 minutes, whisking constantly to ensure no lumps form.

Add the cheese, season to taste with salt and pepper, and mix in the nutmeg. Cook over very low heat, stirring constantly, for 5 minutes. Let cool about 10 minutes.

While the sauce cools, blanch the zucchini slices in boiling salted water 2 minutes only. Immediately drain and refresh under cold running water. Drain well again and pat dry with paper towels.

Mix the egg thoroughly into the cooled sauce, followed by the well-dried zucchini. Pour the mixture into the prepared dish and scatter the bread crumbs over the top.

Bake until bubbling and browned on top, about 15 minutes. Remove from the oven and let "settle" 10 minutes before serving, as the taste and texture are better if the dish is not too hot.

Top: Sauté of Sweet Potato and Bacon; bottom: Asparagus with Lime Zest Butter

Chinese HOISIN SAUCE *is made from soybeans and is flavored with chili peppers, garlic, and rice vinegar. Its sweet flavor works well with vegetables and meat dishes and is particularly suited to barbecue sauces.*

BRAISED RED ONIONS

SERVES 4

2 tbsp butter
4 large red onions, thinly sliced
salt and freshly ground black pepper

Melt the butter in a heavy pan over medium heat. Add the onions and cook gently until translucent.

Season, then cover and simmer over very low heat about 20 minutes. Stir and transfer to a warmed serving dish.

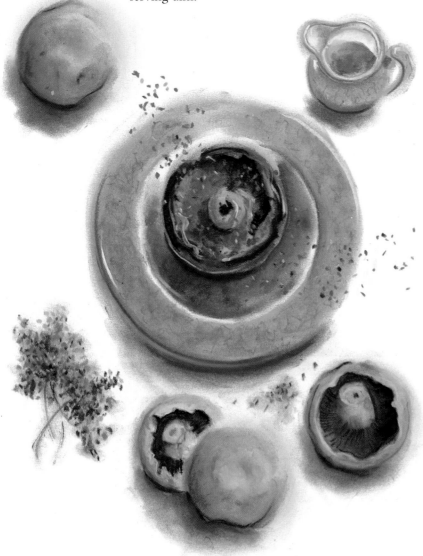

MUSHROOMS WITH HOISIN SAUCE

SERVES 4

1 lb flat, open mushrooms
2 tbsp butter
1 tbsp extra virgin olive oil
salt and freshly ground black pepper
juice of ½ lemon
2 tbsp hoisin sauce
2 tbsp chopped fresh cilantro

Clean the mushrooms well, but do not wash them.

Melt the butter with the oil in a heavy frying pan over medium-low heat and toss the mushrooms, until well coated. Cook gently until tender.

Transfer the mushrooms to a warmed serving plate, leaving the juices in the pan. Season the juices and stir in the lemon juice and hoisin sauce.

Pour this over the mushrooms and sprinkle with the cilantro before serving.

STIR-FRIED ZUCCHINI

SERVES 4

2 tbsp butter
2 tbsp light soy sauce
freshly ground black pepper
8 zucchini, thickly sliced

Melt the butter in a large frying pan over medium heat. Add the soy sauce and some black pepper, followed by the zucchini. Stir the zucchini to coat them evenly in the seasoned butter. Cover the pan and cook over medium heat 5 minutes, shaking the pan frequently.

Transfer to a warmed serving dish.

HERBED CARROTS TOSSED IN LEMON MAYONNAISE

SERVES 4

1 lb carrots, scrubbed, unpeeled, and cut into disks about
½-inch thick
2 tsp herbes de Provence
½ tsp grated zest and 1 tsp juice from a washed lemon
1 tbsp mayonnaise
salt and freshly ground black pepper

Place the carrots in a pan that has a tight-fitting lid. Barely cover with water and add the herbs.

Cover the pan and cook over medium heat until just tender, 15-20 minutes. Shake the pan frequently and add more water from time to time if necessary. Drain, stir in the other ingredients, and season.

POTATOES WITH DANDELION LEAVES AND TOMATO SAUCE

SERVES 4

½ lb potatoes in their skins
salt
½ lb dandelion leaves
4 tomatoes, thinly sliced
¼ cup coarsely chopped stuffed green olives
1 cup warm Quick Tomato Sauce (see page 10)

In a large pan of boiling salted water, cook the potatoes until tender. Drain, let cool slightly, and then slice. Keep warm.

Blanch greens 20 seconds only in boiling salted water. Refresh in cold water, drain, and pat dry.

Arrange the greens in a serving dish and cover with the tomato slices. Sprinkle with olives, arrange the potato slices on top, and pour over the sauce.

STUFFED TOMATOES

SERVES 2

2 large beefsteak tomatoes
1 tbsp butter
½ tbsp extra virgin olive oil
1 purple garlic clove, minced
1 large onion, coarsely chopped
salt and freshly ground black pepper
1 tbsp chopped fresh parsley
1 tbsp chopped fresh chives
2 oz feta cheese, cubed

Preheat the oven to 375°F.

Cut the tops from the tomatoes and reserve them. Scoop out the seeds and pulp to leave an empty cavity in each tomato.

Melt the butter with the oil in a sauté pan over medium heat and add the garlic. Sauté 2 minutes, then add the onion and cook until tender. Season, then sprinkle the parsley and chives into the onions. Stir, then immediately remove from the heat.

Stuff each of the tomatoes with the onion mixture. Then top that filling with the cheese and replace the tops.

Bake 30 minutes, and serve hot.

Small tender DANDELION GREENS *can be gathered wild in the early part of the year; they are also grown commercially. They go well in salads with chopped bacon and ham.*

STRING BEAN BOUQUETS

SERVES 4

1 lb fine string beans
bunch of fresh chives
½ cup canned pimiento, drained and cut into long
thin strips
6 tbsp butter
½ lemon
coarse salt
freshly ground black pepper

Trim all the beans to the same length, leaving the tails on some if necessary.

Plunge the beans into a large pan of boiling salted water and simmer 3-6 minutes, depending on the preferred degree of firmness. Drain and refresh under cold running water. Drain well and pat dry.

In the same water, blanch the chives 30 seconds only. Refresh, drain, and pat dry.

Separate the beans into 6 bundles and tie them together with 2 chives per bundle, securing with two knots. Loop the pimiento strips decoratively around the bundles.

Melt the butter in a frying pan over low heat, then carefully roll the bundles in it until they are thoroughly heated through.

Place on a warmed serving plate. Squeeze the lemon juice over the bundles, then sprinkle with salt and pepper.

NOTE: You can do this sort of ornamental serving with a wide range of vegetables, such as asparagus spears and young leeks. Tying up may also be effected with scallion greens or leek tops that have been cut into long thin strips and blanched. Blanched strips of apple peel or zest from oranges, lemons, and limes are also attractive and provide interesting color in vegetable side dishes.

JAPANESE PICKLED VEGETABLES

SERVES 4

1 head of cauliflower, separated into florets
1 small daikon radish, peeled and sliced (see page 144)
2 carrots, sliced
½ large cucumber, peeled and sliced
1 tsp sugar
pinch of salt
about 2 cups Japanese rice vinegar

Slice the cauliflower florets thinly lengthwise into thin slices. Arrange the cauliflower slices together with the slices of daikon, carrot, and cucumber on a flat serving dish or in a bowl.

Dissolve the sugar and salt in the rice vinegar and pour this over the vegetables. Cover with plastic wrap and marinate 12 hours in the refrigerator.

To serve, drain the pieces of vegetable, reserving the marinade for later use with more vegetables. Arrange in a serving dish.

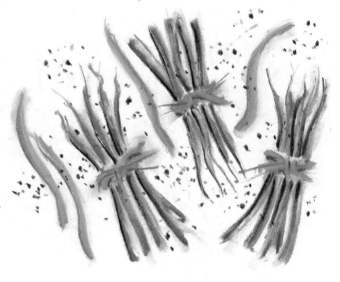

Top: String Bean Bouquets; bottom: Japanese Pickled Vegetables

Stir-frying is the ideal healthy way to cook most vegetables. Use whatever is fresh and in season and try to make the best combination of colors, textures, and flavors.

STIR-FRIED VEGETABLES

SERVES 4 AS AN ACCOMPANIMENT

2 tbsp vegetable oil
1 garlic clove, thinly sliced
1-inch cube of peeled fresh gingerroot, minced
1 hot chili pepper, seeded and chopped (optional)
1 small onion, chopped
1 small carrot, cut across at an angle into slices
½ red, green, or yellow sweet pepper, seeded and cut into uniform bite-sized pieces
¼ lb sugar snap peas or snow peas
½ cup canned straw mushrooms, drained
1 tsp cornstarch
1 tbsp soy sauce
chopped scallions, chives, or fresh cilantro, for garnish (optional)

Heat a wok or large frying pan over medium heat and add the oil. When it is really hot, add the garlic, ginger, and chili, if using, and stir-fry 1 minute.

Add the onion, carrot, and sweet pepper and stir-fry 2–3 minutes longer. Add the sugar snap peas or snow peas and the straw mushrooms and stir-fry 2 more minutes.

Mix the cornstarch with the soy sauce and stir this into ½ cup of water. Pour this liquid over the hot vegetables and let it bubble up and thicken while continuing to stir-fry for a few seconds.

Immediately transfer to a warmed serving dish and garnish with scallions or herbs, if using.

STIR-FRIED BEANS WITH GARLIC

SERVES 4 AS AN ACCOMPANIMENT

2 tbsp vegetable oil
½ tsp salt
4 garlic cloves, coarsely chopped
1-inch cube of peeled fresh gingerroot, minced
1 lb green beans, cut into 3-inch lengths
½ cup chicken stock

Heat a wok over medium heat until hot, add the oil with the salt, garlic, and ginger, and stir-fry 30 seconds. Add the green beans and stock and continue to cook until the beans are just tender and most of the liquid has evaporated, about 4 minutes longer.

Serve at once.

FRIED NOODLES WITH VEGETABLES

SERVES 4 AS AN ACCOMPANIMENT

8 dried Chinese mushrooms
¾ lb Asian noodles
3 tbsp vegetable oil
1 garlic clove, thinly sliced
1-inch cube of peeled fresh gingerroot, minced
1 onion, chopped
1 small carrot, cut across at an angle into slices
½ green sweet pepper, seeded and cut into
bite-sized pieces
¾ cup sliced green cabbage
1 tbsp soy sauce
1 tbsp sesame oil
2 tbsp chopped raw shelled peanuts

Cover the dried mushrooms with hot water and let them soak 30 minutes. Drain and remove the hard stem (this can either be discarded or used to add flavor to stock). Slice the mushroom caps and reserve.

Cook the noodles according to the directions on the package and then drain well.

Heat the oil in a wok or large frying pan over medium heat and stir-fry the garlic and ginger 1 minute. Add the onion and stir-fry 2-3 minutes more. Then add the carrot, sweet pepper, cabbage, and sliced mushroom caps and stir-fry 2-3 minutes.

Add the cooked and drained noodles and continue to cook, 2-3 minutes, tossing all the ingredients together, until the noodles are thoroughly heated.

Stir in the soy sauce and sesame oil and sprinkle with the chopped nuts before serving.

TEMPURA VEGETABLES

SERVES 4 AS AN ACCOMPANIMENT

1 egg + 1 egg yolk, beaten
¾ cup flour
about ½ lb mixed vegetables, such as zucchini, asparagus
tips, broccoli and cauliflower florets, baby spinach leaves,
carrots, and seeded sweet peppers, cut into
bite-sized pieces
vegetable oil, for deep-frying

In a bowl, make a smooth batter with the egg, egg yolk, flour, and about ¾ cup of water.

Dip the pieces of vegetable into the batter, then deep-fry in hot oil in a wok, a few at a time. Drain on paper towels and serve immediately as they are cooked, as they are or with a dipping sauce.

NOTE: Make a dipping sauce for this dish from equal quantities of soy sauce, fish sauce, and dry sherry, with a little grated fresh gingerroot.

The recipes on the following pages are salads with a sufficient protein content – be it from eggs, cheese, nuts, meat, or fish – to make them nourishing and substantial meals in their own right.

Fresh POMEGRANATE seeds are widely used in salads and vegetable purées in the Middle East. Dried seeds are often available when the fresh fruit is more difficult to obtain.

BELGIAN ENDIVE, BLUE CHEESE, AND POMEGRANATE SALAD

SERVES 4

4 large heads of Belgian endive
1 pomegranate
2 cups bean sprouts
3 oz blue cheese, such as Gorgonzola or Danish Blue
4 small garlic cloves, minced
⅔ cup Basic Vinaigrette (see page 14)

Pull the Belgian endive leaves apart and arrange them in a salad bowl. (Break them in pieces if they are very large, but do not cut with a knife as this causes bruising and the base of the leaf turns pink.)

Cut the pomegranate in half and pull out the fleshy seeds with a spoon. Mix the bean sprouts with the endive and then crumble the blue cheese over the top. Sprinkle with the pomegranate seeds.

Mix the garlic into the vinaigrette and dress salad just before serving.

Left: Leafy Green and Red Greek Salad (page 174);
right: Belgian Endive, Blue Cheese, and Pomegranate Salad

Any combination of leaves may be used in the Leafy Green and Red Greek Salad, *such as Romaine with Oakleaf or Red Leaf.*

LEAFY GREEN AND RED GREEK SALAD

SERVES 6

1 head of radicchio
1 head of Oakleaf lettuce
1 head of curly endive
¼ lb feta cheese, crumbled into large pieces
⅔ cup Greek olives, pitted and chopped
⅔ cup Low-calorie Yogurt Dressing (see page 14)
chopped fresh chives, for garnish

Break all the leaves into a salad bowl and mix them together. Add the cheese followed by the olives.
Toss with the dressing and garnish with chives.

MOZZARELLA AND TOMATO SALAD WITH AVOCADO

SERVES 4

2 buffalo or fresh mozzarella cheeses, thinly sliced
2 beefsteak tomatoes, thinly sliced
small basil leaves, for garnish
FOR THE AVOCADO DRESSING
1 large ripe avocado
1 tbsp balsamic vinegar
1 large red onion, minced
4 tbsp olive oil
salt and freshly ground black pepper

First make the dressing: halve and pit the avocado and scoop the flesh into a bowl. Add the vinegar and mash the onion into the avocado flesh.

Gradually add the oil, mixing all the time, until it has all been incorporated. Season to taste.

On a serving plate, arrange the mozzarella and tomato slices in alternating rows. Drizzle dressing over the centers of the rows and garnish with basil leaves.

SPINACH SALAD WITH EGGS AND CROUTONS

SERVES 4

1 lb young spinach leaves
3 eggs, hard-cooked
3 stalks of celery, cut into slices about ¼-inch thick
½ lb croutons
¾ cup freshly grated Parmesan cheese
⅔ cup Hollandaise Sauce (see page 13)
2 tbsp milk
salt and freshly ground black pepper

Remove any stems and coarse ribs from the spinach.

Separate the egg yolks from the whites. Slice the whites finely and push the yolks through a strainer.

Tear the spinach leaves into a bowl. Add the celery followed by the croutons and toss gently. Add the egg whites followed by the Parmesan.

Stir the milk into the Hollandaise sauce, adjust the seasoning, and pour it over the salad. Sprinkle with the egg yolks, toss, and serve.

BROWN RICE SALAD WITH ORANGE, SAGE, AND DATES

SERVES 4

1 washed orange
1 tbsp finely chopped fresh young sage leaves
⅔ cup coarsely chopped dates
3 cups cooked brown rice
FOR THE CASHEW-NUT DRESSING
½ cup low-fat cream cheese
1½ tbsp cashew nut oil
1½ tbsp lemon juice
½ tsp rock salt
freshly ground black pepper
2-3 tbsp Homemade Mayonnaise (see page 13)
½ cup chopped cashew nuts

Pare off the zest from the orange, avoiding any of the bitter white pith, and cut it into thin julienne strips. Stir together with the sage and dates into the rice.

Make the dressing: blend the cream cheese, with with the oil, lemon juice, salt, and pepper. Fold in the mayonnaise, followed by the nuts. If the dressing is too thick, thin it with 1-2 tablespoons of low-fat milk. Toss the salad with the dressing and serve.

SHRIMP AND SHIITAKE MUSHROOM SALAD

SERVES 4

¼ lb dried shiitake mushrooms
¼ lb Chinese egg noodles, cooked
bunch of large scallions, sliced
(including the green tops)
½ lb corn salad (mâche)
freshly ground black pepper
¼ lb peeled cooked small shrimp
1½ tbsp soy sauce
1½ tbsp Japanese rice vinegar
3½ tbsp black sesame seeds, toasted

Soak the mushrooms in water 30 minutes, then drain and squeeze out any excess liquid. Discarding any hard pieces of stem, snip the mushrooms into small pieces with kitchen scissors.

Place the noodles in a salad bowl, then add the mushrooms, scallions, and corn salad. Toss lightly, season with pepper, and add the shrimp.

Dress with a little of the soy sauce and rice vinegar, then sprinkle with the toasted sesame seeds.

Chill 15 minutes before serving, dressed with the remaining soy sauce and vinegar.

S HIITAKE MUSHROOMS *have been cultivated by the Japanese on oak bark for centuries. Dried shiitakes are widely available in gourmet food stores and some supermarkets. They must be soaked in water for 30 minutes before use and stems trimmed off and discarded.*

The sweet and delicate flavor of JAPANESE RICE VINEGAR *is an essential part of many traditional dishes, such as fish sushi. Light cider vinegar may be substituted.*

In QUAIL EGG
AND SMOKED
SALMON SALAD,
*smoked trout or
thinly sliced raw
tuna will work well
as substitutes for
smoked salmon.*

QUAIL EGG AND SMOKED SALMON SALAD

SERVES 6

bunch of watercress, stems removed
2 cooked beets, thinly sliced
1 head of romaine or Oakleaf lettuce
¼ lb smoked salmon, cut into thin strips
3 tbsp butter
6 quail eggs
freshly ground black pepper
⅔ cup Basic Vinaigrette (see page 14)
sprigs of fresh dill, for garnish (optional)
1 large lemon, cut into 6 wedges, for serving

Place the watercress in little piles in the middle of 6 salad plates. Arrange the beet slices around the watercress.

Tear the lettuce leaves into small pieces and arrange them in a ring around the outside of the beet slices.

Arrange 2 strips of smoked salmon in a criss-cross on top of each pile of watercress and arrange the rest around the outside of the rings of lettuce.

Melt the butter in a frying pan over medium heat and fry the quail eggs briefly until the white is just set. Sprinkle them with black pepper and then arrange one egg on top of each pile of watercress.

Dress the leaves and beets with the vinaigrette and serve immediately, garnished with dill sprigs, if using. Serve the lemon wedges separately for the salmon.

SUMMERHOUSE SALAD WITH ORANGE VINAIGRETTE

SERVES 6

1 large head of romaine or Oakleaf lettuce
bunch of watercress, stems removed
2 large avocados
2 large pears, peeled and sliced
1 cup coarsely chopped cooked chicken breast
FOR THE ORANGE VINAIGRETTE
1 tbsp freshly squeezed orange juice, including some flesh
⅔ cup Basic Vinaigrette (see page 14)
salt and freshly ground black pepper

Separate the lettuce leaves into a salad bowl, add the watercress, and toss gently.

Halve and pit the avocados. Using a small spoon, scoop out the avocado flesh and add this to the salad.

Chop the pear slices into the salad and arrange the pieces of chicken on top.

Stir the orange juice and flesh into the basic vinaigrette and adjust the seasoning, if necessary. Pour this over the salad and serve.

Left: Summerhouse Salad with Orange Vinaigrette; right: Corn Salad with Mango and Hazelnuts (page 184)

THAI CHICKEN, SHRIMP, AND FRUIT SALAD

SERVES 4 AS A FIRST COURSE

½ mango or papaya, peeled, pitted or seeded, and cut into bite-sized pieces
1 orange, peeled and sectioned
1 small grapefruit, preferably pink, peeled and sectioned
1 pear, peeled, cored, and cut into bite-sized pieces
16 seedless grapes, halved
8 fresh litchis, peeled and seeded
2 tomatoes, cut into small pieces
⅔ cup halved canned Chinese water chestnuts
¼ cup cooked chicken, cut into bite-sized pieces
¼ lb peeled cooked small shrimp
4-6 shallots, thinly sliced
2 garlic cloves, thinly sliced
vegetable oil, for deep frying
2 handfuls mixed salad leaves
¾ cup roughly chopped salted peanuts, for garnish
fresh cilantro sprigs, for garnish (optional)
FOR THE DRESSING
3 tbsp sugar
juice of ½ lime
1 tbsp fish sauce
1 hot red chili pepper, seeded and chopped
1 garlic clove, minced

The classic THAI CHICKEN, SHRIMP AND FRUIT SALAD *makes a spectacular first course or light meal. Any fruit in season can be used; those given here are merely suggestions.*

In a bowl, lightly mix the fruit, tomatoes, water chestnuts, chicken, and shrimp.

Make the dressing: dissolve the sugar in ⅓ cup of hot water and let it cool. Then mix in the lime juice, fish sauce, chili, and garlic.

Deep-fry the shallot and garlic slices in hot oil in a wok until crisp. Drain on paper towels.

Just before serving, pour the dressing over the salad and mix gently. Cover a serving plate with the leaves and arrange the salad over this. Scatter over the shallots and garlic, the peanuts, and cilantro, if using, to garnish. Serve immediately.

JAPANESE-STYLE CHICKEN AND ASPARAGUS SALAD

SERVES 4 AS A FIRST COURSE

1 tbsp sake, dry sherry, or white wine
½ tsp salt
about ½ lb skinless boneless chicken breast, cut across into thin slices
1 lb asparagus, cut across at an angle into 1½-inch lengths
salad leaves, for serving (optional)
1 tsp very thin matchstick strips of thinly pared zest from a washed lemon, for garnish
FOR THE DRESSING
1 tsp dried English mustard
2 tbsp sake, dry sherry, or white wine
2 tbsp soy sauce

In a small bowl, mix the sake, sherry, or wine with the salt. Toss the chicken slices in this and let marinate 30 minutes.

Bring ⅓ cup of water to a boil in a wok or very small heavy pan. Cook the chicken pieces, stirring constantly, for 1-2 minutes or until just cooked. Using a slotted spoon, transfer the chicken to a bowl and let cool. Reserve the stock left in the wok for making the dressing.

Cook the asparagus in boiling salted water until just tender but still firm, 3-4 minutes. Immediately drain and refresh under cold running water, then drain again. Add to the chicken.

Make the dressing: mix together the ingredients with 1 tablespoon of the reserved stock.

Just before serving, pour the dressing over the salad and toss well to combine thoroughly. Transfer to a serving plate or dish and serve as part of an Asian-style meal. Alternatively, make 4 individual servings piled on beds of salad leaves, if using, and serve as a Western-style first course. Either way, garnish with the lemon zest.

SALAD NIÇOISE

SERVES 4

½ lb tiny fine green beans
½ lb tiny ripe tomatoes, cut in wedges
1 green sweet pepper, seeded and cut into strips
1 English cucumber, cut into thick strips
2 oz canned anchovies, drained
⅓ cup pitted black olives
7 oz canned tuna fish in oil, drained and flaked
4 hard-cooked eggs, shelled and quartered
5 tbsp olive oil
1 tbsp white wine vinegar
1 garlic clove, minced
salt and freshly ground black pepper
2 tbsp chopped fresh flat-leaf parsley

Blanch the beans briefly until just tender and refresh in cold running water. Pat dry.

Mix the vegetables in a large salad bowl (or arrange in separate piles around the bowl). Arrange the anchovies, olives, flaked tuna, and eggs over the top.

Make a dressing by vigorously mixing the oil, vinegar, and garlic with seasoning. Pour this over the salad and sprinkle with parsley.

PROVENÇAL VEGETABLES WITH GOAT CHEESE

SERVES 4

1 small, round goat cheese, weighing about
2½ oz (see below)
¼ lb tiny broccoli florets
¼ lb fine green beans
¼ lb snow peas
2 small zucchini, cut into thick slices
2 large garlic cloves
4 tbsp olive oil
1 tbsp lemon juice

pinch of dried thyme
4 or 5 ripe juicy tomatoes, coarsely chopped
salt and freshly ground black pepper
2 scallions, minced
pine nuts, for garnish (optional)

Select a cheese that is firm but not too dry.

In a large pan of boiling salted water, blanch the vegetables in batches until just tender but still very firm to the bite: 6-7 minutes for the broccoli, 5 minutes for the beans, and 2-3 minutes for the snow peas and zucchini.

Drain each batch of vegetables promptly as they are ready and refresh them under cold running water. Drain well, pat dry, and let cool.

Make the dressing: put the cheese, garlic, oil, lemon juice, and thyme in a blender or food processor. Mix until smooth.

Add the tomatoes in small batches, processing each until smooth. Add just enough to give the dressing a rich consistency that is thick but liquid enough to coat the vegetables. Season well.

Put the cooled vegetables in a large bowl and pour over the dressing. Toss well to coat all the ingredients thoroughly. Scatter over the scallions and garnish with pine nuts, if using.

In its native South of France, SALADE NIÇOISE commonly also contains fava beans and artichokes. Elsewhere, lettuce and cooked potatoes are popular additions.

PROSCIUTTO AND FRESH FIG SALAD WITH MINT AND LIME CREAM DRESSING

SERVES 6

6 slices of prosciutto
10 fresh mint leaves
juice of 2 limes
18 fresh figs
⅔ cup crème fraîche or sour cream
2 heads of radicchio
salt and freshly ground black pepper
sprigs of mint, for garnish

Cut the prosciutto into strips and cover with plastic wrap to keep it from drying out.

Using a pestle and mortar, bruise and crush the mint leaves in the lime juice. Let the mixture infuse at room temperature about 45 minutes.

Make 2 cuts halfway down each fig from the stem end to make cross-shaped incisions in the top. Press the figs gently in their middles to open up the tops. Place on a plate, cover with plastic wrap, and chill 45 minutes.

Remove the mint from the lime juice and discard. Add a pinch of salt to the juice. Gradually whisk in the crème fraîche, stirring constantly. Adjust the seasoning, if necessary.

Flood 6 plates with the crème fraîche dressing. Arrange 3 figs decoratively on each plate. Arrange the prosciutto strips and the salad leaves around them, garnish with the mint sprigs, and serve immediately.

ASPARAGUS SALAD WITH SPICED HONEY DRESSING

SERVES 4

1 lb large asparagus spears
1 large carrot, peeled
1 small ripe papaya or cantaloupe, peeled, halved, seeded,
and cut into bite-sized pieces
4 small hard-cooked eggs, shelled and quartered, for serving
chopped fresh chives or other herbs, for garnish
FOR THE DRESSING
2 tbsp vegetable oil
2 tbsp lemon or lime juice
1 tbsp filtered honey
¼ tsp salt
¼ tsp hot chili powder or more to taste

Trim off the hard part of the asparagus, cutting away about one-third of each stalk from the cut end. Cut each trimmed spear in half lengthwise, then cut each of these pieces across in two.

Cook the asparagus pieces in boiling salted water until just tender, about 5 minutes. Immediately drain, refresh in cold water, drain well again, and let cool.

Using a swivel-bladed vegetable peeler, cut the carrots into long slivers. Put these in a serving bowl together with the asparagus and the fruit.

Make the dressing by combining the ingredients. Pour this over the salad, toss gently but thoroughly, and divide it among 4 plates.

Arrange 4 egg quarters on each salad and sprinkle with chopped herbs before serving.

CHICKEN SALAD WITH SESAME-CUCUMBER SAUCE

SERVES 4-6

3 skinless boneless chicken breast halves
1 tbsp freshly grated peeled gingerroot
4 scallions, including the green tops
2 small English cucumbers
1 head of Iceberg lettuce, for serving
FOR THE SESAME-CUCUMBER SAUCE
1 tsp peanut oil
1 tsp chili oil
¼ tsp dried English mustard
1 tbsp light soy sauce
2 tbsp tahini paste
1 tbsp rice vinegar
2 tbsp water
salt and freshly ground black pepper
1 tbsp minced green scallion tops
1 tbsp toasted sesame seeds

Place the chicken in a pan with the ginger, scallions, and 3 cups of water and bring to a boil. Cover and simmer gently 12 minutes. Remove from the heat, but let the chicken cool in the stock.

Peel the cucumbers, reserving some of the skin. Halve them, scoop out the seeds, and place the halves on beds of the lettuce arranged on 4 plates.

Using scissors, cut the drained chicken into thin slivers and arrange these in the cucumber. If preparing in advance, cover with plastic wrap, and chill.

Make the sauce: combine all the ingredients except the scallions and sesame seeds in a blender or food processor. Season, then add the scallions and sesame seeds, and toss together. Spoon this over the chicken.

Serve garnished with the reserved cucumber peel cut into thin slivers.

CHICKEN AND WATERCRESS SALAD

SERVES 4

½ ripe cantaloupe, peeled, halved, seeded, and cut into
bite-sized chunks
½ lb cooked chicken, cut into bite-sized pieces
½ bunch (about 2 oz) of watercress
FOR THE DRESSING
1 tbsp lemon juice
3 tbsp corn or sunflower oil
¼ tsp ground ginger or more to taste
salt and pepper

Mix the cantaloupe and chicken in a bowl.

Make the dressing by combining all the ingredients. Season and add a little more ground ginger, to taste. Pour it over the chicken and cantaloupe

Arrange the watercress on top of the salad. (Don't put the dressing on the watercress too early or it will wilt.) Just before serving, mix the watercress into the rest of the salad.

CRISP BACON, BEAN, AND PARSLEY SALAD

SERVES 4

3 cups canned lima beans, drained
6 slices of bacon
10 dried apricots, sliced into thin slivers
3 tbsp coarsely chopped hazelnuts
1½ tbsp coarsely chopped fresh parsley
6 tbsp olive oil
2 tbsp wine vinegar
¾ tbsp coarse-grain mustard
salt and freshly ground black pepper

Rinse the beans under cold running water, drain, and dry on paper towels.

Fry the bacon over medium-high heat until crisp. Drain on paper towels to remove excess fat. Crumble the cooked bacon coarsely into pieces.

Place the beans in a salad bowl. Add the bacon, apricots, hazelnuts, and parsley and toss well.

Pour the oil and vinegar into a screw-top jar. Add the mustard and shake vigorously. Season with salt and pepper and shake again. Pour over the salad and toss well to serve.

ZUCCHINI AND PURPLE BASIL SALAD

SERVES 4-6

1½ lb zucchini, coarsely grated
3 tomatoes, coarsely chopped
2 onions, thinly sliced
1 tbsp poppy seeds
2 tbsp extra virgin olive oil
1 tbsp finely snipped fresh purple basil leaves
1 tbsp tamari sauce
1 tbsp Japanese rice vinegar
freshly ground black pepper

Put the zucchini, tomatoes, onions, and poppy seeds in a salad bowl and gently mix.

Put the oil, basil, tamari, rice vinegar, and pepper in a screw-top jar and shake vigorously. Dress the salad with the mixture, toss well, and serve.

BABY VEGETABLE SALAD IN SOY-SESAME DRESSING

SERVES 4

¼ lb baby carrots
¼ lb baby zucchini
3 oz baby corn
3 oz sugar snap peas
FOR THE DRESSING
2 tsp sesame seeds
1 tbsp lime juice (about ½ lime)
1 tbsp soy sauce
2 tbsp vegetable oil
1 tsp Asian sesame oil

In separate pans, steam or boil the vegetables in lightly salted water until just tender but still firm. Immediately refresh in cold water, drain, and let cool completely in a serving bowl or dish.

Toast the sesame seeds by shaking them in a dry frying pan over medium heat until they begin to turn brown and "jump," about 1 minute.

Combine these with the remaining dressing ingredients and pour this over the vegetables. Toss until they are all well coated, and serve.

WILTED ONION AND CUCUMBER SALAD

SERVES 4

¼ English cucumber, thinly sliced or cut into "ribbons"
with a swivel-bladed vegetable peeler
1 small mild onion, preferably pink, very thinly sliced and
separated into rings
juice of ½ large grapefruit, preferably pink

Put the cucumber and onion slices into a salad bowl. Pour over the fruit juice and mix well. Cover the bowl with plastic wrap and leave at least 12 hours to let the onions "wilt."

The remaining recipes in this chapter are salads to serve beside cheese, egg, meat, or fish dishes, or to which you can add some protein to make them main course salads.

TAMARI SAUCE is a fine Japanese soy sauce made by fermentation. If unobtainable, use a good light soy sauce. If JAPANESE RICE VINEGAR is difficult to obtain, use light cider vinegar.

CORN SALAD
WITH MANGO
AND HAZELNUTS
*can be made using
other exotic fruits,
such as papaya or
pineapple, instead of
mango.*

The recipe for
CHANTERELLE
SALAD *can be
adapted and made
with common
mushrooms, but it
will not have the
same flavor.*

CORN SALAD WITH MANGO AND HAZELNUTS

SERVES 4

1 large ripe mango
¾ lb corn salad (mâche)
1 cup toasted hazelnuts
3 tbsp crème fraîche or sour cream
1 tbsp pickled green peppercorns
1 tsp lime juice
salt and freshly ground black pepper

Peel and pit the mango and coarsely chop the flesh.

Place the corn salad in a salad bowl. Sprinkle the hazelnuts over this and arrange the mango on top.

Mix the crème fraîche with the peppercorns and lime juice. Season and pour over the salad. Toss at the table and serve immediately.

BABY CORN AND SNOW PEA SALAD

SERVES 4

½ lb snow peas
½ lb baby corn
½ cup sliced almonds
½ cup chopped hazelnuts
2 tbsp hazelnut oil, warmed
salt and freshly ground black pepper

Plunge the snow peas and baby corn into a pan of boiling salted water and blanch 2 minutes. Drain and refresh in cold water. Pat dry and let cool.

Place the vegetables in a salad bowl and mix in the nuts. Season the warmed hazelnut oil and pour it over the salad.

CHANTERELLE SALAD WITH BASIL VINAIGRETTE

SERVES 4

2 sprigs of fresh thyme
salt
1 lb fresh chanterelle mushrooms
½ lb croutons
2 large purple garlic cloves, minced
6 large fresh basil leaves, chopped
¼ cup Basic Vinaigrette (see page 14)
¼ cup minced fresh parsley, for garnish

Place the thyme in a pan and add 2 cups of water with some salt. Bring to a boil and boil 5 minutes.

Add the mushrooms, cover, and reduce the heat. Simmer gently 5 minutes. Discard the thyme, drain the mushrooms, and let them cool.

Place the cooled mushrooms and the croutons in a salad bowl and toss lightly. Combine the garlic and

basil with the vinaigrette, then drizzle over the salad.
Garnish with parsley and serve immediately.

SWEET PEPPER SALAD

SERVES 4

1 large red sweet pepper
1 large green sweet pepper
1 large yellow sweet pepper
18 pitted black olives
3 tbsp olive oil
juice of 1 large lemon
3 garlic cloves, minced
3 tbsp minced fresh flat-leaf parsley
salt and freshly ground black pepper

Preheat the broiler. Halve the peppers and remove
their seeds and Broil the pepper halves, skin-side up,
until the skins are black and blistering.

Let cool a little and then peel them. Cut the flesh
into strips and mix in a salad bowl or on a serving
plate.

Finely chop half the olives and halve the others.

Make the dressing by mixing the oil, lemon juice,
chopped olives, garlic, and half the parsley. Season
generously with salt and pepper.

Drizzle the dressing over the peppers and toss
well. Sprinkle the salad with the remaining parsley
and dot with the olive halves. Serve warm or cold.

An optional extra is to add 5 oz of bacon that has
been fried until crisp, well drained, and crumbled.

PUDDINGS AND DESSERTS

The last course of a meal is the one in which even the most conservative of cooks will occasionally indulge themselves in a flight of fancy. Whether it be a simple Rhubarb and Gooseberry Cobbler for the family or an elegant gâteau like the Double Truffle Torte for special guests, there are recipes in this chapter for all occasions.

In the spirit of *The Creative Cook*, old stand-bys are given new life with refreshing and unusual new flavorings, like Apple Brown Betty with Scented Geranium or Orange and Almond Rice Pudding. There are also lots of new ways with fruit, like Spiced Fruit Compote with Mascarpone, and frozen desserts like Zabaglione Ice-cream. The chapter also includes an amazing array of gâteaux, pies, and tarts, such as Key Lime Pie, Chocolate Mousse Tart and Clementine-Strega Cake which are both impressive and tasty, as well as being very approachable for the less-than-experienced cook.

Clockwise from the left: Pear Frangipane Tart (page 189), Crème Brûlée (page 188) and Creamed Rice Pudding (page 188)

Spiced Fruit Compote with Mascarpone makes a simple but elegant dessert. Replace the wine with apple, orange, or pear juice, however, and it becomes a refreshing breakfast treat. Italian mascarpone cheese is available in specialty stores.

Crème Brûlée or "burnt cream," is traditionally caramelized with a salamander heated in an open fire.

CREAMED RICE PUDDING

SERVES 4

2 tbsp butter
5 tbsp pudding rice
2½ tbsp sugar
strip of zest from a washed lemon
1¼ cups milk
1¼ cups light cream
⅛ tsp freshly grated nutmeg
fresh fruit, fruit compote, or cream, for serving

Preheat the oven to 325°F. Use a little of the butter to grease a 3½-cup baking dish.

In a strainer or colander, rinse the rice under running water, then put it into the prepared dish with the sugar, lemon zest, milk, and cream. Stir until the sugar is dissolved.

Bake 1 hour, stirring twice. Dot the remaining butter over the surface and sprinkle with nutmeg. Return to the oven and continue baking until the rice is soft and the top is browned, about 45 minutes. Serve hot or cold, with fruit or cream.

SPICED FRUIT COMPOTE WITH MASCARPONE

SERVES 4

1 lb mixed dried fruit, such as apricots, prunes, apple rings, pears, and figs
3 tbsp light brown sugar
1¼ cups sweet dessert wine
3 whole cloves
1 cinnamon stick
6 oz (¾ cup) mascarpone cheese
grated zest of 2 washed lemons

Put all the ingredients except the cheese and half the lemon zest in a pan with 1¼ cups of water.

Bring to a boil, then lower the heat, cover, and simmer until the fruit is plump and the liquid is syrupy, 45-50 minutes. Discard the cinnamon.

Serve the compote either warm or chilled, with the mascarpone spooned over it and a little of the reserved lemon zest sprinkled over the top.

CRÈME BRÛLÉE

SERVES 6

2¼ cups whipping cream
1 vanilla bean
4 egg yolks
2 tbsp granulated sugar
¼ cup raw or light brown sugar
fresh fruits in season, such as summer berries or exotic fruits, for serving

Put the cream and vanilla bean in a small saucepan. Heat gently until almost boiling. Remove from the heat, cover, and let infuse 30 minutes.

Preheat the oven to 275°F.

Place the egg yolks in a mixing bowl, add the granulated sugar, and beat well to mix. Reheat the cream until almost boiling. Pour this over the egg yolks, beating with a wire whisk at the same time.

Place the bowl over a pan of simmering water and whisk lightly until the mixture thickens enough to coat the back of a spoon. Divide the mixture between six ½-cup ramekins.

Arrange the ramekins in a deep roasting pan and pour in warm water to a depth of 1 inch. Bake 30-35 minutes. Remove the ramekins from the water bath and let cool. Chill at least 1 hour, or up to 24.

Preheat the broiler. Sprinkle the raw or brown sugar over the tops of the ramekins. Broil 3-4 minutes, to melt and caramelize the sugar.

Let cool and then chill at least 2 hours before serving, accompanied by fresh fruits.

PEAR FRANGIPANE TART

SERVES 6

6 tbsp butter, plus more for greasing
7 tbsp vanilla sugar
1 egg + 1 extra yolk, beaten
3 tbsp flour
few drops of almond extract
1 cup ground almonds
3 small, ripe pears
2 tsp lemon juice
crème frâiche or cream, for serving

FOR THE RICH SUGAR PASTRY
(makes about 1 lb)
1⅔ cups flour
pinch of salt
1 stick (8 tbsp) butter, cubed
5 tbsp sugar
2 egg yolks
2 tbsp ice water
1 tsp lemon juice

Preheat the oven to 400°F and grease a deep 9-inch flan ring on a baking sheet or a loose-bottomed tart pan with butter.

Make the pastry: sift the flour and salt into a bowl. Lightly rub in the butter until the mixture resembles crumbs, then stir in the sugar.

Mix together the egg yolks, ice water, and lemon juice. Using a metal spatula, mix this into the flour to form a firm dough.

Turn the dough onto a floured surface and knead lightly. Wrap and chill 20 minutes.

Use the dough to line the prepared flan ring or pan. Prick the bottom and fill with baking beans. Bake 10 minutes. Remove the baking beans and return to the oven 5 minutes longer to cook the base. Reduce the oven temperature to 350°F.

Make the frangipane cream filling: beat together the butter and vanilla sugar until light and fluffy.

Beat in the egg and egg yolk and then stir in the flour, almond extract, and ground almonds. Spread two-thirds of this filling over the bottom of the pastry shell.

Peel, core, and halve the pears, then slice them thinly crosswise. Arrange the slices in the pastry shell and brush with lemon juice.

Spoon the remaining frangipane cream around the pears. Bake the tart until the filling is firm and golden brown, 30-35 minutes.

Serve warm, with crème fraîche or cream.

BAKED SULTANA AND LEMON CHEESECAKE

SERVES 8

4 tbsp butter, plus more for greasing
3 cups crushed graham crackers
confectioners' sugar, for dusting
FOR THE FILLING
1¼ lb cream cheese
7 tbsp sugar
⅔ cup ground almonds
grated zest and juice of 2 washed lemons
½ cup golden raisins (sultanas)
3 eggs, beaten

Preheat the oven to 350°F. Grease the bottom of a deep 8-inch springform cake pan with some butter and line it with wax paper.

Melt the butter in a pan and stir in the graham-cracker crumbs. Mix well and use to line the bottom of the prepared pan, pressing down well with the back of a spoon.

Make the filling: mix all the ingredients and pour into the pan. Bake until just set, 40-45 minutes.

Let cool in the pan, then chill at least 1 hour. Transfer to a serving plate and dredge with confectioners' sugar before serving.

The term FRANGIPANE *was first used of almond-flavored pastry cream in eighteenth-century Paris.*

Beautifully perfumed VANILLA SUGAR *is easily made at home. Just bury a split vanilla bean in granulated sugar, cover, and let stand at least 24 hours (or up to a year, replenishing the sugar as you use it).*

KEY LIME PIE

SERVES 6-8

4 tbsp butter, plus more for greasing
1 lb Rich Sugar Pastry (see page 189)
¼ cup cornstarch
grated zest and juice of 4 washed limes
½ cup granulated sugar
3 egg yolks
FOR THE MERINGUE TOPPING
3 egg whites
pinch of salt
¾ cup superfine sugar

If you can't get the very tart Key limes from Florida, you can use ordinary limes for KEY LIME PIE.

Preheat the oven to 400°F and grease a deep 9-inch loose-bottomed pie pan with butter.

Roll out the pastry dough and use to line the prepared pan. Prick the bottom with a fork and fill with baking beans. Bake 10 minutes, then remove the baking beans and return to the oven. Bake 5 minutes longer to cook the base. Reduce the oven temperature to 350°F.

In a small bowl, mix the cornstarch to a paste with a little of a measured 1¼ cups of water. Put the rest of the water in a saucepan with the lime juice and sugar. Bring to a boil. Pour in the cornstarch mixture, stirring constantly, and cook until smooth and thickened, 2-3 minutes.

Off the heat, stir in the butter and lime zest. Let cool slightly, then add the egg yolks and beat well. Pour into the pastry shell and bake 15 minutes.

Meanwhile, make the topping: put the egg whites in a large bowl with the salt. Beat until stiff, then add half the sugar. Continue beating until standing in stiff peaks. Add the remaining sugar and beat again.

Pile the meringue on to the lime filling to cover it, swirling it into peaks. Return to the oven and bake until the peaks of the meringue are golden, about 15 minutes longer. Serve warm or cold.

PECAN PIE

SERVES 6

FOR THE PASTRY
1 stick (8 tbsp) butter, diced, plus more for greasing
1⅔ cups flour
pinch of salt
3-4 tbsp ice water
lightly whipped cream or vanilla ice-cream, for serving
FOR THE FILLING
1½ cups pecan halves
1 stick (8 tbsp) unsalted butter
¾ cup light brown sugar
3½ tbsp whipping cream
3 tbsp flour, sifted

Preheat the oven to 375°F and grease an 8-inch flan ring on a baking sheet or loose-bottomed tart pan with butter.

Make the pastry: sift the flour and salt into a mixing bowl. Lightly rub in the butter. Using a metal spatula, mix in just enough ice water, a tablespoon at a time, to form a firm dough.

Knead lightly on a floured surface and use to line the prepared ring or pan. Prick the bottom and chill at least 15 minutes.

Fill the pastry shell with baking beans and bake 10 minutes. Remove the beans, return to the oven, and bake 5 minutes longer to cook the bottom.

Meanwhile, make the filling: reserve one-third of the pecans and roughly chop the rest. Melt the butter with the sugar in a pan over medium heat, stirring, and bring to a boil. Beat in the cream and flour. Stir in the chopped nuts and bring back to a boil.

Spoon into the pastry shell and arrange the reserved pecan halves on top. Bake until firm, about 20 minutes. Serve warm or cold, accompanied by lightly whipped cream or vanilla ice-cream.

Top: Pecan Pie; bottom: Key Lime Pie

AUTUMN PUDDING

SERVES 6

2 apples
1 firm pear
2 tbsp lemon juice
¼ lb purple plums, pitted and quartered
¾ lb greengage plums, halved and pitted
½ cup sugar
1 cup sweet wine
1 cinnamon stick, halved
*3 pieces of preserved ginger in syrup, drained
and diced (optional)*
10 large slices of white bread, crusts removed
cream, for serving

Peel, core, and chop the apples and the pear. Put the chopped fruit in a bowl and add the lemon juice. Mix well to prevent the fruit from discoloring.

Put all the fruit in a saucepan with the sugar, wine, cinnamon stick, and ginger, if using. Bring to a boil, stirring frequently, then lower the heat and simmer 15 minutes.

Use 8 slices of bread to line the bottom and sides of a 7-cup pudding basin. Spoon a few tablespoons of the fruit juices over the bread to moisten it and hold it in place, then spoon in the fruit and the rest of the juices.

Use the remaining bread to cover the fruit. Cover the basin with wax paper and a weighted plate. Chill at least 4 hours or overnight.

Unmold the pudding onto a serving plate. Serve with cream, plain or softly whipped.

Autumn Pudding

APPLE AND BERRY CRISP

SERVES 4

1 lb tart apples
1 pint blackberries or loganberries
7 tbsp sugar
½ tsp ground cinnamon
butter, for greasing
cream or custard sauce, for serving
FOR THE TOPPING
1¼ cups flour
6 tbsp butter, diced
6 tbsp raw or light brown sugar
1 tsp grated zest from a washed lemon

Preheat the oven to 350°F and grease a baking dish with butter.

First prepare the topping: sift the flour into a mixing bowl and rub in the butter until the mixture resembles fine crumbs. Stir in the sugar and lemon zest and set aside.

Peel, halve, core, and thinly slice the apples. Place the slices in a bowl with the berries, sugar, and cinnamon and toss lightly to mix.

Transfer the mixture to the dish and sprinkle over the topping mixture to cover completely.

Bake until the top is golden brown, about 35 minutes. Serve hot with cream or custard sauce.

APPLE AND BERRY CRISP *lends itself to a wide range of variations. Try replacing the berries with sliced nectarines, peaches, plums, rhubarb, or even raisins.*

The COBBLER originated among the early American settlers and consists of a fruit filling topped with simple pastry dough and baked.

RHUBARB AND GOOSEBERRY COBBLER

SERVES 4

1 lb rhubarb, cut into 1-inch chunks
1½ cups gooseberries
6 tbsp light brown sugar
1 bay leaf
butter, for greasing
whipping cream, for serving
FOR THE COBBLER TOPPING
1¼ cups self-rising flour
pinch of salt
3 tbsp butter
2½ tbsp sugar
about ½ cup milk, plus extra for glazing
1 tbsp light brown sugar, for sprinkling

Preheat the oven to 425°F, and lightly grease a shallow 1¼-quart baking dish with butter.

Put the fruits in a pan with the sugar and bay leaf. Cook over medium heat, stirring frequently, until the fruit is almost tender, 12-15 minutes. Remove the bay leaf and spoon the fruit in an even layer into the prepared baking dish.

Prepare the topping: sift the flour and salt into a mixing bowl. Rub in the butter and stir in the sugar. Add enough milk to form a firm dough.

Turn the dough onto a floured surface, knead lightly, and roll out to a thickness of ½ inch. Using a 2½-inch cookie cutter, stamp out rounds or other shapes.

Arrange these on top of the fruit and brush with milk to glaze. Sprinkle with the brown sugar and bake until the cobbler topping is well risen and golden brown, about 15 minutes.

Serve hot, with cream.

CHOCOLATE SPONGE PUDDINGS★

SERVES 6

6 tbsp butter, plus more for greasing
3 oz semisweet chocolate, cut into pieces
½ cup granulated sugar
2 eggs★
(★see page 2 for advice on eggs)
⅓ cup sour cream
¾ cup self-rising flour, sifted
confectioners' sugar, for dusting
FOR THE CHOCOLATE SAUCE
4 oz semisweet chocolate
2 tbsp butter
3 tbsp rum or brandy

Preheat the oven to 350°F. Grease 6 timbale molds or custard cups with butter and then line their bottoms with wax paper.

Put the chocolate in a small saucepan with ½ cup of water. Stir over low heat until melted and smooth. Remove from the heat.

In a mixing bowl, beat the butter and granulated sugar until light and fluffy. Beat in the eggs, one at a time. Stir in the chocolate mixture, then fold in alternating spoonfuls of the sour cream and flour.

Spoon the mixture into the prepared molds. Place them on a baking sheet and bake until just firm to the touch, about 15 minutes.

Meanwhile, prepare the sauce: put the chocolate and butter in a small saucepan with 3 tablespoons of water. Stir constantly over low heat until smooth and melted. Stir in the rum or brandy.

Unmold the puddings onto individual serving plates. Dredge with a little confectioners' sugar and serve with the chocolate sauce.

LEMON PUDDING

SERVES 4

1 stick (8 tbsp) butter, plus extra for greasing
½ cup sugar
finely grated zest of 2 washed lemons
2 eggs, beaten
1¼ cups self-rising flour
¼ cup golden syrup, light molasses, or maple syrup
cream or custard sauce, for serving

Grease a 5-cup pudding basin with butter and line the bottom with a disk of wax paper.

Beat together the butter, sugar, and lemon zest until light and fluffy. Beat in the eggs, a little at a time, and then fold in the flour.

Spoon the syrup into the bottom of the prepared basin. Spoon in the lemon sponge batter.

Cover the basin with a layer of pleated wax paper and with foil. Secure tightly with string. Place in a large pan and add enough water to come three-quarters up the basin. Cover tightly, bring to a simmer, and steam the pudding until firm, 1½–2 hours, replenishing the water as necessary.

Unmold onto a serving plate and serve accompanied by cream or custard sauce.

French lemon tart,
TARTE AU
CITRON, *is one of
the glories of
Provençal cooking.
The riper and more
fragrant the lemons,
the better the filling
will taste. Make an
orange or tangerine
tart in the same
way, using 3 large
juicy oranges or 8
tangerines in place of
the lemons and
adding 1 tablespoon
of grated zest to the
pastry.*

TARTE AU CITRON

SERVES 6-8

1⅔ cups flour, plus more for dusting
¾ cup confectioners' sugar, plus more for dusting
1 stick (8 tbsp) butter, softened, plus more for greasing
4 eggs
pinch of salt
few drops of vanilla extract
5 washed lemons
½ cup granulated sugar
⅔ cup finely ground almonds
⅔ cup whipping cream

Sift the flour and confectioners' sugar into a bowl and work the butter in lightly with your fingertips. Make a well in the center and add 1 of the eggs, the salt, vanilla, and the grated zest of 1 lemon. Gradually bring the flour in from the edges and mix to a smooth dough. Chill the dough about 30 minutes.

Preheat the oven to 350°F and grease a 10-inch loose-bottomed tart pan with butter.

Roll out the dough on a lightly floured surface, and use it to line the pan. Do not remove any overhang. Chill briefly until firm.

Line with foil or wax paper, weight with dried beans, and place on a baking sheet. Bake about 10 minutes. Remove from the oven, take off weights and paper and trim the edges. Return to the oven and bake 10 minutes longer.

Meanwhile, finely grate the zest of 2 of the remaining lemons and extract the juice from all the lemons. In a large bowl, beat the remaining eggs with the granulated sugar until thick enough to form a ribbon trail. Stir in the lemon zest and juice, together with the almonds and cream.

Pour this filling into the baked pastry shell as soon as it comes from the oven. Return to the hot baking sheet in the oven and bake 30 minutes.

Preheat the broiler. Sprinkle the top of the tart liberally with sifted confectioners' sugar and flash under the broiler to caramelize it. Serve hot or warm.

ORANGE AND ALMOND RICE PUDDING

SERVES 6

1 tbsp butter
¾ cup short-grain rice
nearly 1 cup sliced almonds
7 tbsp sugar
1 quart milk
finely grated zest and juice of 2 large washed oranges
juice of 1 small lemon
⅔ cup crème fraîche or heavy whipping cream
⅛ tsp ground cinnamon
1 tbsp orange flower water, rum, or orange liqueur
(optional)

Preheat the oven to 350°F and grease a large baking dish with the butter. Rinse the rice thoroughly and finely crush half the almonds.

Put the rice, sugar, milk, and orange zest in a large pan and bring to a boil, stirring constantly.

Immediately transfer to the prepared baking dish and stir in the crushed almonds, orange juice, lemon juice, cream, cinnamon, and orange flower water, rum or liqueur, if using.

Bake about 1 hour, until the rice is tender, stirring from time to time during the first 30 minutes.

About three-quarters of the way through, spread the remaining almonds on a baking sheet and put them in the oven to toast lightly.

Serve the rice pudding with the toasted almonds sprinkled on top, along with a little more cinnamon.

YOGURT, DATE, AND HONEY CHEESECAKE

SERVES 8-12

3 tbsp butter, melted
6 sheets of phyllo pastry
1¼ cups thick plain yogurt
6 tbsp skim milk
3 tbsp rice or potato flour
⅓ cup ground almonds
⅓ cup mild-flavored honey
1 cup ricotta cheese
3 eggs, lightly beaten
⅓ cup raisins
⅓ cup chopped dates
grated zest and juice of 1 small washed lemon
grated zest and juice of 1 small washed orange
2 tbsp orange flower water or almond liqueur
confectioners' sugar, to finish

Preheat the oven to 375°F and grease a 10-inch loose-bottomed tart pan with some of the butter.

Trim the sheets of phyllo so that they are about 12-inches square. Line the pan with them, brushing each with butter and putting it at an angle of about 60 degrees to that beneath it to fan out the corners.

Mix the yogurt and milk in a large pan and sift in the flour. Then add the almonds and honey. Bring almost to a boil, stirring constantly. The mixture should become quite thick. Let cool slightly.

Transfer to a large mixing bowl and add the cheese and all but 1 tablespoon of the beaten eggs. Beat in well. Stir in most of the fruit, reserving some for decoration, together with the citrus zest and juice and the orange flower water or liqueur.

Pour into the pastry shell, brush the top lightly with the reserved beaten egg and bake for about 45 minutes, or until a good light golden brown.

Dust with confectioners' sugar and decorate with the reserved fruit before serving.

TIRAMISÙ★

SERVES 6-8

12 ladyfinger cookies
1 tsp instant coffee
2 tbsp brandy
2 tbsp Marsala wine
3 eggs, separated★
(★see page 2 for advice on eggs)
3 tbsp sugar
¾ lb (1½ cups) mascarpone cheese
3 oz semisweet chocolate

Cut the ladyfingers in half lengthwise. Line the bottom of a deep glass serving bowl with half the ladyfingers, cut-side uppermost.

Dissolve the coffee in 2 tablespoons of boiling water and mix the brandy and Marsala into it. Use a pastry brush to paint the ladyfingers with this.

Beat the egg yolks with the sugar until the mixture is thick and pale. Then beat the cheese into this mixture a spoonful at a time.

Whisk the egg whites until standing in stiff peaks and fold into the cheese mixture.

Grate half the chocolate into tiny pieces. Spread half the cheese mixture over the ladyfingers and sprinkle with half of the chocolate pieces. Repeat the layers.

Finish by smoothing the top of the cheese mixture and chill at least 4 hours or overnight.

Just before serving, grate the remaining chocolate finely over the top. Use within 24 hours.

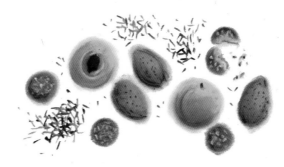

The Italian coffee-flavored dessert, Tiramisù, has become a great restaurant favorite in recent years. It often disappoints, however, having been made with custard rather than thick, rich mascarpone cheese. For more flavor and crunch, spread the layers of ladyfingers with some apricot preserves and stud the top with tiny amarettini cookies.

PISTACHIO BAKLAVA

MAKES ABOUT 40 PIECES

1 stick (8 tbsp) butter, melted
½ cup blanched almonds
½ cup walnut pieces
15 sheets of phyllo pastry
2 cups chopped pistachios
1 tbsp sugar
½ tsp ground cinnamon
FOR THE SYRUP
2¼ cups sugar
1 cinnamon stick, broken into pieces
1 tbsp mild-flavored honey
2 whole cloves
½ tsp finely grated lemon zest
juice from ½ small washed lemon
2 tbsp orange flower water

The Middle-Eastern nut pastry cake, BAKLAVA, is made with a mixture of almonds, walnuts, and pistachios. Here the pistachios predominate, but the nuts may be mixed in any proportion. It is important that the nuts are not ground too finely.

GRANITAS are Italian ices in which the formation of crystals is encouraged to give a refreshing grainy texture.

First make the syrup: mix all the ingredients except the orange flower water with 1 cup water in a saucepan. Place over medium heat and stir until the sugar has dissolved. Then bring to a boil and boil, without stirring, until the syrup is slightly thickened, about 4 minutes. Discard the spices and stir in the orange flower water. Let cool and then chill.

Preheat the oven to 325°F and grease the bottom and sides of a deep 8-inch square cake pan generously with some of the melted butter.

Toast the almonds either on a baking sheet in the oven as it warms or in a frying pan. Put them in a food processor or mortar with the walnuts and grind to the consistency of small bread crumbs.

Cut the sheets of pastry roughly to fit the pan. Layer 3 sheets in the bottom of the pan, brushing each with butter and trimming as necessary. Keep the other sheets covered with a damp cloth.

Mix together the pistachios, ground nuts, sugar, and cinnamon. Sprinkle one-quarter of this mixture over the pastry base in the pan.

Continue with layers of buttered phyllo and nuts until all are used up, finishing with a layer of 3 sheets of pastry. Brush this well with butter and sprinkle the top with 1 tablespoon of water.

Bake 45 minutes, then increase the heat to 425°F and continue baking until the baklava is puffed and lightly golden, 10-15 minutes longer.

As soon as the baklava comes out of the oven, pour the chilled syrup all over it. Let cool in the pan.

Slice in diagonal cuts about 2 inches apart and then do the same at right angles to cut the baklava into diamond-shaped pieces for serving.

COFFEE GRANITA

SERVES 4

6 oz dark-roasted coffee beans, ground
7 tbsp sugar
2 tbsp coffee liqueur, such as Kahlúa or Tia Maria
(optional)
light cream, for serving
candy coffee beans, for decoration (optional)

Put the coffee and sugar in a pot or large pitcher and pour in 5 cups of boiling water. Stir, cover, and let infuse in a warm place about 30 minutes.

Stir again and strain through a strainer lined with cheesecloth or a coffee filter paper.

Stir in the liqueur, if using, and freeze the mixture in a mold or ice cube trays 3-4 hours, without stirring.

Serve topped with a little cream and decorated with a few candy coffee beans.

NOTE: this is very refreshing and not too sweet; those with a sweet tooth may like to add more sugar to the freezing mixture.

Left: Pistachio Baklava; right: Zabaglione Ice-cream (page 201) with fresh raspberries

ZABAGLIONE ICE-CREAM★

SERVES 6

12 egg yolks★
(★see page 2 for advice on eggs)
9 tbsp sugar
1¼ cups Marsala wine
1¼ cups whipping cream
fresh strawberries, raspberries, or chopped toasted
hazelnuts, for decoration

In a bowl, beat the egg yolks together with the sugar until pale and thick. Stir in the Marsala and mix well.

Set the bowl over a saucepan of just simmering water. Stir constantly until the custard begins to thicken. Immediately remove from the heat and set the base of the bowl in cold water to stop the cooking, still stirring constantly. Let cool completely.

Whip the cream until standing in soft peaks and fold in the custard.

Freeze for about 6 hours in ice trays in the freezer, taking out and stirring vigorously with a fork halfway through to break up any ice crystals that have formed. Use within 48 hours.

Serve in tall elegant sundae glasses, decorated with fruit or nuts.

NOTE: this is a very rich ice-cream, but you can lighten it by adding the stiffly beaten whites of 2 or 3 of the eggs to the mixture. (The remaining egg whites can be used to make meringues to serve with the ice-cream.)

BAKED FIGS STUFFED WITH WALNUTS

SERVES 4

12 ripe fresh figs
2 oz walnut halves
3 tbsp mild-flavored honey or light brown sugar
3 tbsp Madeira or sweet sherry wine
½ cup cream cheese

Preheat the oven to 400°F.

Cut a tiny slice off the base of each fig so that it will sit stably. Make 2 cuts down through their tops, about 1-inch deep, at right angles to one another. Ease the figs open with a spoon, squeezing their middles at the same time, if necessary.

In a food processor or mortar, grind most of the walnut halves coarsely, reserving the better-looking pieces for decoration. Do not over-process.

In a bowl mix the honey or sugar, Madeira or sherry, and ground nuts into the cream cheese. Spoon this into the opened figs and arrange them in a baking dish. Bake until the cheese is bubbling, 15-20 minutes. Arrange the reserved walnuts halves on the tops of the figs and serve.

NOTE: toasted almonds or hazelnuts work equally well in this dish, as does mascarpone cheese.

ZABAGLIONE *is a frothy Italian custard made from egg yolks beaten with sugar and alcohol. Usually served hot in tall glasses, it is most commonly flavored with Marsala, but some versions use sparkling white wine or even liqueurs.*

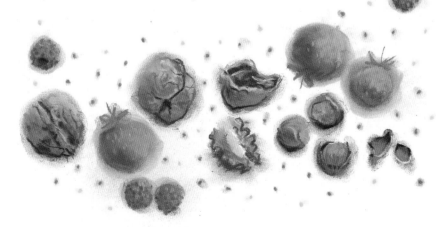

Baked Figs Stuffed with Walnuts

MASCARPONE AND RASPBERRY DESSERT CAKE

SERVES 8-12

32 ladyfingers
½ cup Marsala wine
1½ cups raspberries, thawed if frozen
3 oz Amaretti cookies, crushed
unsweetened cocoa powder, for dusting
FOR THE MASCARPONE CREAM
3½ tbsp custard powder or cornstarch
2 egg yolks
1¼ cups milk
1¼ cups confectioners' sugar, sifted
1 lb 2 oz mascarpone cheese

First start making the mascarpone cream: in a large bowl, mix the custard powder and egg yolks with a little of the milk. Heat the remaining milk with a little of the sugar to just below boiling point and pour this over the custard. Return this mixture to the pan and cook, stirring constantly, until thickened. Transfer to a bowl, cover, and let cool.

Meanwhile, line the bottom and sides of an 9-inch springform cake pan with nonstick silicone paper.

Finish the mascarpone cream by beating the cheese with the rest of the sugar. Beat this into the cold custard until smooth and light in texture.

Set 16 ladyfingers in the bottom of the prepared pan and sprinkle over half the Marsala. Spread with half the mascarpone cream, then sprinkle the raspberries on top. Repeat the layers of ladyfingers and mascarpone cream.

Cover the cake with a round of parchment and chill at least 8 hours, but preferably overnight.

Set the cake on a plate. Remove the sides of the pan. Turn the cake upside down on another plate and remove the base and base paper. Turn the cake back the right way up on the serving plate. Remove the top and side papers. Smooth the top and sides.

Press some of the crushed Amaretti cookies on the sides to cover them and sprinkle the rest on top of the cake. Chill until required.

Dust heavily with cocoa powder just before serving.

CHESTNUT MOUSSE CAKE WITH VANILLA CREAM

SERVES 8-12

10 tbsp unsalted butter, softened, plus more for greasing
1 cup + 2 tbsp sugar
1 lb canned unsweetened chestnut purée
grated zest of ½ washed lemon
3 extra large eggs, separated
⅔ cup whipping cream
2-3 drops vanilla extract, or to taste

Preheat the oven to 350°F and grease a 10-inch round cake pan with butter.

Cream the butter and sugar until pale. Beat in the chestnut purée together with the lemon zest, followed by 2 of the egg yolks. (Use the remaining egg yolk to enrich a sauce.)

Beat the egg whites until stiff but not dry and fold them into the mixture. Pour the resulting batter into the prepared pan.

Bake until a skewer inserted into the middle of the cake comes out clean, 55-60 minutes.

Toward the end of this time, whip the cream with the vanilla extract until stiff.

Let the cake cool in the pan - it will shrink a little as it cools and crack slightly. Serve the cake cut in wedges and accompanied by vanilla cream.

CŒUR À LA CRÈME WITH SUMMER BERRIES★

SERVES 4

6 oz fresh cream cheese, softened
1 cup whipping cream
1 tbsp sugar
1 extra large egg white, beaten until stiff but not dry★
(★see page 2 for advice on eggs)*
1 lb prepared seasonal soft fruits
extra sugar, for serving (optional)

The traditional French summer dessert, CŒUR À LA CRÈME, *is made from fresh cheese and cream set in distinctive heart-shaped molds that have drainage holes in their bases. Such molds are now available from kitchenware stores in this country.*

Mix the cheese with the cream and the sugar. Mix in 1 tablespoon of the egg white to soften the mixture, then carefully fold in the rest.

Dampen 4 squares of cheesecloth and use these to line 4 heart-shaped cœur à la crème molds. Spoon the mixture into the molds and smooth the tops.

Place these on a large plate to catch the liquid that will drain out of the holes in the bottoms of the molds. Let drain in the refrigerator several hours, or overnight.

To serve: unmold each by inverting it on a plate, and surround with fruit. Sprinkle the fruit with extra sugar, if desired.

Left and foreground: Cœur à la Crème with Summer Berries; top right: Raspberry Fool (page 207)

The basic RASPBERRY FOOL recipe (see page 207) can be varied according to what summer fruit is available. Try making it with strawberries, blackberries, or any ripe soft fruit. The amount of sugar added can be adjusted to taste, depending on the tartness of the fruit.

GOLDEN TART WITH ORANGE THYME

SERVES 6

10 tbsp unsalted butter, cut into small pieces, plus
more for greasing
1⅓ cups flour
½ tsp salt
4 egg yolks
½ cup fresh bread crumbs, preferably a mixture of white
and whole wheat
¼ cup golden syrup or light corn syrup
2 tbsp sliced almonds
2 tbsp grated zest and the juice from ½ washed lemon
1 tbsp minced fresh orange-scented thyme leaves

Preheat the oven to 400°F and grease a 9½-inch loose-bottomed tart or quiche pan with butter.

Sift the flour with the salt into a bowl. Add the butter and rub it in with the fingertips until the mixture resembles bread crumbs. Using a fork, mix the egg yolks in lightly, together with enough cold water to make a firm dough.

On a cold lightly floured surface, knead the dough 2 minutes and then roll it out to a thickness of about ⅛ inch. Use it to line the prepared pan and prick the bottom gently with a fork.

Mix the remaining ingredients together and spread them evenly in the pastry shell. Use the pastry trimmings to decorate the top of the tart.

Bake on the middle shelf of the oven, until golden, 25–30 minutes. Serve hot, warm, or cold.

Left: Apple Brown Betty with Scented Geranium; right: Golden Tart with Orange Thyme

APPLE BROWN BETTY WITH SCENTED GERANIUM

SERVES 4-6

9 slices of stale whole wheat bread, crusts removed
4 tbsp softened butter
2 lb tart apples, peeled, cored, and sliced
3 tbsp light molasses
1 tbsp minced scented geranium leaves
plain yogurt, custard sauce, or cream, for serving

Preheat the oven to 325°F.

Spread the slices of bread generously with butter and cut each slice into quarters.

Place a layer of one-third of the bread quarters over the bottom of a baking dish. Cover this with half the apple, drizzle one tablespoon of molasses over, and then sprinkle over half of the geranium leaves.

Repeat with a second similar layer, and finish with a layer of overlapping bread quarters to cover. Spread this with the remaining molasses.

Bake 50 minutes, then increase the temperature to 375°F, and continue baking until crisp and golden brown, 10 minutes longer. Serve hot, warm, or cold with yogurt, custard sauce, or cream.

MARIGOLD AND APRICOT SORBET★

SERVES 4-6

3 tbsp sugar
1¼ cups canned apricot halves in syrup, drained
1 egg white, beaten until stiff★
(★see page 2 for advice on eggs)
juice of 1 lemon
petals from 2 marigold (calendula) heads

Dissolve the sugar in ⅔ cup water in a saucepan. Bring to a boil and boil until it is syrupy, stirring constantly.

Let cool.

Purée the apricots in a blender or food processor, then strain this purée. Stir in the egg white and lemon juice. Then mix this into the syrup.

Put the mixture into an ice-cream machine or in ice-cube trays with half the marigold petals sprinkled into it. If using an ice-cream machine, follow the manufacturer's instructions; otherwise place the trays in the freezer until the sorbet is just set, whisking several times with a fork to disperse large crystals as it freezes.

Serve in chilled glass dishes, decorated with the remaining marigold petals.

RASPBERRY FOOL

SERVES 4

1½ cups raspberries
1 tbsp sugar, or more to taste
1¼ cups whipping cream
mint or lemon balm leaves, for decoration (optional)

Reserving a few perfect berries for decoration, mash the fruit with the sugar. (Do not use a food processor; the texture is nicer if the purée isn't too smooth.)

Whip the cream until stiff, then fold this into the purée. Chill well.

Serve decorated with the reserved whole berries and the leaves, if using.

APRICOT-CHOCOLATE TART

SERVES 6

FOR THE PASTRY
1¼ cups flour
1 stick (8 tbsp) butter, cut into small pieces
2 tbsp sugar
1 tsp almond extract
1 egg
FOR THE FILLING
2 egg yolks
7 tbsp sugar
¼ cup flour
1¼ cups milk
1 oz semisweet chocolate
¼ cup whipping cream
1 lb apricots, halved
2½ tbsp sliced almonds, toasted
¼ cup apricot preserves

To make the pastry: sift the flour into a bowl, add the butter, and rub it in finely with your fingertips. Stir in the sugar, almond extract, and egg and mix together with a fork to form a firm dough.

Knead the dough on a lightly floured surface until it is smooth. Roll it out thinly and use to line a 9-inch round loose-bottomed fluted tart pan. Chill 30 minutes.

Preheat the oven to 400°F.

Bake the pastry shell "blind" until lightly browned at the edges, 15-20 minutes.

While the shell is baking make the filling: in a bowl, whisk together the egg yolks, 2 tablespoons of the sugar, the flour, and 1 tablespoon of the measured milk until smooth. In a saucepan, bring the remaining milk and the chocolate to a boil, whisking, then pour over the egg mixture, whisking constantly over low heat. Return the mixture to the saucepan and cook gently, whisking well, until the custard has thickened.

Remove the saucepan from the heat and whisk in the cream. Pour the custard into the pastry shell and leave until cold.

Place the remaining sugar in a saucepan with ⅓ cup of water and bring to a boil, stirring. Add the apricot halves, cover, and cook gently until tender, 2-3 minutes. Using a slotted spoon, remove the apricots from the syrup and arrange them over the custard filling. Scatter the almonds on top.

Add the apricot preserves to the syrup in the saucepan and bring to a boil. Boil 1 minute, then strain into a bowl. Let cool slightly.

Pour the apricot syrup evenly over the apricots to glaze and then let cool.

PRUNE AND ARMAGNAC TART

SERVES 6

FOR THE PASTRY
¾ cup flour
6 tbsp butter, cut into small pieces
2 tbsp sugar
1 egg yolk
FOR THE FILLING
20 plump pitted prunes
¼ cup Armagnac or brandy
1 tbsp honey
1 tbsp light brown sugar
½ cup whipping cream
2 eggs
3 tbsp hazelnuts, halved
FOR DECORATION
confectioners' sugar

To make the pastry: sift the flour into a bowl, add the butter, and rub it in finely with your fingertips. Stir in the sugar and egg yolk and mix together with a fork to form a firm dough.

Knead the dough on a lightly floured surface until it is smooth. Roll it out thinly and use to line an 8-inch round loose-bottomed fluted tart pan. Chill 30 minutes. Preheat the oven to 400°F.

Bake the pastry shell "blind" until lightly browned at the edge and cooked on the bottom, 10-15 minutes.

While the shell is baking make the filling: place the prunes and Armagnac or brandy in a small saucepan and warm gently over low heat, taking care not to over-heat. Cover and leave until cold.

Beat the honey, sugar, cream, and eggs together until well blended. Strain the Armagnac or brandy into the mixture and place the prunes in the shell.

Stir the filling, pour it over the prunes, and return the tart to the oven to bake 20 minutes. Scatter the hazelnuts over the top and continue baking until the filling has set, about 10 minutes longer. Dust with confectioners' sugar and serve warm or cold.

ROSÉ PEAR TART

SERVES 6

FOR THE PASTRY
¾ cup flour
6 tbsp butter, cut into small pieces
½ cup finely chopped walnuts
2 tbsp sugar
1 egg

FOR THE FILLING
1¼ cups rosé wine
1 cup sugar
5 small pears, peeled, quartered, and cored
2 egg yolks
¼ cup flour
1 tbsp rose water
1¼ cups milk
¼ cup whipping cream
2 tsp unflavored gelatin

To make the pastry: sift the flour into a bowl, add the butter, and rub it in finely with your fingertips. Stir in the walnuts, sugar, and egg and mix together with a fork to form a firm dough.

Knead the dough until smooth. Roll it out thinly and use to line an 8-inch square loose-bottomed fluted tart pan. Chill 30 minutes.

Preheat the oven to 400°F.

Bake the pastry shell "blind" until lightly browned at the edges, 15-20 minutes.

While the shell is baking make the filling: place the wine and ¾ cup of the sugar in a pan and heat gently, stirring, until the sugar has dissolved. Add the pears and bring to a boil. Cover and cook over low heat until tender, 10-15 minutes. Let cool.

In a bowl, whisk together the egg yolks, remaining sugar, the flour, and rose water until smooth. Bring the milk to a boil in a saucepan and pour it over the egg mixture, whisking all the time. Return the mixture to the saucepan and cook over low heat, whisking well, until the custard has thickened. Remove from the heat and whisk in the cream. Pour into the pastry shell and let cool.

Using a slotted spoon, transfer the pears to a large plate. Blend the gelatin with 2 tablespoons of water and stir this into the wine syrup until dissolved. Leave until almost set.

Meanwhile, cut half of the pear quarters into about 4 thin slices each, keeping the quarters together with the rounded sides on the right hand side. Slice the remaining pear quarters in the same way, with the rounded sides on the left.

Arrange 5 of the pear quarters on the custard filling and press lightly to spread them evenly; place another 5 quarters cut in the other direction and spread similarly. Repeat the process with the remaining pear halves in different directions.

When the gelatin has begun to set, spoon it over the pears and chill until set. Remove from the pan for serving.

NORMANDY APPLE TART

SERVES 6

FOR THE PASTRY
1 cup flour
6 tbsp butter, cut into small pieces
2 tbsp sugar
2 egg yolks
FOR THE FILLING
1 stick (8 tbsp) unsalted butter, softened
½ cup + 2 tbsp sugar
3 egg yolks
2 tbsp whipping cream
1¼ cups ground almonds
2 tbsp crumbled lavender flowers
4 apples, peeled, halved, and cored
¼ cup apricot preserves, boiled and strained

Normandy, being the apple-growing region of France, strongly features apples in its traditional cookery. There are many variations of this tart and the addition of the sweet scent of lavender is particularly rewarding.

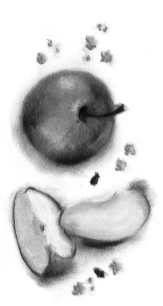

Make the pastry: sift the flour into a bowl, add the butter, and rub in finely with your fingertips. Stir in the sugar and egg yolks and mix to a firm dough.

Knead the dough until smooth. Roll it out thinly and use to line a 9-inch round loose-bottomed fluted tart pan. Chill 30 minutes. Preheat the oven to 400°F.

To make the filling: in a bowl, beat together the butter and ½ cup of the sugar until light and fluffy. Add the egg yolks one at a time, beating well after each. Stir in the cream and fold in the almonds.

Scatter the lavender over the bottom of the pastry shell. Then spread the almond mixture over these.

Slice the apple halves very thinly, keeping the halves together. Place one half in the center of the filling and arrange the remaining 7 evenly around it. Press each apple half gently to spread out the slices.

Bake 15 minutes, then sprinkle the remaining sugar over the apples. Reduce the oven temperature to 350°F and continue baking until the filling is lightly browned, 40-45 minutes longer.

Let cool before removing the tart from the pan. Brush the top evenly with the apricot preserves.

ROSE CUSTARD TARTLETS

MAKES 8

FOR THE PASTRY
¾ cup flour
6 tbsp butter or margarine, cut into small pieces
⅔ cup ground almonds
5 tbsp sugar
1 egg, beaten
FOR THE FILLING
2 eggs + 2 extra yolks
2 tbsp rose water
1 tbsp flour
¾ cup milk
1¼ cups light cream
1 pint wild strawberries or stoned cherries

To make the pastry: sift the flour into a bowl. Add the butter or margarine and rub it in finely with your fingertips. Stir in the ground almonds, sugar, and egg and mix with a fork to form a firm dough.

Knead the dough on a lightly floured surface until it is smooth. Roll it out thinly, and use to line eight 4½-inch loose-bottomed fluted tartlet molds. Chill 30 minutes.

Preheat the oven to 400°F.

Bake the pastry shells "blind" until lightly browned at the edges, 10-15 minutes. Reduce the oven temperature to 350°F.

Place the eggs, egg yolks, rose water, and flour in a bowl and whisk until smooth. Whisk in the milk and cream and pour the mixture into the pastry cases. Dot with the fruit.

Return the tartlets to the cooler oven to bake until the filling has just set, 45-50 minutes. Let cool before serving.

A Rose Custard Tartlet

CARROT AND PASSION FRUIT LAYER CAKE

SERVES 12-16

1¼ cups raisins
1¼ cups sunflower oil, plus more for greasing
1⅔ cups flour
2 tsp baking powder
1 tsp baking soda
1 tsp salt
2 tsp ground cinnamon
4 eggs
2 tsp pure vanilla extract
1 cup + 2 tbsp granulated sugar
1¼ cups light brown sugar
2 cups chopped walnuts
1 lb carrots, finely grated and excess moisture squeezed out
FOR THE PASSION FRUIT ICING
4 passion fruit, halved
2 cups confectioners' sugar, sifted
1 tsp lemon juice
2 sticks (1 cup) butter, softened
½ cup cream cheese

Put the raisins in a small saucepan with just enough water to cover and simmer until they are well plumped up, about 10 minutes. Let cool completely and then drain thoroughly.

Preheat the oven to 350°F. Grease three 9-inch round cake pans with oil and line the bottoms with wax or parchment paper.

Sift the flour, baking powder, soda, salt, and cinnamon together. Beat the eggs, vanilla, sugars, and oil in a bowl until thick. Fold in the flour mixture, followed by the walnuts, raisins, and carrot.

Transfer the batter to the prepared pans and bake until risen and just firm to the touch, about 25 minutes. Let the cakes cool in the pans, then carefully unmold them on wire racks.

Make the passion fruit icing: place the pulp from the passion fruit in a saucepan with 2 tablespoons of the sugar, the lemon juice, and 2 tablespoons water. Simmer until the pulp loosens from the seeds, 2–3 minutes. Pass the contents of the pan through a fine strainer and let cool.

Beat the butter until smooth, then beat in the remaining icing sugar, a little at a time. Beat in the cream cheese and stir in the passion fruit purée.

Use a little of this mixture to sandwich the cakes together, then use the rest to cover the top and sides of the cake.

PAVLOVA PALETTE

SERVES 12-16

4 egg whites (about ¾ cup)
pinch of salt
1 cup + 2 tbsp superfine sugar
2 tsp cornstarch
1 tsp vinegar
1 tsp pure vanilla extract
2½ cups whipping cream, whipped into soft peaks
selection of prepared fruits in season
confectioners' sugar, for dusting

Preheat the oven to 300°F.

Draw a circle on a piece of 10-inch nonstick silicone paper and set it on a baking sheet.

Beat the egg whites with a pinch of salt until stiff, then beat in the superfine sugar, 1 tablespoonful at a time, adding the cornstarch with the last spoonful. Quickly beat in the vinegar and vanilla.

Transfer the mixture to the paper and spread it evenly, making a slight dip in the center. Bake 1 hour, then switch off the oven and leave the meringue in the oven to cool completely.

Spread the whipped cream over the top of the cold pavlova, then cover with an abstract arrangement of fruits. Dust with confectioners' sugar.

A classic of Antipodean cooking that has become an international favorite, the PAVLOVA *meringue cake was devised in honor of the great Russian prima ballerina when she toured Australia early this century.*

DOUBLE TRUFFLE TORTE★

SERVES 16-20

FOR THE CAKE LAYERS
½ cup cake flour, plus more for dusting
½ cup + 2 tbsp sugar, plus more for dusting
2 tbsp cornstarch
¼ cup unsweetened cocoa powder, plus more for dusting
4 eggs
butter, for greasing
FOR THE DARK TRUFFLE LAYER
3 oz semisweet chocolate
2 tbsp milk
1 stick (8 tbsp) unsalted butter
½ cup + 2 tbsp sugar
¾ cup unsweetened cocoa powder, sifted
3 egg yolks★
(★see page 2 for advice on eggs)
1 cup crème fraîche or whipping cream
FOR THE WHITE TRUFFLE LAYER
3 oz white chocolate
1 stick (8 tbsp) unsalted butter
½ cup + 2 tbsp sugar
¾ cup ground almonds
3 egg yolks
1 cup crème fraîche or whipping cream

Preheat the oven to 375°F. Butter three 8-inch layer cake pans and line the bottoms with wax or parchment paper. Dust the sides with a mixture of equal parts flour and sugar, then shake out any excess. Sift the flour, cornstarch, and cocoa together.

Place the eggs and sugar in a large bowl set over a saucepan of simmering water and beat until thick and foamy (the beaters should leave a thick trail in the mixture).

Fold in the flour mixture and divide among the pans. Bake until just firm to the touch, 10-15 minutes. Unmold and let cool on wire racks.

Line the bottom and sides of an 8-inch springform cake pan with a 3½-inch collar of nonstick silicone paper.

Make the dark truffle layer: melt the chocolate with the milk and stir until smooth. Let cool.

Beat the butter and sugar together in a bowl until light and fluffy, then beat in the chocolate mixture, cocoa, egg yolks, and crème fraîche or cream.

Place one cake layer in the prepared pan and spread the dark truffle mixture on top. Set a second cake layer on top and press lightly. Chill.

Make the white truffle layer: melt the chocolate and stir until smooth. Let cool.

Beat the butter and sugar together in a bowl until light and fluffy, then beat in the chocolate, ground almonds, egg yolks, and crème fraîche or cream.

Spread the white truffle mixture on top of the second cake layer and cover with the last layer. Press down lightly and chill 24 hours.

Unmold and dust with cocoa powder before serving, cut in very thin wedges.

The candies known as chocolate TRUFFLES, *due to their physical similarity to the equally delicious little black truffle fungus, are traditionally given as Christmas gifts in France. They are classically flavored with rum or praline, but brandy, Scotch, Champagne, and vanilla truffles are also common.*

PEAR GALETTE

SERVES 8

FOR THE PASTRY
1 cup finely ground, toasted almonds
6 tbsp butter
3 tbsp sugar
¾ cup + 2 tbsp flour
pinch of salt
FOR THE FILLING
2 lb pears, peeled, cored, and chopped
1 tbsp apricot preserves
finely grated zest of ½ washed lemon
1 tbsp diced mixed candied peel
2 tbsp dried currants
2 tbsp golden raisins (sultanas)
FOR DECORATION
about ½ cup whipped cream
8 toasted skinned hazelnuts
confectioners' sugar, for dusting

Make the pastry: work all the ingredients in a food processor until evenly combined. Chill 20 minutes.

Cut the dough in half and roll out each piece to form a 9-inch round on a circle of nonstick silicone paper. Chill on baking sheets for 20 minutes.

Preheat the oven to 375°F and bake the pastry rounds until golden, about 20 minutes. Cut one into 8 even wedges. Let cool completely.

Make the filling: place the ingredients in a pan and cook over medium heat, stirring occasionally, until the pears are soft and all the juice has evaporated, about 15 minutes. Let cool.

Just before serving, place the pastry round on a plate and spread with filling. Set the wedges on top and dust with confectioners' sugar. Decorate with piped "shells" of cream and top with hazelnuts.

Left to right: Marzipan Petal Cake (page 219), Pear Galette, and Coconut Cheesecake with Strawberry Coulis (page 218)

COFFEE-WALNUT GÂTEAU

SERVES 12

2 tbsp espresso coffee granules dissolved in 2 tbsp
boiling water
6 eggs
1 cup + 2 tbsp sugar
1⅓ cups finely ground walnuts
1½ cups cake flour
1 tsp baking powder
2 tbsp walnut oil
¼ cup apricot preserves
12 candied coffee beans
butter, for greasing
FOR THE COFFEE BUTTERCREAM
1 tbsp espresso coffee granules
½ cup milk
4 egg yolks
½ cup + 2 tbsp sugar
2 sticks + 1 tbsp unsalted butter, diced

Preheat the oven to 350°F. Butter two 8-inch round cake pans and line with wax or parchment paper.

Mix a batter as on page 215, adding coffee to the eggs and sugar, and walnuts to the sifted flour. Fold in the walnut oil. Divide between the pans and bake 25 minutes. Cool in the pans, then unmold on racks.

Make the buttercream: in a small pan over very low heat, dissolve the coffee in the milk. Beat the egg yolks and sugar in a bowl, then pour on the milk and stir well. Return to the pan and cook gently until thick enough to coat the back of a spoon. Strain, cover, and cool. Beat in butter, a little at a time, to make a thick buttercream.

Split each cake into 2 layers and sandwich the pairs together with a little buttercream. Put the two cakes together with preserves. Reserving 6 tablespoons, use the rest of the buttercream to cover the top and sides. Pipe 12 rosettes of buttercream around the top. Top each with a coffee bean.

The stirred custard for the coffee buttercream used in the COFFEE WALNUT GÂTEAU *can also be thickened by cooking it in the microwave oven for 3 minutes, whisking after each minute.*

In French cooking, a COULIS is a thin purée or sauce of raw or cooked vegetables or fruit. Fruit coulis are popular accompaniments to all sorts of desserts, especially frozen ones.

COCONUT CHEESECAKE WITH STRAWBERRY COULIS

SERVES 8-12

FOR THE BASE
7 tbsp butter, softened
¼ cup sugar
½ cup flour, sifted
1 tsp baking powder
1 extra large egg, beaten
½ cup dried shredded coconut

FOR THE FILLING
½ lb cream cheese
3 eggs, separated
½ cup + 2 tbsp sugar
3 tbsp flour
⅔ cup canned coconut milk
1 tbsp lemon juice

FOR THE STRAWBERRY COULIS
1 pint ripe strawberries, hulled
½ cup confectioners' sugar
squeeze of lemon juice

FOR DECORATION
⅔ cup whipping cream, whipped to soft peaks
2 fresh strawberries, quartered
1 tbsp shredded coconut, toasted

Make the base: beat the ingredients together in a bowl until creamy. Using a spatula, spread a thin layer of the mixture on the sides of a 9-inch nonstick springform cake pan. Spread the rest on the bottom. Chill at least 20 minutes. Preheat the oven to 325°F.

Make the filling: beat the cream cheese, egg yolks, and half the sugar in a bowl until smooth, then beat in the flour and coconut milk.

Beat the egg whites until fairly stiff, then beat in the lemon juice, a little at a time. Beat in the remaining sugar a spoonful at a time. Fold this into the cheese mixture and transfer to the prepared pan.

Bake until lightly golden, about 35 minutes.

Switch off the oven and let the cheesecake cool in it for 10 minutes before removing. Let cool completely.

Make the strawberry coulis: put the strawberries in a blender or food processor and purée until smooth. Sweeten and add lemon juice to taste. Then pass through a fine strainer to remove seeds, if desired.

Unmold the cheesecake and decorate with rosettes of whipped cream, strawberry quarters, and a little toasted coconut. Serve with the strawberry coulis.

LEMON LAYER SYRUP CAKE

SERVES 10-12

1¼ cups sugar, plus more for dusting
¾ cup flour, plus more for dusting
2 washed lemons
4 eggs
2 tbsp lukewarm water
7 tbsp cornstarch or potato flour
1 tsp baking powder
butter, for greasing

FOR THE FILLING AND TOPPING
2½ cups whipping cream
3 tbsp confectioners' sugar
½ cup minced pistachio nuts
8 fresh strawberries, for decoration

Preheat the oven to 375°F. Butter a 9-inch round cake pan and line the bottom with wax or parchment paper. Dust the sides of the pan with a little sugar and flour. Shake out any excess.

Finely grate the zest of one lemon and pare the zest of the other. Extract the juice from them both.

In a large bowl set over a saucepan of simmering water, beat the eggs with the lukewarm water, ¾ cup of the sugar, and the grated lemon zest until thick and mousse-like (the beaters should leave a thick trail in the mixture). Remove from the heat.

Sift the flour, cornstarch, and baking powder together and carefully fold into the mixture. Transfer to the prepared pan and bake until risen and just firm to the touch, about 25 minutes.

Let cool in the pan, then unmold on a wire rack. When cold, split into 3 layers.

Place the pared lemon zest and all the lemon juice in a pan with the remaining sugar and 1¼ cups of water. Heat gently until the sugar dissolves, then boil until the liquid is reduced to about ¾ cup. Strain this syrup and let it cool. Brush the syrup over one of the cut surfaces of each cake layer.

Make the filling: whip the cream with the sugar to stiff peaks. Use a generous third of this to sandwich the cake layers back together.

Cover the top and sides of the cake with most of the remaining cream. Press the pistachios into the sides of the cake. Using a pastry bag fitted with a star tip and filled with the remaining cream, pipe a ring of shells around the rim of the cake.

Chill until required, then decorate with fruit.

MARZIPAN PETAL CAKE★

SERVES 10

2 tbsp butter, melted, plus more for greasing
½ cup + 2 tbsp sugar, plus more for dusting
½ cup cake flour, plus more for dusting
4 eggs
finely grated zest from ½ washed lemon
3½ tbsp cornstarch
½ tsp baking powder
¼ cup ground almonds
FOR THE FILLING AND TOPPING
1 lb 2 oz white marzipan
about 5 tbsp egg whites (about 2 eggs)★
(★see page 2 for advice on eggs)
about ½ cup raspberry preserves
⅔ cup sliced almonds, lightly toasted

Preheat the oven to 350°F. Grease an 8½-inch springform cake pan with butter, then line the bottom with wax or parchment paper. Coat the sides with a little sugar and flour and shake out any excess.

In a large bowl set over simmering water, beat the eggs, sugar, and lemon zest until thick and mousse-like. Remove from the heat and continue beating until cool.

Sift the flour, cornstarch, baking powder, and ground almonds together and fold them into the mixture, followed by the melted butter.

Transfer the batter to the prepared pan and bake until risen and golden and just firm to the touch, about 25 minutes. Let cool in the pan, then unmold on a wire rack. (This cake is best made the day before.)

Make the filling: place half the marzipan and 3 tablespoons of the egg white in a food processor and work until smooth and soft enough to spread.

Split the cake into 2 layers and then sandwich the layers together with about 6 tablespoons of the preserves. Set it on a baking sheet.

Use the marzipan-egg white mixture to cover the top and sides of the cake, then press the toasted almonds all over the sides to cover them completely.

Preheat the oven to its highest setting.

Put the rest of the marzipan in a food processor with 5 tablespoons of egg white and work until smooth enough to pipe. Using a pastry bag fitted with a small star tip and starting in the center of the cake, pipe about 10 loops of the marzipan mixture to the outside edge to create the impressions of the petals of a flower. Pipe a rosette in the center.

Bake the cake until golden brown, about 10 minutes. Then remove from the oven and let cool. Fill each "petal" with about ½ teaspoon of preserves and let it cool completely.

WHITE MARZIPAN, *unlike the yellow variety, has no coloring added. Made from sugar, ground almonds, glucose syrup, and invert sugar syrup, it must always be kneaded thoroughly before using or rolling.*

The curd cheese RICOTTA is popular in all sorts of Italian dishes. Its delicious sweet flavor makes it a popular dessert on its own with fruit or honey. Use strained cottage cheese if you can't find ricotta.

The bittersweet Italian liqueur STREGA is brewed using over 70 herbs.

ITALIAN HAZELNUT CAKE

SERVES 10-12

¾ cup skinned hazelnuts
1 stick (8 tbsp) butter, softened, plus more for greasing
½ cup + 2 tbsp sugar
4 eggs, separated
½ cup ricotta cheese
2 tsp finely grated zest from 1 washed lemon
3 tbsp flour, sifted
pinch of salt

FOR DECORATION
4 oz semisweet chocolate, melted
6 tbsp apricot preserves, warmed
1¼ cups whipped cream, whipped to soft peaks
confectioners' sugar, for dusting

Preheat the oven to 400°F and toast the nuts 15-20 minutes. Let cool, then grind them to a fine powder.

Reduce the oven setting to 375°F. Grease a 10-inch layer cake pan or tart pan with butter and line the bottom with wax or parchment paper.

Cream the butter with two-thirds of the sugar in a large bowl until almost white, then beat in the egg yolks, cheese, and lemon zest. Fold the hazelnuts and flour into the creamed mixture.

Beat the egg whites with a pinch of salt until standing in soft peaks. Beat in the remaining sugar and then fold this into the creamed mixture.

Transfer the batter to the prepared pan and bake about 25 minutes. Let cool in the pan, then transfer to a wire rack.

To decorate: spread the chocolate thinly on a marble slab or smooth plastic work surface and let it set. Using a large knife held at a 45-degree angle to the surface of the chocolate and with the blade facing away from you, scrape curls from the chocolate and set these on a tray in the refrigerator to harden.

Spread the surface of the cake with preserves, then top with whipped cream and the chocolate curls. Finally, dust with confectioners' sugar.

CLEMENTINE-STREGA CAKE

SERVES 16

FOR THE FRUIT LAYER
¾ lb candied whole clementines (mandarins)
½ cup + 2 tbsp sugar
⅔ cup Strega liqueur
FOR THE CAKE LAYERS
½ cup soft tub margarine or 1 stick (8 tbsp) softened
butter, plus more for greasing
½ cup + 2 tbsp sugar
2 eggs
¾ cup self-rising flour
⅓ cup unsweetened cocoa powder, sifted
FOR THE CHOCOLATE MIXTURE
1½ cups chocolate-hazelnut fudge sauce
10 oz semisweet chocolate, melted

First make the fruit layer: place the clementines in a saucepan and just cover with water. Bring to a fast boil, then remove from the heat and let cool in the liquid. Drain, reserving ½ cup of the cooking liquid.

Mince the fruit or work in a food processor, then mix it with the reserved liquid and the sugar in a saucepan. Cook over medium heat, stirring occasionally, until thick and syrupy (rather like marmalade), 10-15 minutes. Remove from the heat and stir in two-thirds of the Strega. Let cool completely.

Preheat the oven to 375°F. Grease two loaf pans, measuring about 9 x 5 x 3 inches, with butter and line the bottoms with wax or parchment paper.

Make the cake layers: cream the margarine or butter and sugar together until almost white, then beat in the eggs one at a time. Divide the mixture in half and fold ½ cup of the flour into one portion and the remaining flour and cocoa powder into the other.

Spread one batter in each pan, making a dip in the center of each. Bake until risen and just firm to the touch, about 20 minutes. Let cool on wire racks, then trim the crusts to give two layers each about ¾-inch thick.

Line one of the loaf pans with plastic wrap. Prepare the chocolate mixture by mixing four-fifths of each of the ingredients together. Pour half of this mixture into the bottom of the pan and freeze until solid.

Set one cake layer on top of the frozen chocolate layer and moisten with half of the remaining Strega. Top with the fruit mixture, followed by the other cake layer, and moisten with the last of the Strega. Spread the remaining chocolate mixture on top and freeze until solid, about 1 hour.

Prepare the remaining chocolate mixture ingredients. Unmold the cake and spread the sides with the mixture.

Chill until set, then cut the cake into thin slices for serving.

Top: Italian Hazelnut Cake; bottom: Clementine-Strega Cake

NORFOLK TREACLE TART

SERVES 8

FOR THE PASTRY
1¼ cups flour
1 stick butter, cut into small pieces
1 tbsp lemon juice
FOR THE FILLING
⅔ cup golden syrup or light corn syrup
2 tbsp butter
6 tbsp light cream
2 eggs, beaten
grated zest and juice from 1 washed lemon
1⅓ cups fresh white bread crumbs

To make the pastry: sift the flour into a bowl, add the butter, and rub it in finely with your fingertips. Stir in the lemon juice and 2 tablespoons of cold water and mix together with a fork to form a firm dough.

Knead the dough on a lightly floured surface until smooth. Roll it out thinly and use to line a 9-inch round tart or quiche dish, reserving the pastry trimmings. Chill 30 minutes.

Preheat the oven to 400°F.

To make the filling: place the golden syrup in a saucepan and heat gently until liquid. Remove the pan from the heat, add the butter, and stir until melted. Then beat in the cream, eggs, lemon zest, and juice until well blended.

Sprinkle the bread crumbs over the bottom of the pastry shell and pour the syrup mixture over the top. Roll out the pastry trimmings, cut into thin strips, and use to make a lattice design over the top.

Bake until the pastry is golden brown and the filling has set, 40-45 minutes. Let cool and serve warm or cold.

Clockwise from the top: Fruit Bakewell Tart; Rum and Butterscotch Tart (page 224); Norfolk Treacle Tart

FRUIT BAKEWELL TART

SERVES 6

FOR THE PASTRY
¾ cup flour
4 tbsp butter or margarine, cut into small pieces
1 tsp sugar
FOR THE FILLING
3 tbsp red currant jelly
½ cup each red currants, white currants,
and black currants
6 tbsp butter or margarine, softened
7 tbsp sugar
⅔ cup ground almonds
6 tbsp self-rising flour
2 eggs, beaten
1 tsp almond extract
⅓ cup sliced almonds
FOR DECORATION
confectioners' sugar

Make the pastry: sift flour into a bowl, add the butter or margarine, and rub in finely. Stir in the sugar and 2 tablespoons of cold water. Mix to a firm dough. Knead until smooth. Roll out thinly and use to line an 8-inch round loose-bottomed fluted tart pan. Chill 30 minutes. Preheat the oven to 350°F.

To make the filling: spread the red currant jelly over the bottom of the shell. Reserve a few stems of each type of fruit, and remove the remainder from their stems. Scatter over the jelly.

Beat together the butter or margarine, sugar, ground almonds, flour, eggs, and almond extract 1-2 minutes. Spread this mixture over the fruit in the pastry shell. Scatter the sliced almonds evenly over the top and bake until the filling has risen and feels firm when pressed lightly in the center, about 45-50 minutes.

Cool in the pan, then remove carefully. Dust with confectioners' sugar. Decorate with the reserved fruit.

BAKEWELL TART *is named after the town of Bakewell in Derbyshire, England. The layers were traditionally separated by crushed raspberries or raspberry preserves, to add moisture.*

GOLDEN SYRUP *can be found in some supermarkets and many specialty markets. You can substitute corn syrup or light molasses.*

KENTISH
STRAWBERRY
TART *consists of a
strawberry trifle
enclosed in a light,
crisp almond pastry.
Trifles were very
popular in Victorian
England. They were
made using light
sponge cakes soaked
in sherry, brandy, or
Madeira, layered
with fruit – Kentish
strawberries being
the most popular –
and covered with a
rich egg custard
sauce.*

RUM AND BUTTERSCOTCH TART

SERVES 6

FOR THE PASTRY
1¼ cups flour
1 stick (8 tbsp) butter
2 tbsp sugar
1 egg
FOR THE FILLING
½ cup packed dark brown sugar
4 tbsp butter
¼ cup flour
1¼ cups milk
⅔ cup light cream
2-3 tbsp dark rum
FOR DECORATION
whipped cream
chocolate-coated coffee beans

To make the pastry: sift the flour into a bowl, add the butter, and rub it in finely with your fingertips. Stir in the sugar and egg and mix together with a fork to form a firm dough.

Knead the dough on a lightly floured surface until smooth. Roll it out thinly and use to line a 9-inch round tart or quiche dish. Chill 30 minutes.

Preheat the oven to 400°F.

Bake the pastry shell "blind" until lightly browned at the edges and cooked at the base, 15-20 minutes.

While the shell is cooling, make the filling: place the sugar, butter, flour, milk, and cream in a saucepan. Whisking constantly over medium heat, bring to a boil. Simmer until the sauce is thick and smooth, 1-2 minutes. Stir in the rum.

Pour the filling into the pastry shell and leave until cold. Decorate the top with whipped cream and chocolate-coated coffee beans.

KENTISH STRAWBERRY TART

SERVES 8

FOR THE PASTRY
¾ cup flour
⅔ cup ground almonds
1 stick (8 tbsp) butter, cut into small pieces
2 tbsp sugar
1 tsp almond extract
1 egg
FOR THE FILLING
1 egg + 1 egg yolk
1 tsp pure vanilla extract
2½ tbsp sugar
3 tbsp flour
1¼ cups milk
3 tbsp strawberry preserves
10 ladyfingers, cut into half
2 tbsp Madeira wine
1½-2 cups strawberries, sliced
1¼ cups whipping cream, whipped
FOR DECORATION
strawberry slices and strawberry leaves

Make the pastry: sift the flour into a bowl, stir in the almonds, add the butter, and rub in finely. Stir in the sugar, almond extract, and egg and mix to a firm dough.

Knead the dough until smooth. Roll it out thinly and use to line a 11- x 7-inch rectangular fluted tart or quiche dish. Chill 30 minutes.

Preheat the oven to 400°F.

Bake the pastry shell "blind" until lightly browned at the edges, 15-20 minutes.

While the shell is baking, make the filling: in a bowl whisk together the egg, egg yolk, vanilla extract, sugar, and flour until well blended. Place the milk in a saucepan and bring it to a boil. Whisking constantly, pour the milk over the egg mixture. Return to the pan and continue whisking over low heat until the custard thickens. Let cool.

Spread the preserves in the pastry shell. Dip the ladyfingers into the Madeira, turning to coat well. Arrange them over the jam. Cover with strawberry slices.

Fold two-thirds of the whipped cream into the custard and spread evenly over the strawberries.

Place the remaining cream in a pastry bag fitted with a small star tip. Pipe ropes of cream across the tart and decorate with strawberry slices and leaves.

IRISH APPLE TART

SERVES 6

FOR THE PASTRY
½ cup + 2 tbsp flour
2 tbsp butter, cut into small pieces
1 tsp sugar
½ lb baking potatoes, cooked and puréed
FOR THE FILLING
1½ lb apples, cored, peeled, and thinly sliced
2½ tbsp sugar
1 tsp ground cloves
⅔ cup sour cream
2 tsp honey

To make the pastry: place the flour in a bowl, add the butter and rub it in finely with your fingertips. Stir in the sugar and potato and mix to a soft dough.

Roll out the dough thinly and use to line a 9-inch round tart or quiche dish.

Preheat the oven to 375°F.

Mix together the apples, sugar, and cloves and pile the mixture in the pastry shell. Bake until the apples are almost tender, 20-25 minutes.

Stir the apples, spread the sour cream over the top, and drizzle with honey. Bake until the cream has set, 5-10 minutes longer. Serve warm or cold.

Kentish Strawberry Tart

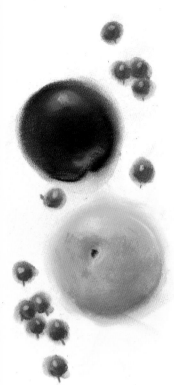

PLUM AND SOUR CREAM TART

SERVES 6

FOR THE PASTRY
1¼ cups flour
1 stick (8 tbsp) butter, cut into small pieces
2 tbsp sugar
3 tbsp sour cream
FOR THE FILLING
⅔ cup crushed amaretti cookies
¼ cup sour cream
¼ cup packed light brown sugar
½ lb red plums, halved and pitted
½ lb yellow plums, halved and pitted
¼ cup red currant jelly

To make the pastry: sift the flour into a bowl, add the butter, and rub it in finely with your fingertips. Stir in the sugar and sour cream, and mix together with a fork to form a firm dough.

Knead the dough on a lightly floured surface until it is smooth. Roll it out thinly and use to line an 8-inch round loose-bottomed fluted tart pan, reserving the trimmings. Chill 30 minutes.

Preheat the oven to 375°F.

To make the filling: in a bowl, mix together the crushed cookies, sour cream, and brown sugar. Spread the mixture in the pastry shell and arrange the plums on top, alternating the colors.

Roll out the pastry trimmings thinly and cut out 12 thin strips. Arrange these over the plums in a lattice design. Trim off the ends and press the strips onto the edge of the pastry shell.

Bake until the pastry is lightly browned and the plums are tender, 35-40 minutes. Let cool.

Heat the red currant jelly until melted, then pour it in between the pastry lattice to glaze the plums. Let set.

PEACH AND PASSION FRUIT TART

SERVES 8

FOR THE PASTRY
1¼ cups flour
1 stick (8 tbsp) butter, cut into small pieces
2 tbsp sugar
1 egg
FOR THE FILLING
2 eggs
½ cup whipping cream
5 tbsp sugar
strained juice from 3 passion fruits
6 peaches, peeled and halved
¼ cup pistachio nuts, shelled
¼ cup apricot preserves, boiled and strained

To make the pastry: sift the flour into a bowl, add the butter, and rub it in finely with your fingertips. Stir in the sugar and egg, and mix together with a fork to form a firm dough.

Knead the dough on a lightly floured surface until it is smooth. Roll it out thinly and use to line a 9-inch round tart or quiche dish. Chill 30 minutes.

Preheat the oven to 400°F.

Bake the pastry shell "blind" until lightly browned at the edge and cooked on the bottom, 10-15 minutes. Reduce the oven temperature to 325°F.

While the shell is baking make the filling: place the eggs, cream, sugar, and passion fruit juice in a bowl. Beat together until well blended.

Pour the mixture into the pastry shell and return it to the oven to bake until the filling has set, 30-40 minutes. Let cool.

Arrange the peaches over the custard filling and decorate with pistachio nuts. Brush the top with the apricot preserves and let set.

MINTED CURRANT TART

SERVES 6

FOR THE PASTRY
¾ cup flour
6 tbsp butter, cut into small pieces
2 tbsp sugar
1 egg yolk
FOR THE FILLING
2½ cups red currants
2½ cups white currants
2 sprigs of fresh mint
¼ cup cornstarch
½ cup + 1 tbsp sugar
FOR DECORATION
sprigs of fresh mint

To make the pastry: sift the flour into a bowl, add the butter, and rub in finely with your fingertips. Stir in the sugar and egg yolk, and mix to a firm dough.

Knead the dough until it is smooth. Roll it out thinly and use to line an 8-inch round loose-bottomed fluted tart pan. Chill 30 minutes.

Preheat the oven to 400°F.

Bake the pastry shell "blind" until lightly browned at the edges, 15-20 minutes.

While the shell is baking, make the filling: place half each of the red currants and white currants with the mint in a saucepan with 1 cup of water. Bring to a boil and simmer 2 minutes. Pour the pan contents into a strainer set over a bowl and rub through the fruit, discarding the stems and seeds.

Blend the cornstarch with ¼ cup of water in a saucepan. Add the strained fruit purée, stir well, and bring to a boil. Let cool 5 minutes, then stir in the sugar and pour the mixture into the pastry shell. Leave until cold.

Decorate the top of the tart with the remaining red currants and white currants and fresh mint sprigs.

TARTE FRANÇAISE

SERVES 8

¾ lb frozen puff pastry, thawed
FOR THE FILLING
6 tbsp apricot preserves, boiled and strained
6 oz cream cheese
3 tbsp plain yogurt
1 tbsp honey
1 tsp pure vanilla extract
1 lb mixed soft fruits, such as cherries, raspberries,
strawberries, apricots, peaches, plums, pitted and sliced
as necessary

Roll out the pastry on a lightly floured surface to make an oblong about 12 x 8 inches. Lightly flour the pastry surface and then fold the pastry in half lengthwise to make a long narrow oblong.

Measure 1 inch down from the top of one narrow edge and cut across the fold to within 1 inch of the open edge. Repeat at the bottom.

Cut a line 1 inch in from the open edge to join up with the side cuts. Remove the center piece from the "frame," open out the pastry, and roll out and trim to match the size of the pastry "frame."

Place the oblong on a dampened baking sheet, brush the edges with water, and place the frame on top. Press the edges together to seal well. Cut up the edges with a knife to form flakes. Mark a design on the top of the edges. Prick the bottom and chill 30 minutes.

Meanwhile, preheat the oven to 425°F.

Bake the pastry shell until risen and golden brown, 15-20 minutes. Cool on a wire rack and then brush the bottom with some apricot preserves.

Beat the cream cheese, yogurt, honey, and vanilla together in a bowl until well blended. Spread the mixture evenly in the pastry shell and cover with an arrangement of soft fruits. Brush well with the remaining preserves and let set.

MARINATED MELON FILLED WITH FRUIT

SERVES 6-8

1 large cantaloupe
1 small ripe mango
3 oz sweet grapes, preferably muscat
¾ lb (about 3-4 cups) mixed summer fruit, including sweet
cherries, raspberries, strawberries, and red currants
2 tbsp lemon juice
1 tbsp rose or orange flower water
2 tbsp kirsch, maraschino or Grand Marnier
2-3 tbsp sugar
small pinch of salt

Cut a thin slice off the base of the cantaloupe so that it will sit stably. Cut a "lid" off the top. Scoop out and discard the seeds. Then scoop out the flesh with a melon baller or spoon, taking care not to pierce the skin.

Peel the mango and chop the flesh into pieces the same size as the pieces of melon. Reserving a few on their stalks for decoration, remove the seeds from the grapes if necessary and halve if large.

Mix the melon flesh with the prepared mango and grapes and half the summer fruit. Mix the lemon juice, rose or orange flower water, and 1 tablespoon of liqueur and stir in all but 1 tablespoon of the sugar and the salt until dissolved. Use to dress the fruit, tossing gently to coat well. Let macerate in the refrigerator at least 2 hours.

Dissolve the remaining sugar in the remaining liqueur and swirl this mixture around the inside of the melon shell. Put the "lid" back on the melon shell and chill with the other fruit.

Just before serving, pile the fruit mixture into the chilled melon shell along with the macerating juices. Arrange the remaining summer fruit so that it spills decoratively from the top.

Melon shells make a delightful way of serving a whole range of dishes in summer. Make ice-cream using the mashed melon flesh mixed with 5 beaten egg yolks and 7 tbsp sugar. Stir the mixture over low heat until thick and then fold in 2 cups whipped cream. Flavor with lemon or lime juice and port wine, if desired. Freeze in an ice-cream machine. Pile into the well-chilled melon shell, and serve with fruit or raspberry purée. Alternatively, mix the melon flesh with citrus sections and chopped fresh mint or chunks of avocado, apples, and grapes. Dress with a light vinaigrette made with lemon or lime juice and serve in the melon shells as a refreshing first course.

CRUSTY APPLES WITH ORANGE AND CRANBERRY SAUCE

SERVES 4

2 cups fine fresh white bread crumbs
1 tbsp sugar
¼ tsp ground cinnamon
2 apples, such as Granny Smiths, peeled,
cored, and very thinly sliced
flour, for coating
1 extra large egg, beaten
6 tbsp unsalted butter
FOR THE SAUCE
⅔ cup fresh orange juice
1 tsp arrowroot, dissolved in a little water
2 tbsp cranberry sauce

Mix together the bread crumbs, sugar, and cinnamon. Dip the apple rings first in flour, then in beaten egg, and then in the bread crumb mixture, shaking off any excess each time.

Gently heat the butter in a large frying pan (or two smaller ones – or work in batches) over medium heat and fry the apple rings, turning them once, until they are crisp and golden. Keep them warm, if necessary.

Meanwhile, make the sauce: combine the ingredients in a small saucepan and heat, stirring constantly, until the sauce thickens.

Pour a little sauce on each of 4 warmed plates. Top these pools of sauce with a circle of overlapping cooked apple rings and drizzle the remaining sauce over them. Serve at once.

Left: Crusty Apples with Orange and Cranberry Sauce;
right: Honey and Lemon Dream Pudding (page 231)

HONEY AND LEMON DREAM PUDDING

SERVES 6

10 tbsp unsalted butter, plus more for greasing
½ cup sugar
⅓ cup filtered honey
5 eggs, separated
½ cup flour
grated zest and juice of 2½ washed lemons
1¼ cups milk

Preheat the oven to 350°F and generously grease a shallow 2-quart ovenproof dish with butter.

In a large bowl, cream the butter and sugar together until pale. Beat in the honey followed by the egg yolks. Stir in the flour, followed by the lemon zest and juice and then the milk. The mixture may look a little curdled at this stage.

Beat the egg whites until stiff but not dry, and fold these into the mixture.

Pour into the prepared dish and set it in a large roasting pan. Pour boiling water into the pan to come halfway up the sides of the dish.

Bake until the sponge topping is golden and feels firm to the touch in the middle, 35–40 minutes.

This pudding is best served straight from the oven but is also good cold, when the sauce sets to a thick consistency.

CHOCOLATE MOUSSE TART★

SERVES 6

FOR THE PASTRY
1¼ cups flour
1 stick (8 tbsp) butter or margarine, cut into small pieces
2 tbsp sugar
1 egg yolk
FOR THE FILLING
6 oz semisweet chocolate
½ oz white chocolate
3 eggs, separated★
(★see page 2 for advice on eggs)
2 tbsp dark rum

To make the pastry: sift the flour into a bowl, add the butter or margarine and rub it in finely with your fingertips. Stir in the sugar, egg yolk, and 1 tablespoon of water and mix to a firm dough.

Knead the dough until it is smooth. Roll it out thinly and use to line a 14- x 4-inch rectangular loose-bottomed fluted tart pan or form set on a baking sheet. Chill 30 minutes.

Preheat the oven to 400°F. Bake the shell "blind" until lightly browned at the edges, 15-20 minutes.

While the shell is cooling make the filling: place the semisweet and white chocolate in separate clean, dry bowls over hot water. Stir occasionally until melted. Stir the egg yolks and rum into the semisweet chocolate until well blended and thick.

Beat the egg whites in a clean bowl until stiff. Gradually add the egg white to the semisweet chocolate mixture, folding it in gently.

Pour the semisweet chocolate mixture into the pastry shell and shake gently to level. Place the melted white chocolate in a paper piping cone, fold down the top, and snip off the point.

Pipe parallel lines of white chocolate across the chocolate filling. Draw a toothpick across the white chocolate lines to feather them. Let it set.

CHESTNUT TART

SERVES 6

FOR THE PASTRY
1¼ cups flour
6 tbsp butter or margarine, cut into small pieces
1 tbsp chocolate fudge sauce
FOR THE FILLING
15 oz canned unsweetened chestnut purée
1 cup cream cheese
2 tbsp Marsala wine
4 oz white chocolate, melted
⅔ cup light cream
2 oz semisweet chocolate, melted
FOR DECORATION
white and dark chocolate curls

To make the pastry: sift the flour into a bowl, add the butter or margarine and rub it in finely with your fingertips. Stir in the fudge sauce and 2-3 tablespoons of cold water and mix to a firm dough.

Knead the dough until it is smooth. Roll it out thinly and use to line a 9-inch round loose-bottomed fluted tart pan. Chill 30 minutes.

Preheat the oven to 400°F. Bake the pastry shell "blind" until lightly browned at the edges, 15-20 minutes. Let it cool on a wire rack.

While the shell is cooling make the filling: place half the chestnut purée, the cheese, and Marsala in a food processor and process until smooth. Stir in the white chocolate until well blended.

Place the remaining chestnut purée and the cream in the food processor and process until smooth. Add the semisweet chocolate and blend well.

Spread half the semisweet chocolate mixture in the pastry shell and spread the white chocolate mixture over it.

Put the remaining semisweet chocolate mixture in a piping bag fitted with a plain tip. Pipe a lattice on top and decorate with chocolate curls.

MOCHA-WALNUT TART

SERVES 6

FOR THE PASTRY
¾ cup flour
6 tbsp butter, cut into small pieces
½ cup finely chopped walnuts
2 tbsp light brown sugar
1 egg
FOR THE FILLING
1¼ cups milk
2 oz semisweet chocolate
4 tbsp unsalted butter
1 tsp instant coffee granules
1 tbsp cornstarch
2 egg yolks
2 tbsp Tia Maria
⅔ cup light cream
FOR DECORATION
⅔ cup whipping cream, whipped to soft peaks
chocolate-coated coffee beans and chocolate curls

To make the pastry: sift the flour into a bowl, add the butter, and rub it in finely. Stir in the walnuts, sugar, and egg and mix to a firm dough.

Knead the dough until it is smooth. Roll it out thinly and use to line a 9-inch round loose-bottomed tart pan. Chill 30 minutes.

Preheat the oven to 400°F.

Bake the pastry shell "blind" until lightly browned at the edges, 15-20 minutes.

While the shell is baking make the filling: place the milk, chocolate, butter, and coffee in a pan and heat gently until the chocolate has melted. Blend the cornstarch, egg yolks, and liqueur together, add this to the pan, and bring to a boil, stirring. Simmer 1 minute. Off the heat, stir in the cream and pour into the pastry shell. Leave until cold.

Pipe the whipped cream over the tart and decorate with chocolate-coated coffee beans and curls.

PECAN-CHOCOLATE TART

SERVES 8

FOR THE PASTRY
1⅓ cups flour
½ tsp baking powder
10 tbsp butter or margarine, cut into small pieces
5 tbsp sugar
grated zest of 1 washed lime
1 egg
FOR THE FILLING
¾ cup sugar
6 tbsp butter or margarine, softened
2 eggs, beaten
1 tbsp cornstarch
2 cups ground pecans
3 oz semisweet chocolate, chopped into small pieces
2 tbsp chocolate liqueur
FOR DECORATION
pecan halves

To make the pastry: sift the flour and baking powder into a bowl, add the butter or margarine, and rub it in finely with your fingertips. Stir in the sugar, lime zest, and egg and mix to a firm dough.

Knead the dough until it is smooth. Roll it out thinly and use to line a 10-inch round tart or quiche dish, reserving the trimmings. Chill 30 minutes.

Preheat the oven to 375°F.

To make the filling: place the sugar and butter or margarine in a bowl and beat until light and fluffy. Add the eggs a little at a time, beating well after each addition. Fold in the cornstarch, ground pecans, chocolate, and chocolate liqueur until evenly blended.

Pour the mixture into the pastry shell. Use the pastry trimmings to make a lattice across the top. Bake until the filling has set, 40-50 minutes.

Decorate with pecan halves and serve warm or cold, cut in wedges.

ITALIAN CHEESE TART

SERVES 6

FOR THE PASTRY
¾ cup flour
6 tbsp butter or margarine, cut into small pieces
2 tbsp sugar
grated zest of 1 washed lemon
1 egg white
FOR THE FILLING
⅓ cup chopped candied fruits
1 oz semisweet chocolate, chopped into small pieces
2½ tbsp raisins
1 tbsp Marsala wine
1 cup ricotta or cream cheese
2 tbsp sugar
1 egg, separated, + 1 extra egg yolk

To make the pastry: sift the flour into a bowl, add the butter or margarine, and rub it in finely with your fingertips. Stir in the sugar, lemon zest, and egg white and mix to a firm dough.

Knead the dough until it is smooth. Roll it out thinly and use to line a 7-inch round loose-bottomed fluted tart pan. Chill 30 minutes.

Preheat the oven to 400°F.

Bake the pastry shell "blind" until lightly browned at the edges, 10-15 minutes. Reduce the oven temperature to 350°F.

While the shell is baking make the filling: place the candied fruits, chocolate, raisins, and Marsala in a bowl and stir well to mix.

Place the cheese in another bowl. Add the sugar and egg yolks and beat well. Beat the egg white in a third bowl until stiff. Fold this into the cheese mixture, together with the mixed fruits. Spread the filling in the pastry shell.

Bake in the cooler oven until the filling has set and the pastry is golden brown, 45-50 minutes. Let cool in the pan.

BELGIAN TART

SERVES 6

FOR THE PASTRY
½ cup cream cheese
4 tbsp butter, softened
1⅓ cups flour
3½ tbsp cornstarch
2 tbsp sugar
FOR THE FILLING
2 tbsp shredded coconut
2 tbsp light brown sugar
3 tbsp apricot preserves
2 nectarines, sliced
FOR DECORATION
strips of fresh coconut
nectarine slices

To make the pastry: place the cream cheese and butter in a bowl and beat until smooth. Stir in 2 tablespoons of water, the flour, cornstarch, and sugar and mix with a fork to form a firm dough.

Knead the dough on a lightly floured surface until it is smooth. Roll out two-thirds thinly and use to line an 8-inch round loose-bottomed fluted tart pan. Chill 30 minutes.

Preheat the oven to 400°F.

Make the filling: shred the remaining dough and trimmings on a coarse grater. Mix together the coconut and sugar in a bowl.

Spread the apricot preserves over the bottom of the pastry shell and cover with the sliced nectarines. Top with the grated pastry dough and sprinkle with the coconut mixture.

Bake until lightly browned, 35-40 minutes. Serve warm or cold, decorated with strips of coconut and slices of nectarine.

Left: Mascarpone and Raspberry Dessert Cake (page 202); right: Chocolate Refrigerator Cake (page 241)

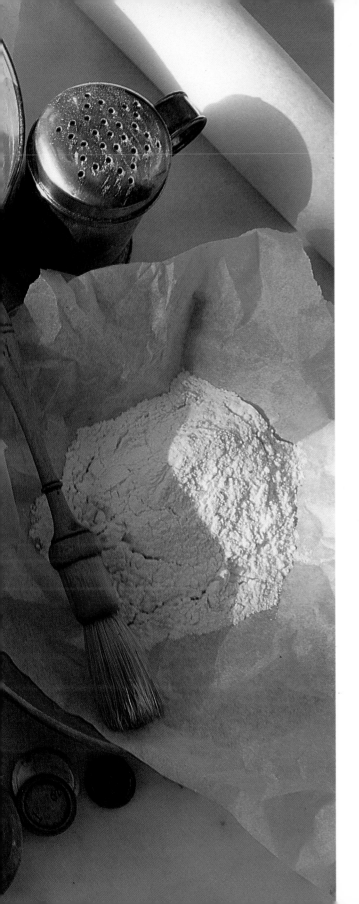

BAKING

The varied recipes in this section are for all those occasions when you wish you had a piece of cake or a little something to offer friends when they drop in for tea or coffee. The recipes are characterized by an amalgamation of unusual textures and exciting flavors to memorable effect, like German Poppy Seed and Strawberry Cake or Spanish Olive Oil and Date, Pear, and Walnut Cake. All are reasonably easy to make and the instructions are so clear and uncomplicated that it is almost impossible not to produce wonderful results every time – be it something as simple-sounding as Fudge Brownies or as exotic as Red Berry Griestorte. So if you want to make an impressive cake for an elegant afternoon tea at home or simply have something nice in the pantry for coffee in the morning, like a mature gingerbread, dip into this chapter and enjoy every last crumb.

MOIST CHOCOLATE SQUARES

MAKES 9

5 tbsp butter, softened, plus more for greasing
4 oz semisweet chocolate, broken into pieces
3 eggs, separated
¾ cup ground almonds
½ cup + 2 tbsp confectioners' sugar, sifted
1 tbsp flour, sifted
pinch of salt
unsweetened cocoa powder, for dusting
confectioners' sugar, for dusting

Preheat the oven to 350°F. Grease a 7½-inch square cake pan with butter and line the bottom with wax or parchment paper.

In a small bowl, melt the chocolate with 2 tablespoons of water, either in a microwave oven or set over a saucepan of simmering water.

Remove from the heat and beat in the butter until evenly incorporated. Beat in the egg yolks one at a time. Then stir in the ground almonds, confectioners' sugar, and flour.

Beat the egg whites with a pinch of salt until stiff. Then carefully fold into the chocolate mixture.

Transfer to the prepared pan and bake until risen and just firm to the touch, about 20 minutes.

Let cool in the pan. Trim the edges, if necessary, and then cut into 9 squares. Dust with cocoa powder and confectioners' sugar.

RUM BABAS

MAKES 8

2 tbsp dark rum
⅓ cup seedless raisins
⅓ cup dried currants
1 stick (8 tbsp) butter, melted, plus more for greasing
1 package quick-rise dry yeast
1⅔ cups strong plain or plain flour
4½ tbsp sugar
4 eggs, beaten
FOR THE SYRUP
¾ cup caster sugar
5 tbsp dark rum

Mix the 2 tablespoons of rum and the dried fruit in a bowl, cover, and let soak at least 1 hour or up to 24 hours.

Grease 8 large (about ⅔ cup) individual brioche molds with butter.

Mix the yeast, flour, and sugar in a large bowl. Beat in the butter and eggs until the batter is light in texture. Beat in the fruit and rum.

Half-fill the molds with the batter, then cover and let rise in a warm place until the batter reaches the top of the molds.

Preheat the oven to 400°F.

Bake the babas until golden brown and just firm to the touch, 15–20 minutes. Let cool a little, then unmold into a shallow dish.

Make the syrup: in a small saucepan set over medium heat, dissolve the sugar in ⅞ cup of water. Once the sugar is completely dissolved, bring to a simmer and simmer 5 minutes. Stir in the rum and remove from the heat.

Immediately pour the hot syrup over the babas and leave until they have absorbed all the syrup.

COCONUT AND CHERRY MACAROONS

MAKES 10

2 egg whites
¾ cup confectioners' sugar, sifted
1¼ cups dried shredded coconut
1⅓ cups ground almonds
⅓ cup chopped candied cherries
1 tbsp dark rum or dry sherry wine

Preheat the oven to 300°F and line a baking sheet with nonstick silicone paper.

Combine all the ingredients in a bowl and then shape the mixture into 10 round cakes.

Place these on the baking sheet. Bake until lightly golden, about 20 minutes.

Let cool on a wire rack.

FUDGE BROWNIES

MAKES 9

6 tbsp butter, diced, plus more for greasing
3 oz best-quality white chocolate, broken into pieces
2 eggs
½ tsp pure vanilla extract
¼ tsp salt
1¼ cups light brown sugar
¾ cup self-rising flour
1 cup chopped walnuts

Preheat the oven to 350°F. Grease an 8-inch square pan with butter and line the bottom with wax or parchment paper.

Place the chocolate and butter in a bowl set over simmering water and heat gently until they have just melted.

Beat the eggs, vanilla, salt, and sugar together in another bowl until thickened. Then stir in the flour and melted chocolate mixture, followed by the walnuts.

Transfer the batter to the prepared pan. Bake until risen and just firm to the touch, about 30 minutes. Let cool in the pan and then cut into 9 square pieces.

BROWNIES *are classics of American baking. Chopped nuts, such as pecans, or shredded coconut are often added to the mixture.*

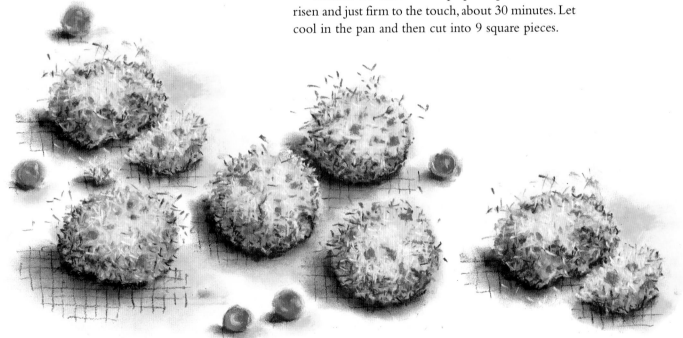

If preferred, the traditional Austrian layer cake, GRIESTORTE, can be made as two smaller cakes rather than one big one as described here.

SEMOLINA is ground from hard durum wheat. It is available, in fine, medium, and coarse grinds, from Italian stores, health-food stores, and some supermarkets.

GREAT GRAPEFRUIT CAKE

SERVES 8-12

½ cup soft tub margarine
½ cup + 2 tbsp granulated sugar
2 eggs
1½ cups self-rising flour
½ tsp baking powder
pinch of salt
finely grated zest of 1 washed grapefruit
juice of 2 grapefruit
½ cup confectioners' sugar
butter or vegetable oil, for greasing

Preheat the oven to 350°F. Grease an 8-inch square pan with butter or oil and line the bottom with wax or parchment paper.

Place the margarine, granulated sugar, eggs, flour, baking powder, salt, and grapefruit zest in a large bowl and beat well with a wooden spoon for 1-2 minutes, until the mixture has a "soft dropping consistency." Transfer to the prepared pan and level the surface of the batter. Bake until risen and just firm to the touch, about 30 minutes. Let cool in the pan.

Place the grapefruit juice and confectioners' sugar in a saucepan and bring to a boil. Boil until slightly syrupy, about 3-4 minutes. Prick the top of the cake all over with a skewer and pour the syrup over it. Let cool completely in the pan.

Unmold the cake and cut it into fingers. Dust with extra confectioners' sugar, if desired.

PEAR GRIESTORTE WITH ALMONDS AND GINGER

SERVES 12-16

butter, for greasing
flour, for dusting
1 cup + 2 tbsp granulated sugar, plus more for dusting
6 eggs, separated
grated zest and juice of 1 washed lemon
⅔ cup fine semolina
⅓ cup ground almonds
1 tbsp ground ginger
3 drops of pure vanilla extract
6 ripe pears, peeled and sliced
2 cups whipping cream, whipped to soft peaks
sprigs of mint, for garnish
confectioners' sugar, for dusting (optional)

Preheat the oven to 350°F.

Grease two 8-inch round layer cake pans with butter and line their bottoms with disks of wax paper (this is unnecessary if using non-stick pans). Butter the paper and then dust the paper and the sides of the pans with flour followed by granulated sugar.

In a large bowl, beat the egg yolks and granulated sugar together until pale, creamy, and light. Add the lemon juice and continue beating until the mixture thickens. Stir in the semolina, almonds, ginger, and lemon zest and mix thoroughly. Beat the egg whites to stiff peaks and gently fold them into the batter.

Spoon into the prepared pans and bake 30-40 minutes. The cakes will rise dramatically owing to the proportion of egg to starch. Do not open the oven door or the cakes will subside!

Let the cakes cool, then split them across horizontally. Stir the vanilla extract and some of the pear slices into the whipped cream. Put all the cake layers together with this mixture and then top with the remaining pear slices. Dust with confectioners' sugar, if desired, and decorate with mint.

CHOCOLATE REFRIGERATOR CAKE★

SERVES 12

½ cup walnut pieces
½ cup blanched almonds
⅓ cup golden raisins (sultanas)
⅓ cup chopped candied cherries
2 cups graham-cracker crumbs, firmly packed
5 oz semisweet chocolate, melted
1 extra large egg, beaten★
(★see page 2 for advice on eggs)
3-4 tbsp dark rum, or more to taste
FOR DECORATION (OPTIONAL)
whipped cream
2 maraschino or candied cherries, cut into thin wedges

Preheat the oven to 350°F and line an 8-inch tart pan with foil. Place the nuts on a baking sheet and toast them in oven until golden, about 20 minutes.

Roughly chop the toasted nuts and combine them with the fruit and graham-cracker crumbs in a large bowl. Stir in the chocolate. Add the egg and 3-4 tablespoons rum. Check the taste and add a little more rum, if desired.

Press the mixture into the prepared pan and chill at least 4 hours or preferably overnight.

Unmold the chilled cake and cut into 12 wedges. If desired, top each wedge with a swirl of whipped cream and a piece of cherry.

MINCEMEAT CAKE

SERVES 8

⅔ cup soft tub margarine
⅔ cup light brown sugar
2 eggs
¾ cup self-rising flour
½ cup whole wheat self-rising flour
½ tsp baking powder
1 tbsp warm water
1 cup mincemeat
butter or vegetable oil, for greasing
FOR THE ICING
1½ cups confectioners' sugar, sifted
2 tbsp tangerine juice

Preheat the oven to 325°F. Grease an 8-inch round cake pan with butter or oil and line the bottom with wax or parchment paper.

In a large bowl, combine all the ingredients for the cake and beat well with a wooden spoon for about 2 minutes, until the batter has a "soft dropping consistency." Transfer to the prepared pan and level the surface.

Bake until risen and just firm to the touch, about 40 minutes. Let cool in the pan and then transfer to a wire rack to cool completely.

Make the icing by mixing the confectioners' sugar with the juice until smooth. Spread this over the top of the cake. Let it set.

Toasting the nuts before adding them to the CHOCOLATE REFRIGERATOR CAKE adds an extra depth of flavor. If desired, replace the almonds and walnuts with an equal quantity of other nuts such as pecans, hazelnuts, brazils, or macadamia nuts.

MINCEMEAT CAKE is a clever way of using up mincemeat left over after the holidays.

VERY GINGERBREAD WITH LEMON ICING

SERVES 9-16

1 stick (8 tbsp) butter, plus more for greasing
¾ cup + 2 tbsp all-purpose flour
pinch of salt
1 tsp apple pie spice
1 tbsp ground ginger
¾ cup + 2 tbsp whole wheat flour
5 tbsp raw brown sugar
⅓ cup chopped preserved stem ginger
⅓ cup dark molasses
⅓ cup light corn syrup
1 tsp baking soda
½ cup warm milk
1 extra large egg, beaten
FOR THE LEMON ICING
½ cup confectioners' sugar, sifted
2½ tsp lemon juice

Preheat the oven to 350°F. Grease an 8-inch square cake pan with butter and line the bottom with wax or parchment paper.

Sift the all-purpose flour, salt, and spices into a large bowl, then stir in the whole wheat flour, brown sugar, and chopped ginger.

In a saucepan, warm the butter, molasses, and corn syrup together until the butter just melts.

Dissolve the baking soda in the milk and add this to the dry ingredients together with the syrup mixture and egg. Beat the batter well until smooth.

Transfer to the pan and bake until risen and firm to the touch, 40-45 minutes. Cool slightly in the pan, then unmold and cool completely on a wire rack.

Make the icing: mix the confectioners' sugar and lemon juice in a bowl until thick and smooth. Drizzle this over the cake in a random pattern and let set. Cut into squares to serve.

WARM CINNAMON CAKE

SERVES 8-10

1⅔ cups flour
1 tbsp baking powder
½ tsp salt
½ cup + 2 tbsp sugar
½ cup shortening or soft tub margarine
1 egg
6 tbsp milk
butter, for greasing
vanilla ice-cream, for serving (optional)
FOR THE TOPPING
3 tbsp flour
3 tbsp sugar
1 tbsp ground cinnamon
3 tbsp shortening or soft tub margarine

Preheat the oven to 400°F. Grease a 10-inch round cake pan with butter and line the bottom with wax or parchment paper.

First, make the topping by sifting the dry ingredients together and rubbing in the fat.

Then make the cake: sift the dry ingredients into a bowl and add the shortening, egg, and milk. Beat 1 minute with a wooden spoon until smooth and then transfer to the prepared pan.

Sprinkle evenly with the topping and bake until well risen, about 25 minutes. (Don't be tempted to press it with your finger to check if it's cooked – the sugar in the topping will be very hot!)

Serve straight from the oven, plain or with vanilla ice-cream.

Left: Very Gingerbread with Lemon Icing; right: Warm Cinnamon Cake

ESPRESSO COFFEE GRANULES *are freeze-dried to give a more authentic coffee taste. Available from most supermarkets, they are very useful for adding a good flavor to cakes and frostings. Always dissolve them in a little boiling water before use.*

ONE-STEP COFFEE LAYER CAKE

SERVES 8

¾ cup soft tub margarine
¾ cup + 2 tbsp sugar
3 eggs
1½ cups self-rising flour
1 tsp baking powder
pinch of salt
1 tbsp espresso coffee granules, dissolved in 1 tbsp
boiling water
butter or vegetable oil, for greasing
candied coffee beans, for decoration
FOR THE FILLING
6 tbsp butter, softened
1 tbsp espresso coffee granules, dissolved in 1 tbsp
boiling water
1½ cups confectioners' sugar, sifted
FOR THE ICING
¾ cup confectioners' sugar, sifted
1½ tsp espresso coffee granules, dissolved in 2½ tsp
boiling water

Preheat the oven to 350°F. Grease two 8-inch layer cake pans with butter or oil and line the bottoms with wax or parchment paper.

Place all the ingredients for the cake in a large

bowl and beat well with a wooden spoon for 1-2 minutes until mixed to a "soft dropping consistency".

Divide the batter between the pans and bake until risen and just firm to the touch, about 25 minutes. Let cool slightly in the pans, then transfer to wire racks and let cool completely.

Make the filling: beat the butter in a bowl until soft and almost white, then stir in the coffee solution and beat in the confectioners' sugar. Use two-thirds of this mixture to put the cake layers together.

Make the icing: mix the confectioners' sugar and coffee solution until smooth and then spread this over the top of the cake. Let set. Using a pastry bag fitted with a medium star tip, pipe 8 rosettes of the remaining filling around the rim of the cake and decorate each one with a candied coffee bean.

ANNIE'S FAT-FREE FRUIT LOAVES

MAKES 2, SERVES 20-24

3 cups golden raisins (sultanas)
1¼ cups cold tea
1 egg, beaten
1¼ cups light brown sugar
2½ cups self-rising flour
butter, for greasing

Soak the raisins in the tea overnight.

Preheat the oven to 325°F. Grease two loaf pans, about 5 x 4 x 2 inches, with butter and line the bottoms with wax or parchment paper.

Beat all the ingredients together until evenly combined. Divide the batter between the pans and bake until risen and firm to the touch, about 1¼ hours (a fine metal skewer inserted into the center will come out clean and hot to the touch).

Let cool in the pans, then unmold on a wire rack. Serve cut into slices, with or without butter.

TUTTI-FRUTTI CAKE

SERVES 8

¾ cup soft tub margarine
¾ cup + 2 tbsp sugar
3 eggs
1½ cups self-rising flour
pinch of salt
1 tsp baking powder
⅓ cup minced assorted candied fruits, such as cherries and
angelica
butter or vegetable oil, for greasing
FOR THE FILLING
⅔ cup whipping cream, whipped to soft peaks
¼ cup apricot preserves

Preheat the oven to 350°F. Grease two 8-inch layer cake pans with butter or oil and line the bottoms with wax or parchment paper.

Place all the ingredients for the cake except the candied fruits in a large bowl and beat well with a wooden spoon for 1-2 minutes, until the batter has a "soft dropping consistency."

Divide the batter between the two pans and level the surface. Sprinkle the candied fruit evenly over the surface of one of the cakes.

Bake the cakes until risen and just firm to the touch, about 25 minutes. Let cool slightly and then unmold and transfer to wire racks.

Make the filling by combining the cream and apricot preserves and use this to put the cake layers together with the fruit-topped cake layer uppermost.

NOTE: for a more professional finish, bake the cake 10 minutes before sprinkling over the candied fruits.

Center: Tutti-frutti Cake; top and bottom: Annie's Fat-free Fruit Loaves

COCONUT CAKE

SERVES 8

1½ sticks (¾ cup) butter, softened, plus more for greasing
¾ cup + 2 tbsp sugar
3 tbsp warm water
3 eggs
1 cup + 2 tbsp self-rising flour
¾ cup dried shredded coconut

Preheat the oven to 350°F. Grease an 8-inch round cake pan with butter and line the bottom and sides with a double thickness of wax or parchment paper.

Cream the butter and sugar until almost white. Beat in the water, 1 tablespoon at a time. Then beat in the eggs one at a time.

Sift in the flour, then add all but 2 tablespoons of the coconut. Fold this into the creamed mixture until evenly combined.

Transfer to the prepared pan and level the surface. Sprinkle with the remaining coconut and bake until risen and golden and just springy to the touch, about 45 minutes.

Let cool slightly in the pan and then unmold on a wire rack.

Dried shredded coconut gives COCONUT CAKE *a moist, crumbly texture that is further enhanced by leaving the cake to mature a couple of days. Wrap it carefully and store in a cool dry place.*

BANANA LOAF *tastes better if made using well-ripened bananas with blackening skins. The cake also develops in flavor if wrapped and stored a few days before eating.*

BANANA LOAF

SERVES 10-12

1 stick (8 tbsp) butter, diced, plus more for greasing
2 cups self-rising flour
½ tsp salt
¾ cup + 2 tbsp sugar
¾ cup golden raisins (sultanas)
½ cup chopped pecans
¾ cup candied cherries, halved
2 eggs, beaten
2 cups mashed ripe bananas

Preheat the oven to 350°F. Grease a loaf pan, about 9 x 5 x 3 inches, with butter and line the bottom with wax or parchment paper.

Sift the flour and salt into a large bowl and rub in the butter until the mixture resembles fine crumbs.

Stir in the sugar, raisins, nuts, and cherries until evenly coated with the mixture.

Add the eggs and banana to the mixture and beat well until evenly incorporated.

Transfer to the prepared pan and bake until risen and just firm to the touch, about 1 hour 10 minutes. Let the cake cool in the pan, then unmold on a wire rack.

SUNSHINE MARBLE CAKE

SERVES 8-12

1½ sticks (¾ cup) butter, softened, plus more for greasing
¾ cup + 2 tbsp sugar, plus more for dusting
1¼ cups flour, plus more for dusting
3 tbsp orange juice
finely grated zest from 1 large washed orange
3 eggs, separated
2¼ tsp baking powder
⅓ cup ground almonds
1½ tbsp hot water
pinch of salt

Preheat the oven to 350°F. Grease a 8¾-inch (1½-quart capacity) kugelhopf mold with butter. Sprinkle liberally with sugar and flour and shake well to coat the inside of the mold evenly. Shake out any excess.

Cream the butter and sugar until almost white, then divide the mixture into two equal portions.

To one portion, add the orange juice, a little at a time. Then add the orange zest and egg yolks and beat thoroughly.

Sift half the flour with 1½ teaspoons of baking powder and fold this into the orange mixture together with half the ground almonds.

To the other portion of butter mixture, add the hot water and beat well.

Sift the remaining flour, baking powder, and ground almonds together.

Beat the egg whites with a pinch of salt until stiff. Then fold alternate spoonfuls of them and the sifted flour mixture into the hot water and butter mixture.

Place alternate spoonfuls of the orange batter and this white mixture in the prepared mold.

Bake until risen and just firm to the touch, about 40 minutes. Let the cake cool in the mold until just cool enough to handle, then immediately unmold on a wire rack.

BLACKBERRY AND APPLE RIPPLE CAKE

SERVES 8-10

1½ sticks (¾ cup) butter, softened, plus more for greasing
1 cup sugar
3 eggs
1½ cup self-rising flour
nearly 2 cups blackberries
2 apples, peeled, cored, and grated

Preheat the oven to 350°F. Line the bottom of a 9-inch round cake pan with wax or parchment paper and grease it with butter.

Reserve 2 tablespoons sugar. Cream the butter with the remaining sugar in a large bowl until almost white, then beat in the eggs one at a time until thoroughly incorporated. Fold in the flour.

Spoon about two-thirds of the batter into the prepared pan.

Mix the blackberries, apples, and reserved sugar. Spoon this over the cake batter and then drop spoonfuls of the remaining cake batter over the top in a random pattern.

Bake until risen and golden and just firm to the touch, about 1 hour. Let cool in the pan.

The two-tone marbling effect in SUNSHINE MARBLE CAKE *is produced by separating eggs and using the yolks in one batter and the whites in the other.*

Any soft berry fruits, such as raspberries, loganberries, or blueberries, can be used in place of the blackberries in the BLACKBERRY AND APPLE RIPPLE CAKE.

JEWELED FRUITCAKE

SERVES 16

2 sticks (1 cup) butter, softened, plus more for greasing
1 cup ground almonds
1⅔ cups light brown sugar
1¼ cups beaten egg (5 extra large eggs)
1¼ cups flour
1 tbsp apple pie spice
3 cups raisins
3 cups golden raisins (sultanas)
1 cup diced mixed candied peel
3 tbsp orange juice
¼ cup sherry wine or dark rum
1½ cups candied cherries

FOR DECORATION

4-6 tbsp apricot preserves, warmed and strained
6 candied cherries
2 candied pears, quartered
3 candied orange slices, halved
3 candied pineapple slices, halved
2 wedges of candied apple
2 slices of candied kiwi, halved
3 tbsp whole blanched almonds, toasted

Preheat the oven to 300°F. Line the bottom and sides of a 9-inch round cake pan with a double thickness of greased parchment paper, then wrap the outside with a thick layer of brown paper or newspaper.

Place the ground almonds in a frying pan and cook over medium heat, stirring all the time, until evenly toasted. Let cool.

Cream the butter and sugar together in a large bowl until pale and fluffy. Beat in the egg a little at a time until evenly combined.

Fold in the flour, spice, and ground almonds. Then stir in the fruit, orange juice, and sherry or rum and mix thoroughly. Lastly, stir in the cherries.

Transfer the batter to the prepared pan and level the surface.

Bake until just firm to the touch, about 3 hours (a fine metal skewer inserted into the center should come out piping hot and clean). Let cool in the pan.

To decorate: unmold the cooled cake and brush the surface with some of the warmed apricot preserves. Arrange the candied fruit and toasted nuts attractively over the surface of the cake and brush with the remaining preserves.

CHERRY STREUSEL CAKE

SERVES 12-16

1 stick (8 tbsp) butter, softened, plus more for greasing
1 cup sugar
3 eggs
1¼ cups self-rising flour
1⅓ cups ground almonds
1½ cups candied cherries, quartered
⅓ cup sliced almonds

Preheat the oven to 350°F. Grease a 7-inch round cake pan with butter and line the bottom and sides with a double thickness of wax or parchment paper.

Reserve 6 tablespoons sugar. In a bowl, cream the butter and remaining sugar until almost white. Beat in 2 whole eggs, one at a time. Then separate the third egg and add the yolk. Reserve the white for topping.

Combine the flour, half the ground almonds, and the cherries and fold this into the creamed mixture. Transfer to the prepared pan and level the surface.

Make the topping by combining the remaining ingredients and scatter this on the top of the cake.

Bake until risen and golden, 1-1¼ hours (a fine metal skewer inserted into the center of the cake should come out clean and feel piping hot to the touch).

Let the cake cool in the pan, then unmold on a wire rack.

SRI LANKAN FRUITCAKE

SERVES 16

1½ sticks (¾ cup) butter, softened, plus more for greasing
¼ cup raisins, minced
1¼ cups golden raisins (sultanas), minced
⅔ cup diced assorted candied fruits
⅔ cup diced crystallized ginger
⅓ cup diced mixed candied peel
1 cup candied cherries, halved
1 cup minced cashew nuts or blanched almonds
⅔ cup melon and ginger preserves
2 tbsp dark rum
¾ cup + 2 tbsp sugar
3 eggs, separated, + 3 extra yolks
1 tsp finely grated zest from 1 washed lemon
¾ tsp ground cardamom
½ tsp ground cinnamon
½ tsp ground nutmeg
½ tsp ground cloves
1 tbsp pure vanilla extract
⅔ cup semolina flour

Preheat the oven to 300°F. Grease an 8-inch round cake pan with butter and line with a double thickness of parchment paper. Wrap the outside of the pan with newspaper or brown paper.

Combine the fruits, nuts, melon and ginger preserves, and the rum. Cover and let macerate while preparing the cake, or up to 24 hours.

Cream the butter and sugar until almost white then beat in all the egg yolks, one at a time. Then beat in the lemon zest, spices, and vanilla. Stir in the semolina followed by the fruit until evenly mixed.

Beat the egg whites until stiff, then fold them into the fruit mixture.

Transfer to the prepared pan and level the surface. Bake until just firm to the touch, about 2½ hours. Let cool in the pan.

When using CANDIED CHERRIES, *it is always a good idea to rinse and dry them thoroughly to remove excess sugar syrup. Then mix them with some of the flour: this helps prevent them from drifting to the bottom of the cake during baking.*

YVONNE'S YOGURT CAKE

SERVES 8

½ cup vegetable oil or melted butter, plus more for greasing
½ cup plain yogurt
1 cup sugar
2 eggs
1¼ cups flour
1½ tsp baking powder
finely grated zest of 1 washed lemon or 1 tbsp orange
blossom water
strawberry or raspberry preserves or fresh berries, for serving
(optional)

Preheat the oven to 350°F. Grease the bottom of an 8¾-inch round cake pan with oil or butter and line the bottom with wax or parchment paper.

Mix the yogurt and sugar in a large bowl until smooth, then beat in the oil or melted butter and the eggs until well combined.

Sift the flour and baking powder together and beat them into the mixture. Then stir in the lemon zest or orange blossom water.

Transfer the batter to the prepared pan and bake until risen and just firm to the touch, about 45 minutes. Let cool in the pan, then transfer to a wire rack.

Serve with preserves or fresh berries, if using, to accompany morning coffee.

Clockwise from the top: Poppy Seed and Strawberry Cake, Cherry Streusel Cake (page 249), and Yvonne's Yogurt Cake

POPPY SEED AND STRAWBERRY CAKE

SERVES 12

⅔ cup poppy seeds
1 cup milk
2 sticks (1 cup) butter, softened, plus more for greasing
1⅔ cups light brown sugar
3 eggs, separated
1⅔ cups whole wheat flour
1½ tsp baking powder
pinch of salt
6 tbsp strawberry preserves, warmed

Place the poppy seeds and milk in a saucepan and bring to a boil. Then remove from the heat and let infuse at least 20 minutes (leaving it for longer won't matter).

Preheat the oven to 350°F. Grease an 8¾-inch round cake pan with butter and line the bottom and sides with a double thickness of wax or parchment paper.

Cream the butter and sugar together in a large bowl until light and fluffy, then beat in the egg yolks one at a time.

Mix the flour and baking powder together and fold alternate large spoonfuls of this and the poppy seed mixture into the creamed mixture.

Beat the egg whites with a pinch of salt until stiff and then fold into the batter.

Transfer to the pan and level the surface. Bake until risen and just springy to the touch, 1-1¼ hours. Cool in the pan, then unmold on a wire rack.

Brush the top of the cake with the warmed preserves and let cool.

YVONNE'S YOGURT CAKE *is a French plain cake to be eaten for breakfast or with morning coffee, on its own or with preserves.*

Before making POPPY SEED AND STRAWBERRY CAKE, *it is essential to soak the poppy seeds in the milk to soften them; this makes the cake more moist. Any fruit preserves can be used to top the cake, and then it can be served with the corresponding fresh fruit.*

CHOCOLATE SPONGE CAKE

SERVES 8

1 stick (8 tbsp) butter, softened, plus more for greasing
1 cup self-rising flour
1 tsp baking powder
⅓ cup unsweetened cocoa powder
3 tbsp boiling water
3 tbsp light corn syrup
½ cup + 2 tbsp granulated sugar
3 eggs, beaten
⅔ cup whipping cream, whipped to soft peaks
confectioners' sugar, for dusting

Preheat the oven to 350°F. Grease an 8¾-inch round cake pan with butter, then line the bottom with wax or parchment paper.

Sift the flour and baking powder into a bowl. In another bowl mix the cocoa, water, and corn syrup until smooth. In a large bowl, cream the butter and sugar until almost white. Beat in the eggs a little at a time. Fold in the flour, then the cocoa mixture.

Transfer the batter to the pan and bake until risen and just firm to the touch, about 35 minutes.

Let cool slightly, then unmold on a rack. Leave the pan over the cake until cold. To serve, split the cake into 2 equal layers and fill with whipped cream. Dust the top with confectioners' sugar.

When adding the eggs to the CHOCOLATE SPONGE CAKE *mixture, stir in a spoonful of the flour, if necessary, to prevent curdling.*

Traditional to Viennese pastry-making, GRIESTORTE *is commonly made using semolina flour and probably owes its origins to Turkish influence.*

RED BERRY GRIESTORTE

SERVES 8

1 cup + 2 tbsp granulated sugar, plus more for dusting
6 eggs, separated
finely grated zest and juice of 1 washed lemon
⅔ cup rice flour or semolina flour
⅓ cup ground almonds
pinch of salt
about 1½ cups red berries
⅔ cup whipping cream, whipped to soft peaks
butter, for greasing
confectioners' sugar, for dusting

Preheat the oven to 350°F. Grease two 8-inch layer cake pans with butter and line the bottom with wax or parchment paper. Sprinkle the sides of the pans with sugar to coat them evenly. Shake out any excess.

Beat the egg yolks, about ¾ cup of sugar, and the lemon juice in a large bowl until thick and pale. Then stir in the lemon zest, rice or semolina flour, and the ground almonds until smooth.

Beat the egg whites with a pinch of salt until stiff, then beat in the remaining sugar a little at a time.

Fold the egg yolk mixture into the egg whites. Divide the batter between the prepared pans.

Bake until risen and just firm to the touch, about 30 minutes. Let cool slightly in the pans, then unmold on wire racks.

Fold the red berries into the whipped cream and use this to sandwich the cake layers together. Dust the top with confectioners' sugar.

APPLESAUCE CAKE

SERVES 10-12

1 lb tart apples, peeled, cored, and chopped
1 cup + 2 tbsp granulated sugar, plus more for dusting
3 tbsp chopped candied cherries
⅓ cup toasted sliced almonds
3 tbsp dried currants
1 tbsp chopped candied angelica
1 stick (8 tbsp) butter, softened, plus more for greasing
1⅔ cups flour, plus more for dusting
1 egg
1 tsp baking soda
pinch of salt
1 cup confectioners' sugar, sifted
1 tbsp apple juice
candied fruits, for decoration (optional)

Place the apples in a pan with 4 tablespoons of the granulated sugar and cook gently to a purée, about 10 minutes. Continue cooking over medium heat, stirring all the time until really thick, about 5 minutes longer. Let cool completely, then stir in the cherries, almonds, currants, and angelica.

Preheat the oven to 350°F. Grease a 9½-inch ring mold with butter, then dust the inside with a little sugar and flour. Shake off any excess.

Cream the butter and half the remaining granulated sugar until almost white, then beat in the remaining granulated sugar and egg.

Sift the flour, baking soda, and salt together and fold this into the creamed mixture. Stir in the applesauce and transfer the batter to the mold.

Bake until risen and firm to the touch, about 35 minutes. Let cool slightly in the mold, then unmold on a wire rack and let cool completely.

Mix the confectioners' sugar with the apple juice to give a thick, smooth icing and drizzle it over the cooled cake. Decorate with extra candied fruits, if using, and let set.

DATE, PEAR, AND WALNUT CAKE

SERVES 8-10

⅔ cup pitted dates
⅓ cup date syrup or malt extract
½ cup vegetable oil
½ cup plain yogurt or buttermilk
2 eggs
1 cup whole wheat flour
½ tsp baking soda
1 tsp ground cinnamon
½ tsp apple pie spice
¼ cup walnut pieces
2 ripe pears
¼ cup apricot preserves, warmed and strained
butter or vegetable oil, for greasing

Place the dates in a small saucepan with ⅔ cup of water and cook until all the water has evaporated, to produce a soft date purée. Let cool.

Preheat the oven to 350°F and grease a 9-inch springform pan with butter or oil.

Place the date syrup or malt extract in a large bowl with the oil, yogurt or buttermilk, and the eggs and beat until smooth. Then beat in the date purée.

Mix the flour, baking soda, and spices together and fold them into the date mixture with the walnuts. Transfer to the prepared pan.

Peel, quarter, and core the pears. Then cut each quarter into thin slices without cutting completely through the top of each piece. Fan out the slices of each pear quarter and place them attractively on top of the cake batter.

Bake until the cake is risen and just firm to the touch, 45-50 minutes.

Let cool in the pan, then transfer to a wire rack. Brush with the warmed and strained apricot preserves and let cool.

INDEX